Paths to the Professoriate

Strategies for Enriching the Preparation of Future Faculty

Donald H. Wulff, Ann E. Austin, & Associates

JOSSEY-BASS
A Wiley Imprint
www.josseybass.com

Published by Jossey-Bass
A Wiley Imprint
989 Market Street, San Francisco, CA 94103-1741   www.josseybass.com

Jossey-Bass books and products are available through most bookstores. To contact Jossey-Bass directly call
our Customer Care Department within the U.S. at (800) 956-7739, outside the U.S. at (317) 572-3986
or fax (317) 572-4002.

Jossey-Bass also publishes its books in a variety of electronic formats. Some content that appears in
print may not be available in electronic books.

Library of Congress Cataloging-in-Publication Data

Paths to the professoriate : strategies for enriching the preparation of future faculty.— 1st ed.
    p. cm. — (The Jossey-Bass higher and adult education series)
  Edited by Ann E. Austin and Donald H. Wulff.
  Includes bibliographical references and index.
  ISBN 0-7879-6634-7 (alk. paper)
  1. College teaching—United States. 2. College teachers—Training of—United States. 3. Universities
and colleges—United States—Faculty. I. Austin, Ann E. II. Wulff, Donald H. III. Series.
  LB2331.P3625 2004
  378.1'2—dc22
                    2003027456

The Jossey-Bass Higher and Adult Education Series

In Memory of
Marsha L. Landolt
Dean of the Graduate School and Vice Provost (1996–2004)
University of Washington

Whose contributions as scholar, mentor, visionary, leader, and
advocate have greatly enriched graduate education

Contents

Tables

Preface

We can remember the exact moment at which we were struck with the idea of writing this volume. We were sitting beside each other at the 2001 annual conference of the Professional and Organizational Development Network in Higher Education (POD), listening to a keynote address on graduate education by Orlando Taylor, dean of Howard University's Graduate School of Arts and Sciences. Dean Taylor's discussion of challenges and opportunities in preparing future faculty brought to mind the various national research projects and programs emerging in an effort to strengthen the preparation of future faculty. The insights and comments inspired us. At the same time, we knew that information about research studies and action projects concerning the preparation of future faculty resided in disparate parts of the academic community. As we stood up to leave the POD keynote session, we began to discuss the possibilities of creating a volume that would bring together and highlight the thoughtful and innovative work under way.

We realized from the outset of this project the importance of focus. In the past two decades, there has been increasing attention to graduate education. Professional associations, agencies, and foundations such as the Carnegie Foundation for the Advancement of Teaching, the National Science Foundation, The Pew Charitable Trusts, the Spencer Foundation, and the Woodrow Wilson Foundation have sponsored conferences and programs to identify issues of concern in graduate education, frame questions deserving further examination, and offer recommendations for reform. Various questions and issues have fueled interest in graduate education across a range of stakeholders: What are the workforce needs of society and to what extent is graduate education appropriately planning for and addressing those needs? Are doctoral programs preparing graduates to enter a range of positions, including those in business and industry, government agencies, research units, the variety of educational venues, and so on, as well as to assume traditional academic positions? What are the abilities and skills that should be expected of a doctoral graduate? What are the costs and benefits, for individuals, for higher education institutions, and for society at large, of the time and resources spent on graduate education? What are the roles of academics in the communities outside the university or college and how is graduate education preparing scholars for those roles? What are the purposes of graduate education? What are its strengths and weaknesses? Are large-scale reforms or modest adjustments in order?

These questions represent a sampling of the issues that have led employers, foundation and government leaders, university administrators, leaders at the variety of higher education institutions that hire doctoral graduates (including liberal arts colleges, community colleges, and comprehensive institutions), faculty advisors, graduate deans, and graduate students themselves to engage in lively discussion and debate about graduate education. Certainly, questions about graduate education have been voiced for years, but the conversation since the mid-1980s has gained momentum. Many of the programs in this volume have contributed in important ways to these discussions. Although we situate our interest in graduate education in this broad conversation about its purposes, strengths, and issues, we chose to focus this book specifically on one very important purpose of graduate education: preparing the faculty of the future for roles in a variety of institutional types.

Two kinds of work currently under way are relevant to the preparation of future faculty—and each is very necessary. One body of work consists of research studies done in recent years that pertain to the graduate experience and shed light on paths to the professoriate. Another body of work includes the action projects and strategies that have been designed and implemented to enrich the preparation of future faculty. In this book, we wished to juxtapose research findings that indicate concerns about graduate school preparation for the professoriate with discussions of action projects and strategies intended to address those concerns.

We chose the title of the volume to highlight the variety of paths—experiences during graduate study—that could lead to enhanced preparation for the future professoriate. Although much of the research and many of the action projects described in this volume have been designed to address broader issues in graduate education, they also have important implications for preparing future professors. Through the discussions of their research and action projects, as well as their resulting recommendations, the authors offer many specific strategies—lessons that we believe will be helpful to others working to enhance or establish programs that enrich the preparation of future faculty.

Our Purposes

The purpose of the book is to provide academic leaders, faculty members, and graduate students themselves with research findings, analyses, and recommendations that will help them prepare the future professoriate more successfully. This book highlights and synthesizes the findings from major research studies and action projects that have focused, over the past decade, on improving graduate education and preparing the future faculty. Although there are valuable resources pertaining to graduate education in both the research literature and the publications describing the activities of various associations, institutions, and organizations, there has been no comprehensive effort to bring those pieces together. This volume fills that gap and offers a useful resource for institutional leaders and faculty members. Thus, the key contributions of this book are to synthesize what has been learned about challenges and concerns in graduate education as preparation for faculty careers, to highlight in one place various projects and approaches for improving graduate education, and to identify action strategies for institutional leaders, department chairs, faculty advisors, and graduate students themselves.

Specifically, the book provides the following:

- An overview of the changing context in higher education that is creating concern about graduate education, new expectations for faculty work, new kinds of faculty appointments, and thus a need for new approaches to preparing future faculty

- Summary, synthesis, and comparison of research findings from important recent studies on the graduate experience and its outcomes, particularly in regard to preparing future faculty
- Examples of innovative programs and projects with national impact that respond to calls for reform in graduate education to prepare the future professoriate
- Recommendations to institutional leaders and faculty members for strategies and approaches to ensure that the next generation of faculty is appropriately prepared

To achieve these goals, we sought authors who had conducted significant studies that inform efforts to improve graduate education as well as authors who are conceptualizing and leading significant action projects. In selecting studies to include, we sought those that had gained national attention and have been frequently mentioned among stakeholders concerned about graduate education and the preparation of future faculty. In identifying strategies and programs to highlight in the volume, we also had specific criteria: programs sponsored by associations, agencies, and foundations that had the goal of making a national impact and whose leaders were interested in having their programs described. We were not able to include examples of the many good ideas that individual institutions are developing on their own.

Organization of the Book

We have organized the book in four parts. We begin with an overview chapter and conclude with a synthesis chapter. In between we provide six chapters on research and six chapters on various initiatives in doctoral education.

Part One

Part One, "Introduction," includes the first chapter, which we wrote to set the context for the book. We discuss the increased interest in issues in graduate education in recent years, four of the factors that have contributed to this interest, and specific reasons why attention to the role of graduate education in the preparation of future faculty is so important. Overall, the first chapter provides a rationale for the book's focus on the research and action projects that pertain to graduate education in preparing the future professoriate.

Part Two

Part Two of the volume, consisting of Chapters Two through Seven, is entitled "The Research." Each of the six chapters summarizes the questions and results of a recent study on graduate education and paths to the professoriate. Taken together, the findings are powerful and tend to reinforce each other, because they offer a number of parallels that have emerged from projects using different methodologies.

Part Two begins with Chapter Two, in which Chris Golde and Timothy Dore present highlights from their quantitative survey research on graduate students' perspectives about their experiences. While summarizing key results from the full study, the authors focus in this chapter on comparing the experiences of graduate students in two disciplines, English and chemistry. This comparison illustrates the importance of disciplinary context in shaping doctoral students' experiences and the nature of their preparation for the professoriate.

In Chapter Three, Donald Wulff, Ann Austin, Jody Nyquist, and Jo Sprague discuss their qualitative longitudinal research, funded by The Pew Charitable Trusts and the Spencer Foundation. This qualitative work provides a useful juxtaposition with the Golde and Dore quantitative study. The longitudinal study, taking place over four years, followed a group of doctoral students in two research universities and a group of master's students at a comprehensive institution, all of whom aspired to teaching careers in higher education. The chapter is organized around four research questions about the students' experiences and development as teaching scholars. Emphasizing that most of the participants lacked systematic, developmentally organized preparation, the chapter offers suggestions for improvement based on the study results.

In Chapter Four, Adam Fagen and Kimberly Suedkamp Wells describe a study conducted in 2000 over the Web by a national association of graduate students. Results highlight some of the areas of satisfaction with doctoral education as well as some of the same concerns voiced in the previous two studies (including problems with advising and teaching experiences). The authors also note disciplinary differences in graduate students' experiences.

James Antony and Edward Taylor, in Chapter Five, bring in the important perspective of the nature of graduate experiences for Black doctoral students. They draw on stereotype threat theory to explain the experiences of minority graduate students and offer alternative perspectives to usual theories of socialization. Their chapter is useful in drawing attention to the special challenges and barriers confronting Black students, and most likely, other graduate students of color.

In Chapter Six, Barbara Lovitts summarizes her provocative study on the reasons why students choose to leave doctoral study and the resulting implications for institutions. Because attrition from graduate education is high, her findings and recommendations are helpful to institutional leaders trying to ensure that universities and colleges will have a pool of prepared, committed faculty in the coming decades.

In the final chapter of Part Two, Maresi Nerad, Rebecca Aanerud, and Joseph Cerny draw on data from the national study *PhDs—Ten Years Later.* They discuss perceptions of graduates from six disciplines who have been in the workforce for ten to fourteen years. Using career path analysis and the retrospective evaluations of their survey respondents who reported wanting to be professors, the researchers identify implications and recommendations for enhancing the quality of graduate education for future teaching scholars.

Part Three

Part Three of the volume, "Strategies for Reform," includes Chapters Eight through Thirteen, which highlight important action projects to improve doctoral education. Most of the programs discussed in these chapters were initiated by foundations or associations to encourage institutional programs and efforts across the country; one, though initiated at a single university, has been supported by funding agencies in order to develop the program and support wide national dissemination.

In Chapter Eight, which begins Part Three, Pat Hutchings and Susan Clarke define a major national movement, the scholarship of teaching and learning, and discuss the challenges and opportunities this concept offers for graduate education. They highlight the efforts of The Carnegie Academy for the Scholarship of Teaching and Learning (CASTL) to encourage this form of scholarship, and they provide specific examples of projects organized at various universities and by scholarly associations. The chapter focuses particularly on the implications of the scholarship of teaching and learning for reform of graduate education and preparation of future faculty.

In Chapter Nine, Anne Pruitt-Logan and Jerry Gaff discuss the well-known Preparing Future Faculty Program (PFF). They explain the origins of the program, lay out the principles and components that are integral to it, offer examples from institutions and scholarly associations involved in PFF initiatives, and suggest lessons learned that others working in doctoral education might consider.

Jody Nyquist, Bettina Woodford, and Diane Rogers authored Chapter Ten on Re-envisioning the Ph.D., an initiative sponsored by The Pew Charitable Trusts and located at the University of Washington. They explain the various dimensions of the project, including the extensive ideas and concerns of multiple stakeholders that were gathered early in the program, the landmark conference that brought stakeholders together for a stimulating exchange of ideas around issues in graduate education, and the highly used Web site sponsored by the project to compile, highlight, and make easily available resources and descriptions of reform initiatives under way around the country. They also identify what they call myths, under which much of graduate education continues to operate, and offer recommendations for addressing the challenges of preparing the future professoriate.

In Chapter Eleven, Robert Weisbuch, president of the Woodrow Wilson Foundation, brings his considerable background as a scholar and professor of English to his exploration of the current state of doctoral education. He proceeds, in the main part of the chapter, to present the Woodrow Wilson Foundation's program titled the Responsive PhD Initiative. This project is designed to promote the development of new partnerships among constituencies inside and outside the academy, new paradigms to guide graduate education, new practices for teaching and service in graduate education, and the inclusion of a more diverse group of students in the ranks of graduate programs.

George Walker's Chapter Twelve presents the Carnegie Initiative on the Doctorate, another foundation-supported project designed to strengthen graduate education and prepare future faculty. This multiyear research and action project is conceived as a strategy to support departments engaged in examining and structuring their programs to prepare effectively the next generation of leaders who will be stewards—caretakers—of the disciplines.

Chapter Thirteen, the final chapter in Part Three, is by Karen Klomparens and John Beck. The authors describe Michigan State University's program for improving conflict resolution and the setting of expectations in graduate education. Sponsored in part by the Hewlett Foundation and the Fund for the Improvement of Postsecondary Education, this institutional program has created strategies for teaching graduate students and faculty members new ways to avoid and resolve conflicts that often arise in graduate education. A primary goal of the project is to disseminate conflict resolution and expectation-setting strategies to other institutions interested in improving the graduate experience and in preparing future faculty.

Part Four

Part Four of the volume consists of the concluding chapter, Chapter Fourteen. As co-editors, we summarize and compare the findings of the research studies, highlight lessons learned from the national and institutional projects, offer recommendations to institutional leaders, and provide our vision of future directions for preparing faculty for the twenty-first century.

Audience

We expect this book will be of interest to several different groups in higher education. First, for national program and project leaders who have been engaged in issues of graduate education, the volume will provide a synthesis of important information as they continue to think about how best to move forward. Second, leaders of disciplinary associations will find the information useful in thinking about their roles in the future of graduate education. Third, on campuses, academic leaders, deans of graduate schools, and faculty members who supervise, mentor, and prepare graduate students will be able to use the perspectives and lessons from these national projects in considering how to strengthen their own campus's preparation of the next generation of engaged teaching scholars. The volume also will serve as an important resource for faculty developers who work with teaching assistant (TA) and new faculty preparation programs on their campuses and deal on a daily basis with many of the issues identified.

Researchers who study higher education issues will be interested in what the volume says about the implications of changing contexts and the resulting developments in faculty roles, as well as the suggestions for important future research directions that could make a real difference in institutional efforts to prepare future faculty. Of course, a very important audience consists of graduate students who themselves are pursuing careers as faculty members. We hope they will be drawn in as they read about stories and experiences like their own. They are likely to learn about the larger context in which their graduate education occurs and strategies they can use to optimize their own paths to the professoriate.

Acknowledgments

A volume such as this one needs good ideas and quality research, for sure. For such ideas and research, we express our gratitude to the contributors. They worked with enthusiasm and graciousness in responding to our requests, and exemplified, through their hard work, their commitment to strengthening the preparation for the professoriate through enriched graduate education. Colleagues, we thank all of you for your efforts to blend the descriptions and accomplishments of your research and programs with our vision for this volume.

A book also requires countless hours devoted to organizational details, editing, proofreading, and preparing materials. For these details, we are especially indebted to three individuals. Madelle Quiring, secretary lead at the Center for Instructional

Development and Research (CIDR) at the University of Washington, was especially instrumental in the early stages of organizing the volume. She created mail merges, typed and mailed contracts, and created files to keep us organized. As the project continued, Emily Nicklett, secretary senior at CIDR, assisted with organizational details and proofreading. She was adept at holding all the details in her mind until, one by one, they were resolved. We also acknowledge the contributions of Maile Chapman, who stepped in at the last moment to make suggestions on the manuscripts, do some final proofreading, and prepare all the final documents. Finally, we thank CIDR support staff team members Patricia Hadfield, Paul Bronson, and Marc Comstock for keeping the office running and supporting Madelle, Emily, and Maile as they carried out their duties for the volume. To all of you, we express our heartfelt gratitude for your patience and contributions.

We also express particular appreciation to our colleagues Jody Nyquist and Jo Sprague, with whom we worked closely for several years on our longitudinal study of teaching scholars (discussed in Chapter Three). Many of our insights about the role of graduate education in paths to the professoriate began in the course of our many discussions about our study's data. Both Jody and Jo have contributed immensely throughout their careers to supporting teaching assistants and strengthening the preparation for their futures as teaching scholars. Thank you, Jody and Jo, for the many hours of thoughtful discussion and collaboration that have contributed to our thinking about issues of graduate education.

We thank also the graduate students with whom we each have worked throughout our years in academia, both those with whom we have collaborated on research and those who have provided us with insights about their graduate experiences. They have enriched our lives and helped us understand aspects of their own. We hope this book will provide ideas and insights that contribute, though modestly, to the preparation of the next generation of faculty. To all of you students, we express our appreciation and best wishes for success in future careers.

David Brightman also receives our thanks. As higher education editor at Jossey-Bass, he was excited about this project and supportive of it from our first meeting with him. Throughout the project, he was always available, responsive to questions, and helpful in making specific suggestions. It has been a pleasure to work with you, David.

Finally, we express gratitude to each other as colleagues. We have worked as equal partners on this book, and each of us appreciates the years of experience, dedication, thoughtfulness, and collegiality the other has brought to the collaboration. We have learned from each other and we have certainly laughed—lots—amidst the hard work done to complete the project.

DONALD H. WULFF   ANN E. AUSTIN
University of Washington   Michigan State University

About the Authors

Donald H. Wulff is director of the Center for Instructional Development and Research, assistant dean in the graduate school, and affiliate graduate faculty in the Department of Communication at the University of Washington in Seattle. In these roles, he is responsible for a centralized campus program for instructional development in which he works closely with administrators, departments, faculty, and graduate teaching assistants. He has devoted the last twenty-three years to teaching, consulting, researching, and publishing on issues of teaching and learning in higher education, with his most recent research being a collaborative study on the development of graduate students as prospective teaching scholars. He previously co-edited or co-authored four volumes on preparation of graduate students for teaching roles and one volume on instructional-faculty development. In addition, he has served in leadership positions in various national educational organizations and on editorial review boards for *Communication Education, Journal for Graduate Teaching Assistant Development, Journal of Higher Education,* and ASHE-ERIC Higher Education Reports. In 1984, he was honored with the University of Washington's Distinguished Teaching Award for his teaching in communication. Wulff received his undergraduate degree from Montana State University, his master's degree in interpersonal communication from the University of Montana, and a Ph.D. in communication from the University of Washington.

Ann E. Austin is professor in the Higher, Adult, and Lifelong Education (HALE) Program at Michigan State University. Her research and teaching focus on faculty careers, roles, and professional development; graduate education reform; the improvement of teaching and learning; and organizational change and transformation in higher education. With colleagues Jody Nyquist, Jo Sprague, and Don Wulff, she co-directed a longitudinal study of graduate students' development sponsored by The Pew Charitable Trusts and the Spencer Foundation. Currently, she is co-principal investigator of the Center for the Integration of Research, Teaching, and Learning (CIRTL), a five-year National Science Foundation–funded effort to improve teaching and learning in higher education in science, technology, engineering, and mathematics. She is the author or co-author of various articles and several books on higher education issues. In 1998, she was a Fulbright Fellow in South Africa, and she served as the 2000–01 president of the Association for the Study of Higher Education (ASHE). In 1998, she was named one of forty Young Leaders of the American Academy by *Change*. She holds degrees from Bates College (B.A., history), Syracuse University (M.S., Higher-Postsecondary Education), and the University of Michigan (M.A., American culture; Ph.D., higher education).

Rebecca Aanerud is associate director of the Center for Innovation and Research in Graduate Education (CIRGE) at the University of Washington. CIRGE undertakes studies on various aspects of graduate education, with particular emphasis on the career and family paths of Ph.D. recipients. Aanerud is also affiliate assistant professor in the Department of Women Studies, where she teaches classes on feminist theory and race theory. She has a number of publications in the field of critical race theory and whiteness studies.

James Soto Antony is associate professor in educational leadership and policy studies and adjunct associate professor in the Department of Sociology at the University of Washington. He also serves as the director of the Graduate Program in Higher Education at the University of Washington. Antony's research examines how higher education influences the socialization and professional development of college students, faculty, and staff. His work has focused on such diverse groups as undergraduates pursuing medical school aspirations, graduate students preparing for faculty careers, and assistant coaches preparing for collegiate head coaching careers. He is currently involved in a multiyear study examining the ways in which higher education and the high-tech industry work together to influence the socialization and professional development of doctoral students in a variety of fields.

John P. Beck is associate professor in the School of Labor and Industrial Relations at Michigan State University (MSU). He is currently associate director of the school, primarily in charge of two of its outreach units, the Labor Education Program and the Project on Innovative Employee Relations Systems (PIERS). In the Labor Education Program, he has taught a variety of labor union leadership courses to union groups throughout and beyond the state of Michigan; in PIERS, he has taught courses on workplace innovation and assisted with a number of joint labor-management workplace transformation efforts. Before joining the staff of MSU, Beck spent five years as the education and research director of the United Paperworkers International Union (UPIU), where he was a charter member of the national joint committee formed between the UPIU and Scott Paper. He also worked on joint program training, design, and evaluation with a number of other paper companies.

Joseph Cerny is professor of chemistry at the University of California–Berkeley. He received a B.S. in chemical engineering from the University of Mississippi in 1957, was a Fulbright Scholar at the University of Manchester, England (1957–1958), and received a Ph.D. in nuclear chemistry at Berkeley in 1961. Remaining at Berkeley, he was chair of the chemistry department (1975–1979); associate director of the Lawrence Berkeley National Laboratory and head of the Nuclear Science Division (1979–1984); provost (1986–1994); then vice chancellor for research (1994–2000) and dean of the graduate division (1985–2000). Based on his fifteen years as graduate dean, Cerny has developed a lasting interest in the evolving career patterns of recent Ph.D.'s, in academia as well as in business, government, and nonprofit venues. With his colleague, Maresi Nerad, he has conducted national surveys on the career outcomes of doctoral education for the six disciplines discussed in their chapter in this volume as well as a recently released national study of the career patterns of art history Ph.D.'s.

Susan E. Clarke is professor of political science at the University of Colorado at Boulder (CU), where she is active in research, teaching, and governance roles in political science. In addition to numerous publications on economic development and local politics, she is the editor of *Urban Affairs Review,* an elected member of the executive council of the American Political Science Association, a recipient of the APSA Women's Caucus Outstanding Mentor award, director of the Preparing Future Faculty political science program at CU, and the only political scientist named as a Carnegie Scholar. She is currently director of the Center to Advance Research and Teaching in the Social Sciences, a campuswide interdisciplinary program. During 2002–03, she was assistant vice chancellor for academic affairs, launching the Provost's Seminar on Teaching and Learning, a campuswide initiative to map, coordinate, and enhance teaching and learning activities at CU. She received her Ph.D. from the University of North Carolina at Chapel Hill.

Timothy M. Dore is assistant professor of chemistry at the University of Georgia (UGA), where he leads an active research program in bio-organic chemistry that seeks to develop new methods of studying cellular function. Dore was the co-investigator for the national Survey on Doctoral Education and Career Preparation, funded by The Pew Charitable Trusts, and co-author of *At Cross Purposes: What the Experiences of Today's Doctoral Students Reveal About Doctoral Education.* In his current position he facilitates career development workshops for doctoral students and runs a seminar series that informs undergraduate science students who aspire to the Ph.D. about opportunities available for doctorate holders and what doctoral study entails and offers practical information about choosing and applying to a program. Dore received a B.S. in chemistry from the University of North Carolina at Chapel Hill in 1990, and a Ph.D. in chemistry from Stanford University in 1998. After postdoctoral work at the Howard Hughes Medical Institute and the University of California-San Diego, he joined the faculty at the University of Georgia in 2000.

Adam P. Fagen is co-chair of the National Doctoral Program Survey and former chair of the ad hoc committee on Faculty-Student Relations for the National Association of Graduate-Professional Students (NAGPS). Having recently completed his doctorate in molecular biology and education at Harvard University, he currently works on education and workforce issues for the National Research Council's Board on Life Sciences. A graduate of Swarthmore College with a B.A. in biology and mathematics, he also holds an A.M. in molecular and cellular biology from Harvard and has been an NSF Graduate Research Fellow and NSF Graduate Teaching Fellow in K–12 Education. Fagen is interested in encouraging a more conceptual approach to introductory college-level science instruction, emphasizing the importance of a research-based approach to education, and ensuring that the training of scientists meets the needs of science and of scientists. Besides participating in graduate student advocacy for NAGPS, Fagen was president of the Harvard Graduate Student Council from 1996 to 1998. He also has participated in a number of discussions on doctoral education, including those organized by the National Research Council, the American Association for the Advancement of Science, and the Council of Graduate Schools.

Jerry G. Gaff is senior scholar at the Association of American Colleges and Universities, where he began directing the Preparing Future Faculty Program (PFF) in 1993. He is also senior consultant at the American Association for Higher Education. He has served on the faculty of four universities and has been dean of the College of Liberal Arts and acting president at Hamline University. Through his research, writing, speaking, and directing educational improvement projects, he has provided national leadership for four initiatives to improve higher education: experimental colleges in the 1960s and 1970s, faculty development in the 1970s and 1980s, general education in the 1980s and 1990s, and PFF. He earned his A.B. degree from DePauw University and his Ph.D. from Syracuse University with a specialization in social psychology.

Chris M. Golde, a senior scholar at The Carnegie Foundation for the Advancement of Teaching, became research director for the Carnegie Initiative on the Doctorate in 2001. Golde was the principal investigator of the national Survey on Doctoral Education and Career Preparation, funded by The Pew Charitable Trusts. She was co-author of the project's summary report: *At Cross Purposes: What the Experiences of Today's Doctoral Students Reveal About Doctoral Education.* While a faculty member at the University of Wisconsin and a scientist at the Wisconsin Center for Education Research, she taught in the higher education program in the Department of Educational Administration. Her research in doctoral education also explored inter- and multidisciplinary graduate education and began with her Ph.D. dissertation on doctoral student attrition. She also had an interest in fostering faculty and staff involvement in undergraduate student life. Golde received an M.A. in sociology in 1993 and a Ph.D. in education in 1996, both from Stanford University. She is a graduate of Brown University (B.A. in linguistics) and Columbia University, Teachers College (M.A. in student personnel administration).

Pat Hutchings is vice president of The Carnegie Foundation for the Advancement of Teaching. Much of her work during the last five years has focused on the scholarship of teaching and learning, a centerpiece of Carnegie's work. Hutchings has written and spoken widely on the investigation and documentation of teaching and learning. Recent publications include: *The Course Portfolio: How Faculty Can Examine Their Teaching to Advance Practice and Improve Student Learning, Opening Lines: Approaches to the Scholarship of Teaching and Learning,* and *Ethics of Inquiry: Issues in the Scholarship of Teaching and Learning.* Before beginning her work at the foundation in 1998, Hutchings served as a senior staff member at the American Association for Higher Education (AAHE), where she directed the Teaching Initiative, working with faculty and campuses to build a culture in which teaching and learning receive serious faculty attention. She was also the founding director of the AAHE Assessment Forum. Earlier, she was a faculty member and chair of the English department at Alverno College in Milwaukee, Wisconsin. Her doctorate is from the University of Iowa.

Karen L. Klomparens is dean of the graduate school and assistant provost for graduate education at Michigan State University (MSU). Earlier, she served as the associate dean for graduate student affairs in the graduate school. As dean, Klomparens oversees all aspects of graduate education at MSU, including curriculum and policy issues, the university's Distinguished Fellowship Program, and the graduate program reviews. She also serves as liaison to more than ninety graduate degree–granting units. She and John Beck have delivered workshops on setting expectations and resolving conflicts as part of this program for eight years. Klomparens is also the director (on leave) of the university's Center for Electron Optics and a professor of botany and plant pathology.

Barbara E. Lovitts is the author of *Leaving the Ivory Tower: The Causes and Consequences of Departure from Doctoral Study.* She has worked as a senior research analyst at the American Institutes for Research, associate program director of the Research in Teaching and Learning Program at the National Science Foundation, and program associate at the American Association for the Advancement of Science. She holds a Ph.D. in sociology from the University of Maryland and is currently an independent researcher.

Maresi Nerad is research associate professor in educational leadership and policy studies and associate dean in the graduate school at the University of Washington. She is also director of the Center for Innovation and Research in Graduate Education. She has spent nearly two decades working in the field of graduate education research. During her many years with the graduate school at the University of California-Berkeley, she researched the career patterns of recent Ph.D.'s in academe and in business, government, and nonprofit venues. With Joseph Cerny, she conducted national surveys described in this volume on the career outcomes of doctoral education for six disciplines as well as a recently released national study of the career patterns of art history Ph.D.'s. Her current national survey, *Social Science Ph.D.'s: Five Years Out,* funded by the Ford Foundation, focuses on the intersection of career paths and family paths of social science Ph.D. recipients. She is the author of *The Academic Kitchen: A Social History of Gender Stratification at the University of California* and numerous articles on graduate education, including "Postdoctoral Appointments and Employment Patterns of Science and Engineering Doctoral Recipients Ten-Plus Years After Ph.D. Completion," "From Rumors to Facts: Career Outcomes of English Ph.D.'s.: Results from the PhDs—Ten Years Later Study," and "Widening the Circle: Another Look at Graduate Women Students."

Jody D. Nyquist is associate dean emerita in the graduate school, senior lecturer emerita in the Department of Communication, and former director of the Center for Instructional Development and Research, at the University of Washington. Her interest in instructional communication led her to explore how one becomes a teaching scholar in higher education, and thus, to a focus on the graduate student experience. She has been principal investigator for two major grants, one from The Pew Charitable Trusts and the Spencer Foundation on the stages of TA development and another from The Pew Charitable Trusts to develop the Re-envisioning the Ph.D. Project. She has edited several volumes on TA training and has written numerous articles and a book on TA-RA development and preparation. She has served on the boards of over fifty universities, organizations, independent schools, and nonprofit agencies in the United States and lectured in universities throughout this country and in Europe, Australia, and Saudi Arabia. In 1992, she was a Fulbright Scholar in New Zealand. She has received numerous awards for her work in communication and higher education. Nyquist's undergraduate and graduate work were completed at the University of Washington, where she has been a faculty member since 1969.

Anne S. Pruitt-Logan is professor emerita in educational policy and leadership at The Ohio State University. Her forty-year career in education ranges from appointment as secondary school guidance counselor to her recently completed appointment as Scholar in Residence at the Council of Graduate Schools, where she codirected—with Jerry Gaff—the Preparing Future Faculty initiative. Along the way she achieved appointment as professor of education at Case Western Reserve University and held administrative positions at Fisk University and Albany State College in Georgia. At The Ohio State University she also served as associate dean of the graduate school, associate provost, and director of the Center for Teaching Excellence. She was on the board of trustees of both Case Western and Central State University, Ohio. She was an early contributor to the literature on equity and access issues for women and minorities in U.S. higher education, has given congressional testimony on behalf of fellowship programs for women and minorities, served on NSF's Committee on Equal Opportunities in Science and Engineering, and held lengthy consultancies with the Southern Regional Education Board and the Southern Education Foundation.

She received her bachelor's degree at Howard University and her master's degree and doctorate at Teachers College, Columbia University.

Diane L. Rogers was project manager for the Re-envisioning the Ph.D. Project at the University of Washington's graduate school. Her interest in graduate education issues evolved from her mix of experience in both academic and corporate sectors and in small colleges and institutions, where she has served as academic dean, professor, business officer, and accreditation advisor. For over fifteen years she has been involved in corporate organizational development, focusing on training and process improvement. She has consulted with for-profit and nonprofit organizations in strategic assessment, diagnosis, and implementation of transformation efforts and has taught on-line courses. In addition to an M.B.A. in management, Rogers has a Ph.D. in organizational leadership from Regent University, in Virginia Beach, Virginia. Her recent research has focused on mentoring in senior leadership positions. She is currently an organizational consultant and teaches courses in management and organizational leadership.

Jo Sprague is professor of communication studies at San Jose State University, where she has also held appointments in the Office of Faculty Affairs and the Center for Faculty Development and Support. Throughout her career, she has assumed leadership roles on campus and in professional associations. Her chapters, articles, and conference presentations have covered a range of topics related to the intersection of communication and instruction. Throughout her work with teaching assistants in communication and new faculty members across the university, her special interest has been in why people are drawn to academic careers and how their initial experiences shape their professional beliefs and practices. Her textbook, *The Speaker's Handbook,* is in the sixth edition. Along with colleague Jody Nyquist, she has published articles exploring the theoretical and research bases for a developmental perspective on the teaching assistant role. Most recently, in collaboration with Nyquist, Ann Austin, and Don Wulff, she was a senior researcher for a longitudinal study of graduate students' development sponsored by The Pew Charitable Trusts and the Spencer Foundation.

Sprague received her undergraduate degree in speech from Northern Illinois University and her M.A. and Ph.D. in communication from Purdue University.

Edward Taylor is associate professor in educational leadership and policy studies at the University of Washington, teaching in the Graduate Program in Higher Education. He is also co-director of the Center for Educational Leadership and an affiliate faculty member of the Center for Multicultural Education. He currently serves on the board of regents of Gonzaga University. Taylor's scholarly interests are in critical race theory and education policy, race identity, and the history and social context of higher education. He is the author of several articles and chapters on race and higher education. His work has been recognized internationally, recently taking him to South Africa to work with various leaders and students throughout that nation's system of education.

George E. Walker is senior scholar at The Carnegie Foundation for the Advancement of Teaching, where he directs the Carnegie Initiative on the Doctorate. During the initial period of this project (2002–2003), he continued as vice president for research and dean of the graduate school at Indiana University. Walker, who received his Ph.D. in theoretical physics from Case Institute of Technology, is a fellow of the American Physical Society and has twice received the teaching award for outstanding contributions to graduate education in the Department of Physics at Indiana University. He has served major leadership roles in the Council of Graduate Schools, the Midwest Association of Graduate Schools, the Association of American Universities-Association of Graduate Schools, the National Association of State Universities and Land-Grant Colleges, and the Council on Research Policy and Graduate Education. Improving the development of scholar-teachers in Ph.D. programs is a special emphasis of his efforts. He is a member of the advisory committees for the Responsive PhD Program and the Re-envisioning the Ph.D. Project. Through his national roles, Walker advocates the twin goals of excellence and access as necessary components in American higher education.

Robert Weisbuch is president of the Woodrow Wilson Foundation. Before joining the foundation, he spent twenty-five years at the

University of Michigan, where he served as chair of the Department of English, associate vice president for research, associate dean for faculty programs, and interim dean at the Rackham School of Graduate Studies. While dean of the graduate school he established a fund to improve the mentoring of graduate teaching assistants, created humanities and arts awards for faculty, and made diversity an integral criterion in evaluating program quality. He also headed a two-year initiative to improve undergraduate education. He is a graduate of Wesleyan University and holds his Ph.D. in English from Yale University. He has received awards for both teaching and scholarship at the University of Michigan and is the author of books on Emily Dickinson and the stormy relations between British and American authors in the nineteenth century.

Kimberly M. Suedkamp Wells is co-chair of the National Doctoral Program Survey and a doctoral student in fisheries and wildlife sciences at the University of Missouri-Columbia. She earned a B.S. in renewable natural resources at the University of Arizona and an M.S. in wildlife and fisheries ecology at Oklahoma State University. Her education research interests include women in science and engineering and assessment in graduate education. She is investigating patterns of habitat use, movements, and survival in post-fledging grassland birds in Missouri. She has been active in graduate student advocacy since starting graduate school, serving as president of the Oklahoma State Graduate and Professional Student Association (1999–2000) and later, as president of NAGPS, (2000–2001).

Bettina J. Woodford was founding program officer for the Responsive Ph.D. initiative at the Woodrow Wilson National Fellowship Foundation in Princeton, New Jersey, and the original program manager of the Re-envisioning the Ph.D. Project. She has many years' experience working at the crossroads of academia and the public, private, and nonprofit sectors. Before completing her doctorate, she worked in intercultural training and development and change management for an organizational consulting firm. With a William J. Fulbright fellowship, she conducted doctoral research on political linguistics in Barcelona, Spain. Woodford holds a Ph.D. in communication from the University of Washington and is currently a writer and higher education consultant based in Seattle.

Paths to the Professoriate

Part One

Introduction

During the last few years, the calls for reform in graduate education, and ultimately, in preparing future faculty to be more successful in meeting the needs of a changing academy and society, have come from many directions and in many forms. Chapter One analyzes the changing context in higher education that is creating new expectations for faculty work and new kinds of faculty appointments, and thus, the need for new attention to the preparation of future faculty. The chapter makes the case that graduate deans, department chairs, faculty advisors, foundation and association leaders, and graduate students themselves must be concerned with enhancing paths to the professoriate.

Chapter One

The Challenge to Prepare the Next Generation of Faculty

Ann E. Austin, Donald H. Wulff

Improving graduate education, and specifically, strengthening the preparation process for future faculty, has become a significant issue in higher education, of importance to a wide-ranging group of stakeholders. In fact, the growing interest in graduate education and the preparation of the future professoriate has been evident over the past decade and a half in an array of conferences, institutional programs, initiatives by professional organizations, funded research, and print and Web material. A quick review of such recent literature, programs, and research shows that, clearly, there is a movement afoot to address the challenges of preparing the next generation of faculty.

This volume provides a summary and synthesis of key information about this movement. Although there are valuable resources in the research literature and publications describing the activities of various associations, institutions, and organizations, there has been no comprehensive effort to bring those pieces together. This volume fills that gap by gathering in one place ideas from major research studies and action projects that have focused, over the past dozen years or so, on improving graduate education and preparing the future professoriate.

This chapter first examines factors that together have contributed to the growing interest in improving graduate education.

Employers, leaders of foundations and government agencies, graduate deans, and doctoral students have added their voices to a call for examining the quality of the graduate experience and its success in preparing students for their future roles as professionals. Then, the chapter turns to the specific interest of this book—graduate education as preparation for an academic career. We make a case for why it is critical at this moment in the history of American higher education to ensure that graduate education is appropriately preparing students who are pursuing paths to the professoriate. In this chapter, we hope to convince readers of the importance of considering strategies for enriching the preparation of future faculty.

Factors Contributing to Interest in Improving Graduate Education

We have identified four of the main factors contributing to the increased recent focus on graduate education: the teaching assistant role, the academic labor market, graduate student attrition rates, and researchers' interest in expanding conceptions of faculty career stages.

The Teaching Assistant Role

Although interest in strengthening graduate education as preparation for a faculty career has gained considerable momentum in the past two decades, signs of concern appeared much earlier. After World War II, when universities increased their emphasis on research productivity and scientific excellence, concerns emerged about both the amount of instruction left to teaching assistants, particularly in introductory courses, and the preparation of teaching assistants for providing quality education when their own education was so heavily focused on preparing them as top-flight researchers. Chase (1970) captured this concern about teaching assistants: "There is a growing awareness—spreading from within academia to interested groups outside—that there are many serious problems associated with the utilization of graduate teaching assistants in contemporary American higher education" (p. 2). Another comment during this period was even more succinct: "It is sometimes wryly noted that college teaching is the only profession requiring no formal training of its practitioners" (Nowlis, Clark, & Rock, 1968, p. iii).

In the spirit of these remarks, over the past two decades the public at large has expressed greater interest in the nature and quality of the undergraduate learning experience as well as the outcomes of that experience. Such public interest, evident in newspapers and legislatures, has contributed to growing attention on the part of university administrators to the quality of teaching provided by teaching assistants who work with large numbers of undergraduate classes.

In response to such concerns, beginning in the 1970s and continuing into the 1980s and 1990s, universities developed increasingly credible programs for preparing graduate students to teach. Originally, such programs focused primarily on initial training designed to prepare those graduate students who had immediate roles as teaching assistants (TAs). Then, over time, many institutions and departments began providing graduate teaching assistants with ongoing training that reflected the recognition that they needed different kinds of information and preparation at different times in their development as teachers.

As faculty developers and TA supervisors gave more attention to preparing teaching assistants, The Pew Charitable Trusts helped build a cross-institutional dialogue about these issues by sponsoring several national conferences on the training and employment of teaching assistants, the first occurring in 1986. Some of these conferences resulted in published proceedings (Chism & Warner, 1987; Lewis, 1993; Nyquist, Abbott, Wulff, & Sprague, 1991). During that same period, the *Journal of Graduate Teaching Assistant Development,* published by New Forums Press, was initiated and complete volumes were written specifically on the issues of TA preparation (for example, Allen & Rueter, 1990; Andrews, 1985; Marincovich, Prostko, & Stout, 1998; Nyquist, Abbott, & Wulff, 1989; Nyquist & Wulff, 1996). Simultaneously, various researchers (among them, Abbott, Wulff, & Szego, 1989; Darling & Dewey, 1989; Nyquist & Sprague, 1992, 1998; Sprague & Nyquist, 1989, 1991; Staton & Darling, 1989) also turned their attention to questions of teaching assistant development, thus contributing to an emerging research base to guide professional practice.

The network of faculty developers, TA supervisors and trainers, foundation leaders, and researchers interested in teaching assistant training and development has been a major factor in the movement to improve the graduate experience, and specifically to prepare graduate students appropriately as future faculty. Indeed, once institutions had initial and ongoing training for TAs in place, they had a base from which to expand efforts to prepare graduate students for their future careers as teachers, not only for their immediate assignments as TAs. In addition, teaching assistant conferences that were held every other year in the late 1980s and early 1990s are now incorporated into discussions and presentations about TA development specifically and preparing future faculty more broadly at many disciplinary and professional conferences.

Labor Market Issues

Besides the growing interest in TA preparation on many campuses, job market issues also emerged as a factor in graduate education. Interest in critiquing and reforming graduate education in the 1990s was likely stimulated by observations, grounded in the tight academic labor market of the 1980s and 1990s, that many doctoral graduates were not being hired into faculty positions. Faculty members and administrative leaders in universities, as well as leaders of scholarly associations and national agencies and foundations, considered what skills and abilities graduate students should master and what kinds of positions they should be prepared to take. Several important reports contributed to an emerging national discussion among relevant stakeholders—including both employers and leaders of government agencies, higher education associations, and foundations—with interests in graduate education. In particular, the Committee on Science, Engineering, and Public Policy published what was called the "COSEPUP Report" (1995), the Association of American Universities published the report of the Committee on Graduate Education (1998), and the National Science Board published a report on science and engineering graduate and postdoctoral education (1997). Then, in 2000, as part of the Re-envisioning the Ph.D. Project sponsored by The Pew Charitable Trusts, Nyquist and Woodford published their report entitled *Re-envisioning the Ph.D.: What Concerns Do We Have?* This report was based on their interviews with stakeholders involved in graduate education, including employers of recent Ph.D. graduates.

The concern was evident throughout these various reports that graduate education in its traditional form was not adequately fulfilling its responsibility to employers, not fully adapting to changing national needs, and not sufficiently preparing graduate students for the world in which they would work. Among the key themes that emerged in a number of the reports were calls for better preparation of graduate students for a range of professional career possibilities (both academic and other), more interdisciplinary work in graduate study, the inclusion of a greater diversity of students, and attention to the length of time required to complete doctoral work. In a frequently quoted sentence in their report entitled *At Cross Purposes: What the Experiences of Doctoral Students Reveal About Doctoral Education,* Golde and Dore (2001) summarized the results of their quantitative research on graduate students' views of their experience: "The data from this study show that in today's doctoral programs, there is a three-way mismatch between student goals, training, and actual careers" (p. 5). Nyquist, Austin, Sprague, and Wulff (2001) reached a similar conclusion in their qualitative study that followed graduate students over four years: "Graduate education does not match the needs and demands of the changing academy and broader society" (p. 5).

Graduate Student Attrition Rates

Another important issue fueling attention to what happens during graduate education has been the attrition rate from graduate school. Based on a thorough review of research, Lovitts (2001) noted that, since the early 1960s, the rate of attrition from doctoral programs in the United States has been estimated consistently at approximately 50 percent. Furthermore, she explained, the rate of attrition for women, while difficult to pin down, is even higher than the overall rate. Not surprisingly, such a high rate concerns academic leaders as well as others interested in the quality and impact of graduate education. Among the questions that arise are why students leave and whether the graduate experience could be changed in ways that would affect the attrition rate. In particular, higher education leaders, faculty, and researchers worry whether graduate students who are especially promising as future professors are choosing to stay or leave.

In response to such concerns and questions, researchers as well as deans and administrators in graduate programs are seeking ways to understand and address the high rate of student attrition. For example, Lovitts (2001) conducted a fascinating study that explored the reasons individuals depart from graduate school. A summary of some of the findings from that study is provided in Chapter Six. Noting such research on graduate attrition, Karen Klomparens, dean of the graduate school at Michigan State University and one of the authors in this volume, has focused on the conflicts experienced by graduate students that seem to arise fairly regularly and may contribute to decisions to leave. As illustrated by these authors who contributed to this volume, as the 1990s continued, concerns about dropout and its sources constituted one important factor contributing to the growing interest in research and programs designed to help improve the graduate experience.

Expanding Conceptions of Faculty Career Stages

The fourth factor pushing educators to reassess what was being done in graduate education was the increasing recognition of the graduate experience as a significant stage in preparation for a faculty career. Beginning in the late 1970s and continuing to the present, researchers of faculty work were realizing that the faculty career begins with the socialization process that occurs during the graduate experience. Previously, research on faculty development had conceptualized the start of the academic career as the first academic appointment. Influenced by theoretical literature on socialization, researchers such as Anderson and Seashore Louis (1991), Austin (2002a), Bess (1978), Golde and Dore (2001), Tierney and Rhoads (1994), and Weidman, Twale, and Stein (2001) turned to examination of the graduate experience as the initial career stage. Some of the research highlighted in this volume resulted in conclusions pertaining specifically to the role of graduate education as a socialization process. Of particular importance, some of this research on how graduate education functions as an initial career stage and a socialization experience has identified concerns that graduate students themselves have about the doctoral experience.

Thus, a significant body of work is now available that provides theoretical perspectives and research-based findings to inform dialogues about graduate education, efforts to improve its quality, and strategies to prepare future faculty more effectively.

In sum, a number of reasons and factors percolated decades ago, gained momentum throughout the 1980s and 1990s, and continue into the present to make the issue of the quality of graduate education, and ideas to improve or reform it, topics of considerable interest to institutional administrators, faculty members, association and foundation leaders, employers, researchers, and graduate students themselves. Calls for reform in graduate education are coming from many directions.

Graduate Education as Preparation for Academic Careers

Although graduate education prepares students for many career options, this book focuses specifically on graduate education as preparation for academic careers. The preparation of the faculty of the future is one of the most significant responsibilities of universities, requiring the best efforts of faculty members and academic leaders. Higher education in the United States is undergoing major change, often described in terms such as "revolution," "reshaping," and "cultural change," making this responsibility particularly challenging. As Yolanda Moses, former president of the American Association for Higher Education (AAHE) observed, the American higher education system is "in the throes of major transformational change" (2001, p. 7).

New faculty today are entering an academic workplace that is changing rapidly and dramatically. The forces affecting higher education are well-known: public skepticism and demands for accountability, the need for fiscal constraint, increasing public expectations for institutional involvement in economic development, the rise of the information society and new technologies, the increasing diversity of students, new kinds of educational institutions, and increasing emphasis on learning outcomes. Because of these pressures on higher education institutions and the changes within them, faculty members must be prepared with a range of abilities and skills. Although faculty members have long needed a number of these abilities and skills, the next generation of faculty must expand their preparation to include new areas of expertise in the context of the changes occurring in higher education (Austin, 2002b).

What will be expected of future faculty? The list of necessary skills and abilities highlights the need for thorough and thoughtful graduate school preparation. The next generation of faculty members must have command of a range of research abilities, appreciation for a variety of ways of knowing, and awareness of the ethical responsibilities researchers will encounter. Faced with a diverse array of students, they must understand how teaching and learning processes occur, and they must be effective teachers. They must know how to use technology in their teaching and understand the meaning and practice of engagement and service appropriate for their institutional type. Faculty members must be effective in communicating to diverse audiences, including government and foundation leaders, members of the community, parents and students, institutional leaders and colleagues. Furthermore, they must know how to work effectively, comfortably, and collaboratively with various groups both inside and outside the academy. The next generation of faculty also must understand how to be responsible institutional citizens, comprehending the challenges facing higher education and the implications of these challenges for their roles in the academy and as academics in society. Boyer (1990), for instance, in his now widely cited treatise, suggested, "for America's colleges and universities to remain vital a new vision of scholarship is required. What we are faced with, today, is the need to clarify campus missions and relate the work of the academy more directly to the realities of contemporary life" (p. 13). Others, such as Richlin (1993), who wrote about new approaches to scholarship, followed through with suggestions for helping educators think about the role of graduate education in preparing students for faculty roles in a changing academy.

The next generation of faculty members needs more than simply an expanded set of abilities and skills. These new faculty members also must be prepared for a variety of faculty appointments (Austin, 2002b; Finkelstein & Schuster, 2001; Finkelstein, Seal, & Schuster, 1998), including part-time, contract, and term appointments as well as tenure-stream and full-time appointments. In fact, scholars increasingly are appointed into term and part-time appointments rather than traditional full-time tenure-stream positions. Furthermore, although they are trained in research universities, new faculty members ultimately find employment in a range of institutional types, including community colleges, comprehensive institutions, and liberal arts colleges. The specific expectations for faculty work—including the balance of teaching, research, and service responsibilities, the kind of interactions that are customary with students, and the roles of a faculty member in the academic community and in society—vary by institutional type. A graduate student who has observed faculty work and roles in the research university should not expect this model to be the norm in other types of institutions.

It may be argued that, given the changing expectations for faculty work and the range of types of faculty positions, it is no longer adequate or appropriate for current faculty members to prepare graduate students as "clones" of themselves. Gaff, Pruitt-Logan, and Weibl (2000) suggested that, although the nineteenth-century model of graduate education grounded in German models of research and scientific discovery is widespread, "it is inadequate for the challenges confronting the professoriate of the twenty-first century." They argued that "a mismatch exists between doctoral education and the needs of colleges and universities that employ new Ph.D.'s" (p. 3).

In a recent address to a national higher education association, Austin (2002b, p. 128) summarized the challenge for those preparing the future professoriate:

> Various pressures and expectations external to and within higher education are creating a time of significant change. The changes within the academy have a direct impact on the work and lives of faculty members. New expectations require the next generation of faculty members to have a range of abilities, skills, knowledge, and understanding that goes beyond what entering faculty members typically have needed. The preparation of the next generation of faculty members cannot be "business as usual."

In addition to contextual changes that affect the nature of faculty work, there is a very practical reason for thinking seriously about the preparation of the next group of professors. Universities and colleges are moving into a period when they will be hiring in significant numbers. Finkelstein and Schuster (2001) have pointed out: "The number of retirements, and accordingly, the need for replacements, is increasing rapidly. . . . The continuing aging of the faculty—now it seems, the highest average ever—means huge numbers of retirements looming, leaving wide open the prospect for an even more rapid makeover" (p. 7).

In sum, institutions of higher education are facing new challenges and significant transformation. Faculty work is changing— the expectations, the kinds of appointments, the necessary skills and abilities. Large numbers of retirements will require extensive hiring in the near future. At the same time that the new generation of faculty members must be prepared to enter a changing context, many analysts and observers remain concerned about shortcomings in the current preparation of graduate students for their future work.

In response to these challenges facing higher education institutions and changes in faculty work, various programs and projects have been designed and supported by foundations to address issues in graduate education and improve the preparation of future faculty. Such programs include Preparing Future Faculty (PFF), which is in place at many institutions, Re-envisioning the Ph.D. (sponsored by The Pew Charitable Trusts and hosted at the University of Washington), the Responsive PhD Initiative (a program of the Woodrow Wilson Foundation), and the Carnegie Initiative on the Doctorate to create Stewards of the Discipline. In addition, as noted earlier, many universities have implemented new programs designed to prepare graduate students more successfully not only for their current teaching assistantship positions but also for their future professional roles. As evidence, the Re-envisioning the Ph.D. Web site contains a list of several hundred "Promising Practices" in place at universities committed to enhancing graduate education as preparation for future careers.

Efforts are under way to enhance the preparation of future faculty, and lessons can be learned from the efforts made to date. To continue to address the changes in the academy and the need for new faculty members, university leaders, professors, and leaders of professional associations and foundations must think practically and critically about the paths to the professoriate and strategies for enriching the preparation of future faculty. This book addresses that responsibility.

Conclusion

The thesis of this book is that, given the changing context in higher education, creative attention should be directed to the preparation of the next generation of faculty members. This book provides useful information, resources, lessons, and recommendations for academic leaders and faculty members who are committed to doing their best to prepare the future professoriate. Six chapters provide summaries of major research studies that shed light on aspects of graduate education and the experiences of graduate students, with particular attention to findings that pertain to the role of graduate education in preparing future faculty. Then, six chapters summarize major national initiatives designed to improve graduate education and enrich the preparation of the future professoriate. In the final chapter, we synthesize and compare the findings from the research studies, highlight lessons learned from initiatives to improve the preparation of aspiring faculty members, and suggest future directions of importance in this work. We hope that graduate deans, department chairs, faculty advisors, teaching assistant supervisors, instructional/faculty developers, foundation leaders, and graduate students themselves will find useful this presentation, synthesis, and analysis of the research and initiatives to enrich the preparation of future faculty.

References

Abbott, R. D., Wulff, D. H., & Szego, C. K. (1989). Review of research on TA training. In J. D. Nyquist, R. D. Abbott, & D. H. Wulff (Eds.), *Teaching assistant training in the 1990s*. New Directions for Teaching and Learning, No. 39 (pp. 111–123). San Francisco: Jossey-Bass.

Allen, R. R., & Rueter, T. (1990). *Teaching assistant strategies: An introduction to college teaching*. Dubuque, IA: Kendall/Hunt.

Anderson, M. S., & Seashore Louis, K. (1991). The changing locus of control over faculty research: From self-regulation to dispersed influence. In J. C. Smart (Ed.), *Higher education: Handbook of theory and research* (Vol. VII) (pp. 57–101). New York: Agathon.

Andrews, J.D.W. (Ed.). (1985). *Strengthening the teaching assistant faculty*. New Directions for Teaching and Learning, No. 22. San Francisco: Jossey-Bass.

Association of American Universities. (1998). *Committee on graduate education: Report and recommendations*. Washington, DC: Association of American Universities.

Austin, A. E. (2002a, January-February). Preparing the next generation of faculty: Graduate school as socialization to the academic career. *Journal of Higher Education, 73*(1), 94–122.

Austin, A. E. (2002b, Winter). Creating a bridge to the future: Preparing new faculty to face changing expectations in a shifting context. *Review of Higher Education, 26*(2), 119–144.

Bess, J. L. (1978). Anticipatory socialization of graduate students. *Research in Higher Education, 8,* 289–317.

Boyer, E. L. (1990). *Scholarship reconsidered: Priorities of the professoriate.* Princeton, NJ: The Carnegie Foundation for the Advancement of Teaching.

Chase, J. L. (1970). *Graduate teaching assistants in American universities: A review of recent trends and recommendations.* Washington, DC: U.S. Department of Health, Education and Welfare, U.S. Government Printing Office.

Chism, N.V.N., & Warner, S. B. (Eds.). (1987). *Institutional responsibilities and responses in employment and education of teaching assistants: Readings from a national conference.* Columbus: The Ohio State University, Center for Teaching Excellence.

Committee on Science, Engineering, and Public Policy (COSEPUP) of the National Academy of Sciences, The National Academy of Engineering, and the Institute of Medicine. (1995). *Reshaping the graduate education of scientists and engineers.* Washington, DC: National Academy Press.

Darling, A., & Dewey, M. (1989, November). *Becoming a teaching assistant: An examination of communication experiences with peer leaders.* Paper presented at the annual convention of the Speech Communication Association, San Francisco.

Finkelstein, M. J., & Schuster, J. H. (2001, October). Assessing the silent revolution: How changing demographics are reshaping the academic profession. *AAHE Bulletin, 54*(2), 3–7.

Finkelstein, M. J., Seal, R. J., & Schuster, J. H. (1998). *The new academic generation: A profession in transformation.* Baltimore: Johns Hopkins University Press.

Gaff, J. G., Pruitt-Logan, A. S., & Weibl, R. A. (2000). *Building the faculty we need: Colleges and universities working together.* Washington, DC: Association of American Colleges and Universities and the Council of Graduate Schools.

Golde, C. M., & Dore, T. M. (2001). *At cross purposes: What the experiences of doctoral students reveal about doctoral education.* Philadelphia: A Report for The Pew Charitable Trusts. [www.phd-survey.org]

Lewis, K. G. (Ed.). (1993). *The TA experience: Preparing for multiple roles.* Stillwater, OK: New Forums Press.

Lovitts, B. E. (2001). *Leaving the ivory tower: The causes and consequences of departure from doctoral study.* Lanham, MD: Rowman & Littlefield.

Marincovich, M., Prostko, J., & Stout, F. (1998). *The professional development of graduate teaching assistants.* Bolton, MA: Anker.

Moses, Y. T. (2001). Scanning the environment. *AAHE Bulletin, 53*(10), 7–9.

National Science Board. (1997). *The federal role in science and engineering graduate and postdoctoral education.* (NSB 97-235). Washington, DC: National Science Foundation.

Nowlis, V., Clark, K. E., & Rock, M. (1968). *The graduate student as teacher* (American Council on Education Monograph). Washington, DC: American Council on Education.

Nyquist, J. D., Abbott, R. D., & Wulff, D. H. (Eds.). (1989). *Teaching assistant training in the 1990s.* New Directions for Teaching and Learning, No. 39. San Francisco: Jossey-Bass.

Nyquist, J. D., Abbott, R. D., Wulff, D. H., & Sprague, J. (Eds.). (1991). *Preparing the professoriate of tomorrow to teach: Selected readings in TA training.* Dubuque, IA: Kendall/Hunt.

Nyquist, J. D., Austin, A. E., Sprague, J., & Wulff, D. H. (2001). *The development of graduate students as teaching scholars: A four-year longitudinal study* (Final Report, Grant #199600142). Seattle: University of Washington, Center for Instructional Development and Research.

Nyquist, J. D., & Sprague, J. (1992). Developmental stages of TAs. In J. D. Nyquist & D. H. Wulff (Eds.), *Preparing teaching assistants for instructional roles: Supervising TAs in communication* (pp. 100–113). Annandale, VA: Speech Communication Association.

Nyquist, J. D., & Sprague, J. (1998). Thinking developmentally about TAs. In M. Marincovich, J. Prostko, & F. Stout (Eds.), *The professional development of graduate teaching assistants* (pp. 61–88). Bolton: Anker.

Nyquist, J. D., & Woodford, B. J. (2000). *Re-envisioning the Ph.D.: What concerns do we have?* Seattle: University of Washington, Center for Instructional Development and Research.

Nyquist, J. D., & Wulff, D. H. (1996). *Working effectively with graduate assistants.* Thousand Oaks, CA: Sage.

Richlin, L. (Ed.). (1993). *Preparing faculty for the new conceptions of scholarship.* New Directions for Teaching and Learning, No. 54. San Francisco: Jossey-Bass.

Sprague, J., & Nyquist, J. D. (1989). TA supervision. In J. D. Nyquist, R. D. Abbott, & D. H. Wulff (Eds.), *Teaching assistant training in the 1990s.* New Directions for Teaching and Learning, No. 39 (pp. 37–53). San Francisco: Jossey-Bass.

Sprague, J., & Nyquist, J. D. (1991). A developmental perspective on the TA role. In J. D. Nyquist, R. D. Abbott, & D. H. Wulff, & J. Sprague (Eds.), *Preparing the professoriate of tomorrow to teach: Selected readings in TA training* (pp. 295–312). Dubuque, IA: Kendall/Hunt.

Staton, A. Q., & Darling, A. L. (1989). Socialization of teaching assistants. In J. D. Nyquist, R. D. Abbott, D. H. Wulff (Eds.), *Teaching assistant training in the 1990s.* New Directions for Teaching and Learning, No. 39 (pp. 15–22). San Francisco: Jossey-Bass.

Tierney, W. G., & Rhoads, R. A. (1994). *Faculty socialization as a cultural process: A mirror of institutional commitment* (ASHE-ERIC Higher Education Report No. 93–6). Washington, DC: The George Washington University, School of Education and Human Development.

Weidman, J. C., Twale, D. J., & Stein, E. L. (2001). *Socialization of graduate and professional students in higher education: A perilous passage?* (ASHE-ERIC Higher Education Report, *28*, No. 3). San Francisco: Jossey-Bass, in cooperation with the ERIC Clearinghouse on Higher Education, the Association for the Study of Higher Education, and The George Washington University.

Part Two

The Research

We have conceived this section of the volume to summarize key findings from recent important studies on graduate education as preparation for academic careers. The six studies included—each receiving national attention—have approached the issue of preparing future faculty from a variety of perspectives and methodologies. The research designs range from surveys to in-depth longitudinal qualitative studies. Each study includes student voices as a source for understanding the strengths and challenges in graduate education, but the approaches range from obtaining the early perceptions of students new to the graduate experience to collecting data on students' experiences over time and even to students' perceptions of the graduate experience ten to fourteen years after completion. Despite the range of methodologies and approaches, there are some remarkable consistencies in the findings.

Although we wanted, of course, to give the researchers as much freedom as possible in deciding how they wished to present their studies, we did request that they organize their contributions in similar formats for easier reading and comparison across chapters. Thus, all the chapters include sections on background and purposes of the research, methods, key findings, and implications in the form of specific recommendations that others working in graduate education can consider as they strive to enhance the preparation of future faculty.

Chapter Two

The Survey of Doctoral Education and Career Preparation

The Importance of Disciplinary Contexts

Chris M. Golde, Timothy M. Dore

The 1990s brought considerable attention to doctoral education. As summarized elsewhere in this volume, a number of reports and studies emerged during that period. Notable among them were *In Pursuit of the Ph.D.* (Bowen & Rudenstine, 1992), the so-called COSEPUP report (Committee on Science, Engineering, and Public Policy, 1995), and reports on doctoral education from the Association of American Universities (1998) and the National Science Board (1997). This flurry of attention, we believe, was largely spurred by changes in the academic job market. There were not only fewer tenure-track faculty jobs available than in the past but the promised wave of hiring failed to materialize. At the risk of oversimplifying, we believe that this relatively high level of attention signals a time of sustained distress and change in the doctoral education system. (Compared with other sectors of the American educational system, doctoral study attracts little attention. In the past, there have been similar flurries of attention at other periods of stress and change, including the early 1970s and the post–World War II period.)

Background and Purpose

Notably absent from the reports of the 1990s and the conferences they generated, however, was information about the actual experiences of doctoral students. We sought to remedy this gap by collecting data on the experiences of students in their programs. The Survey of Doctoral Education and Career Preparation was conducted in the summer and fall of 1999, premised on the assumption that students' experiences reveal how the system is functioning—what is working and what is not. A summary report, *At Cross Purposes: What the Experiences of Doctoral Students Reveal About Doctoral Education*, was released in January 2001 (Golde & Dore, 2001).

Rather than repeat information that is already provided in the report, this chapter delves more deeply into the questions of how well doctoral students are being prepared for faculty careers. Although students in eleven arts and sciences disciplines were surveyed, here we focus on the experiences of students in two fields that differ in interesting ways—English and chemistry. Disciplines have different cultures that influence the work faculty members do and how future faculty members are prepared.[1] Thus, explorations of doctoral preparation must take into account and build on the particularities of the various disciplines. We selected English and chemistry because both had large pools of respondents in our data and both are core liberal arts disciplines that are found on all college campuses. They also differ, as we will describe later, in the strategies they use for undertaking doctoral education. These strategies largely reflect differences in the nature of knowledge and how knowledge is produced in each discipline. Chemistry is a team-oriented, laboratory-based science in which knowledge advances incrementally through experiment. English, by contrast, is a relatively solitary scholarly pursuit that relies on writing, reading, and interpretation to illuminate the human condition. By focusing on two disciplines with differing cultures and approaches to knowledge, we emphasize that the nature of the discipline must be considered in analyzing, understanding, and seeking to improve doctoral education.

Methods

Several research questions motivated the project, and two are particularly relevant here:

- Why are doctoral students pursuing the Ph.D.?
- How effective are doctoral programs at preparing students for the careers they pursue, especially faculty careers?

We created a twenty-page survey that we sent to doctoral students at twenty-seven universities and to participants in the Compact for Faculty Diversity. We surveyed students in eleven arts and sciences disciplines. Currently enrolled doctoral students who had spent at least two complete years in their programs composed the survey sample. The resulting data set includes 4,114 completed surveys, a 42.3 percent response rate. Here we focus only on those students who said that, at some point in their careers, they desired a faculty position. Details of the methods, the disciplines, the universities, and the survey instrument can all be found at the project Web site at www.phd-survey.org.

Key Findings

Overall Results

Before delving into the differences in the preparation for faculty careers between chemistry and English doctoral students, we review the general findings of the study about faculty preparation. These data reflect the entire sample of 4,114 survey respondents, of whom 2,505 were interested in faculty careers.

Interest in Faculty Careers

We learned that, despite the decade's worth of attention to the difficulty of securing academic jobs, most arts and sciences doctoral students were primarily interested in faculty careers. Levels of interest varied by discipline, from a high of 88.7 percent in philosophy to a low of 36.3 percent in chemistry (see Table 2.1).

Not surprisingly, students in disciplines with strong connections to industry were least interested, collectively, in faculty careers. Although students believed that their goals were realistic, a third (35.4 percent) of them also reported that their interest in faculty careers had declined since the start of their programs. We attribute this decline to the clearer view of faculty life that becomes available to students when they are in graduate school.

Table 2.1. The Career Interests, Goals, and Available Resources of Doctoral Student Respondents

Variable	All Respondents (%)	English (%)	Chemistry (%)
Interested in a faculty job at any point in the future	63.0	76.7	36.3
Definite interest in faculty career as next step	47.9	66.5	19.8
Realistic to see faculty career as next step	48.2	42.7	40.4
Decline in interest in faculty career as next step since start of program	35.4	32.9	41.7
Workshop on academic job search available	57.7	82.0	49.0
Workshop on career opportunities outside academia available	45.6	50.6	49.0
Advisor would support any career path chosen	70.7	70.7	68.2
Advisor provides information on possible career paths	42.0	36.6	42.5
Interested in working at (realistic to work at):*			
Community college	3.9 (16.6)	52.1 (72.8)	6.0 (25.1)
Liberal arts college	54.3 (30.5)	98.0 (92.4)	58.5 (45.7)
Comprehensive university	43.8 (26.8)	98.2 (86.0)	34.2 (27.2)
Research university	54.1 (19.6)	84.7 (53.2)	34.5 (14.0)

Sample: Except as noted, the sample is of all students responding; all = 4,114, English = 506, chemistry = 574.

*The sample for the data reported in this part of the table included only those who indicated interest in ever being a faculty member; all = 2,505, English = 391, chemistry = 200.

Note: For items on career interests, percentages indicate those respondents saying "yes" or "definitely"; other choices were "perhaps/possibly" and "no/not at all." For items on workshops, percentages indicate those respondents saying "yes"; other choices were "no" and "don't know." For items on advisor, percentages indicate respondents saying "strongly agree" or "agree"; other choices were "disagree" and "strongly disagree." For items on institutional preferences, percentages indicate respondents saying "very much"; other choices were "somewhat" and "not at all."

Students indicated that they were motivated in their career aspirations by a love of teaching, enjoyment of research, and interest in doing service—the three traditional components of faculty work. They found college campuses appealing places to work and appreciated the lifestyle of faculty; however, the conditions of faculty work gave them pause. They found the tenure process problematic, the workload expectations onerous, the research funding difficult to obtain, and the salaries low.

Preparation for Research

The Ph.D. is a research degree, and there is little argument that doctorate recipients should be trained to conduct sound, rigorous research. Of the various aspects of faculty life, students believed themselves to be best prepared for the research roles (see Table 2.2).

Among prospective faculty, 74.2 percent of students were interested in conducting research, 71.7 percent were confident in their ability to do so, and 65.1 percent reported that they were prepared by their program to do so. Students were not well informed about all aspects of research. Publication is critical in the research process, but fewer than half the students reported being prepared by their programs to publish (42.9 percent), and slightly more (52.4 percent) were confident in their ability to do so. About half (44.7 percent) said they had the opportunity to take progressively more responsible roles in research projects. Although 61.2 percent reported a strong interest in collaborating in interdisciplinary work, only 27.1 percent said that they were prepared by their programs to do so.

Preparation for Teaching

Research is the dominant focus of the doctorate, and it defines the life of most research university faculty, but it is not the primary work activity of most faculty at American colleges. Teaching, according to the Higher Education Research Institute (1999), occupies most of a faculty member's time. On average, faculty spend most of their time on teaching—59 percent—while devoting 23 percent of their time to service and administration and 18 percent to research and scholarship (National Center for Education Statistics, 1999). Teaching is one of the most appealing aspects of faculty life, as well as its core undertaking. We found that 83.2

Table 2.2. Percentage of Doctoral Student Respondents Providing Affirmative Answers on Their Preparation for and Opportunities to Conduct Research

Variable	All Respondents (%)	English (%)	Chemistry (%)
Prepared by program to:*			
Conduct research	65.1	56.1	70.9
Publish	42.9	30.5	56.8
Collaborate in interdisciplinary research	27.1	13.1	43.7
Opportunity:			
Take progressively responsible roles in research	44.7	26.0	55.1
Present research findings at conferences	85.0	83.8	83.1
Encouraged to present at conferences	76.2	84.4	75.4

Sample: Except as noted, the sample is of all students responding; all = 4,114, English = 506, chemistry = 574.

*The sample for the data reported in this part of the table includes only those who indicated interest in ever being a faculty member; all = 2,505, English = 391, chemistry = 200.

Note: For categories labeled "prepared," percentages indicate those respondents saying "very much"; other choices were "somewhat" and "not at all." For categories labeled "opportunity," percentages indicate respondents saying "yes."

percent of the students we surveyed said enjoyment of teaching made them interested in being a professor, and many respondents expressed a deep love for teaching.

More than half (53.6 percent) of students said that their doctoral programs required them to serve as teaching assistants (see Table 2.3). It is important to recognize that such requirements might be motivated by educational concerns and a genuine desire to help students learn how to construct a course, deliver lectures, grade work fairly, and help undergraduates learn. Teaching requirements also serve as mechanisms for financial aid and provide a labor pool of junior instructors for the university. However, serving as a teaching assistant might not fully prepare students for running their own classes. Ideally, students who aspire to become faculty should take progressively more responsible roles in teaching (as many do in research), but slightly fewer than half of the students (49.8 percent) reported that such opportunities were available. Fully prepared teachers have a variety of skills in their repertoire, including advising students and teaching a variety of courses, from introductory undergraduate classes to specialized graduate seminars. Students reported being "very prepared" by their programs to lead discussion sections (57.9 percent), teach lab sections (44.7 percent of science students), and teach lecture courses (36.1 percent). These are the teaching tasks most often performed by doctoral students, so these relatively low percentages are not welcome news. Even smaller proportions of students reported being prepared by their programs to advise students, develop teaching philosophies, incorporate information technology (IT) into the classroom, and create inclusive classroom environments.

Preparation for Service

Service is usually the least respected of the three components of faculty life, and yet in many ways the continued health of American colleges depends on faculty members taking an active role in campus governance and in service beyond the borders of the campus. Students reported strong levels of interest in activities such as spending time with undergraduates outside of class (69.0 percent are interested), serving on a university governing body (52.3 percent), and providing service to the community (52.1 percent). This

Table 2.3. Percentage of Doctoral Student Respondents Providing Affirmative Answers on Their Preparation for and Opportunities to Teach

Variable	All Respondents (%)	English (%)	Chemistry (%)
Required: Teaching assistantship	53.6	59.6	83.8
Opportunity:			
Workshop-seminar on teaching in the discipline	51.2	68.3	45.7
TA training, at least one term	46.4	79.2	28.4
Take progressively responsible teaching roles	49.8	65.1	38.4
Prepared by program to:*			
Teach discussion sections	57.9	77.9	50.0
Teach lab	44.7	NA	59.8
Teach lecture courses	36.1	30.4	36.2
Create inclusive classroom climate	28.0	43.1	21.6
Advise undergraduates	26.8	24.7	32.7
Develop teaching philosophy	26.6	42.9	20.1
Teach graduate courses	23.3	17.6	22.7
Advise graduate students	16.5	12.3	23.9
Incorporate IT in class	14.1	18.6	21.7

Sample: Except as noted, the sample is of all students responding; all = 4,114, English = 506, chemistry = 574.

*The sample for the data reported in this part of the table includes only those who indicated interest in ever being a faculty member; all = 2,505, English = 391, chemistry = 200.

Note: For categories labeled "required" and "opportunity," percentages indicate those respondents saying "yes." For categories labeled "prepared," percentages indicate those respondents saying "very much"; other choices were "somewhat" and "not at all."

positive news was offset by very low proportions of respondents reporting that their programs had prepared them for service roles. Indeed, this aspect of preparation is nearly absent, so we do not discuss it further.

Preparation for Other Professional Responsibilities

The final aspect of the preparation of future faculty that we address is attention to professional responsibility. Many have argued that being a college or university faculty member requires a special commitment that demands principled behavior based on core values. These values, and the ethical choices and behaviors that flow from them, are traditionally transmitted as part of the doctoral apprenticeship experience (Kennedy, 1997; May, 1990). However, we learned that the ethical dimension of faculty and professional life—how to act responsibly and in the best interests of the profession—was not, as is often assumed, part of graduate training. As Table 2.4 indicates, the percentages of students who reported that they had a clear understanding of customary practices in specific areas was as follows: appropriate relations with undergraduates (60.7 percent), using copyrighted material (55.1 percent), generating and using research data (47.4 percent), and taking care of resources, including biosafety human subject and animal care (41.9 percent). Nevertheless, a substantial proportion of students (13 to 30 percent) reported being "not at all clear" on these day-to-day responsibilities of faculty members and researchers. In other areas, the picture was even more disturbing. When we asked them about their knowledge of using research funds appropriately, allocating authorship for papers, submitting papers for publication, and reviewing papers, only 20 to 30 percent of the students reported that they were "very clear" about customary practices.

English

We turn now to a more detailed discussion of doctoral education and the preparation of future faculty in the field of English. Thereafter, we discuss chemistry students, allowing us to conclude with some comparisons and thoughts about the implications of these data. In the discussion that follows, we draw on our extensive work on doctoral education in these fields as well as on program information in

Table 2.4. Percentage of Doctoral Student Respondents Indicating a Clear Understanding of Customary Practices

Variable	All Respondents (%)	English (%)	Chemistry (%)
Appropriate relationships with undergraduates	60.7	61.2	71.1
Use of copyrighted material	55.1	68.2	47.8
Generating and using research data	47.4	33.0	54.5
Grading student work fairly	42.0	49.8	51.4
Resource care (biosafety, human subjects)	41.9	12.8	40.1
Determining and ordering authorship on papers	26.2	24.0	30.5
Appropriate use of research funds	25.8	11.3	33.5
Refereeing academic papers fairly	22.0	13.4	23.6
Patent policies	9.6	2.1	11.7

Note: Survey choices were "very clear," "somewhat clear," and "not at all clear."

Sample: All students responding; all = 4,114, English = 506, chemistry = 574.

each field at the ten largest universities represented in the survey data. Among the respondents to the survey, 506 were studying English, with 391 (77.6 percent) interested in faculty careers. The following demographic data refer only to those interested in faculty careers, as this is the emphasis of this chapter. In regard to the gender ratio, 65.4 percent were female and 34.6 percent male (nearly the opposite of the gender ratio for chemistry). Just over half (59.3 percent) were partnered, and 16.8 percent had dependent children. There were few international students in English studies; fully 94.0 percent of the sample held U.S. citizenship. Of the U.S. citizens, 89.3 percent reported their race-ethnicity as White. The mean age of English student respondents was 32.8 years, reflecting the later start in and the longer duration of the Ph.D. program in English compared with chemistry and many other fields. Few of the English students started a doctorate straight from undergraduate study; only 16.2 percent did so compared with 63.6 percent of the chemists. In fact, over half (53.6 percent) took more than two years off; the mean pause between bachelor's end and doctoral start was 4.0 years. (By comparison, only 16.7 percent of the chemists took two or more years off, and the mean pause was 1.32 years.) About two-thirds (70.5 percent) of the respondents in English had advanced to candidacy (similar to the chemists), and the mean time of enrollment was 5.3 years.

Nature of Doctoral Study in English

Nearly 150 universities grant the doctorate in English language and literature, awarding a total of about one thousand such degrees each year. Over half are granted at the 41 universities whose programs are the largest, those granting at least ten doctorates a year (Laurence, 2002). A doctorate in English is time consuming; the National Research Council reports an average registered time to degree of ten years for the top quartile of programs (Goldberger, Maher, & Flattau, 1995). The study of English usually involves several years of specialized coursework, after which students write a book-length dissertation. (In our survey, 82.5 percent of students indicated that their dissertation would reflect work from one project, rather than several, as is the case for many science students.) Examinations of students are often canonical, with students expected to demonstrate mastery of "Beowulf to Virginia Woolf." After graduation a dissertation is rewritten and (ideally) published as a book by a university press. During the dissertation stage, the life of the English Ph.D. student is fairly solitary, involving library work, thinking, and writing. Among the survey respondents in English, 69.7 percent indicated that their dissertation research was conducted individually, whereas 28.9 percent said their research was done in close collaboration with a faculty member; 95.0 percent said the library was the primary setting for their work. This is noteworthy when compared with the experience of the chemists.

Graduate studies are typically funded by a combination of fellowships and teaching assistantships. English Ph.D. students also often take out loans and graduate with significant debt (Hoffer et al., 2002). Because summers are generally unfunded, students often interrupt their studies to earn money. The reliance of English programs on the teaching assistantship for funding students (in doctoral granting departments 35 percent of undergraduate course sections are taught by graduate students [Laurence, 2001]) has resulted in many departments developing elaborate teaching preparation strategies and sequenced teaching opportunities in which students become increasingly independent instructors. A 1986 survey of doctoral programs showed that 76 percent offered courses in teaching methods (Huber, 1989).

Doctoral study in English is almost entirely geared to the preparation of future faculty. Although many Ph.D. holders work outside of academia, even the possibility of creating the demand for nonacademic positions has been controversial (Leatherman & Wilson, 1998). The phrase "job crisis" is bandied about in English departments, and for good reason. Data from the Modern Language Association (MLA) show that the proportion of new Ph.D. recipients getting tenure-track positions immediately upon receipt of the Ph.D. (English graduates do not do postdoctoral fellowships) was 43 percent in 1977, peaked at 54 percent in 1992, and tapered to 36 percent in 1997 (Laurence, 2002). The rates of attrition are notoriously high in English, as in most humanities, in part because time to degree is long, leading one scholar to compute that his department must admit six students to produce one tenured faculty member (Scholes, 1998).[2]

Interest in Faculty Careers

The data from our survey bear out the perception of graduate study in English as geared primarily to the preparation of new faculty members. Of the respondents in English, 82 percent said that their departments offer workshops on the academic job search (see Table 2.1). Half of the respondents said that their departments offer help in finding nonacademic positions, and 70 percent said that their advisors would support any career path that they chose. The departmental culture reinforces students' desire for faculty positions. Two-thirds to three-quarters (depending on how the question is asked) of English studies students desired a faculty position. About 43 percent saw this career path as realistic, and almost 33 percent reported that their interest in a faculty career had declined since they enrolled. These data reflect a remarkably accurate assessment of the job market for English Ph.D. holders, since about 60 percent ultimately can expect to land tenure-track positions (MLA Ad Hoc Committee on the Professionalization of PhDs, 2002; Nerad & Cerny, 2000); about 85 percent are hired in college teaching positions upon graduation, although only half of those are tenure-track positions (MLA, 2003).

When those interested in faculty positions were asked about which kinds of institutions they wanted to work in and which career paths they thought were realistic, their responses to these two questions differed, but not markedly. Liberal arts and comprehensive colleges were the overwhelming preference, revealing a clear emphasis on and desire to teach, as these are teaching-intensive institutions. Even community colleges—in which only 4 percent of the survey respondents, overall, expressed an interest—were deemed a "very strong" preference by 52.1 percent of the English students. Furthermore, when assessing their chances of employment at a particular type of institution, very high proportions of English students interested in an academic career felt they had realistic employment possibilities in liberal arts colleges and comprehensive universities, and to a slightly lesser extent, community colleges. Half thought it realistic that they would obtain a position at a research university. Again, this shows a remarkable savvy or perhaps fortuitous sorting of the graduate students as a group: federal data show that tenure-track English faculty are distributed 32 percent each at doctoral and master's granting institutions, respectively, 13 percent at baccalaureate granting colleges, and 23 percent at community colleges (National Center for Education Statistics, 1999).

Preparation for Research

Inquiry in English is often referred to as "scholarship" rather than "research." It tends to be based on analysis of texts or the use of texts, and is more a matter of understanding and interpretation than discovery. It is relatively rare for students to apprentice to faculty members (this is typical in the humanities and very different from the sciences). The data (see Table 2.2) bear out this observation; only a quarter of the respondents reported the opportunity in their programs to take progressively more responsible roles in research. Scholarly work (like experimental research) is presented at conferences and then published. Most of the students were encouraged to present, but fewer than a third said that their programs had prepared them to publish work. And only a small proportion (13 percent) felt that they were prepared to participate in interdisciplinary research collaborations, although over half were interested in doing so (53.9 percent).

Preparation for Teaching

It is in the preparation of future faculty members as teachers that English excels compared with other disciplines; the structures and opportunities seemed to be in place for most of the students we surveyed. Of the eleven fields in the study, workshops or seminars on teaching in the discipline were most common in English (68.3 percent of the respondents in English said that the opportunity was available). Furthermore, 80 percent of the English respondents said that there was a teaching assistant (TA) training course lasting at least a term. Even more encouraging, two-thirds said that they had the opportunity to take progressively more responsible roles in teaching.

The results of these opportunities and requirements can be seen in the data (Table 2.3). Of those interested in faculty careers, relatively high proportions believed that their programs had prepared them for many of the tasks and roles of teaching. In particular, a high proportion of English students said that they were prepared to lead discussion sections and small seminar-style composition and literature courses, which is what most English TAs do. Nearly half felt prepared to create an inclusive classroom environment and to develop a teaching philosophy—neither of which are skills that the student population as a whole (particularly the science students) felt competent in. Nevertheless, teaching graduate courses, advising students, and using instructional technology in the classroom were still areas in which most students did not feel prepared.

Preparation for Other Professional Responsibilities

The ethical dimensions of academic life, whether conducted by students or faculty members, seem from our data (see Table 2.4) to be too often neglected as part of the doctoral preparation process. To the extent that the majority of students felt that they clearly understood customary practices, it was generally in areas that were covered in written policy and in areas that they might confront in their lives as students. The future ethical dilemmas that they will face as faculty members seem not to be part of the conversation during doctoral preparation. In English, the three most clearly understood domains are appropriate relations with undergraduates, appropriate use of copyrighted material, and grading student work fairly. Three domains that seem outside the ken of students in English are the use of research funds, resource care, and patent policies. It may be said that these are beyond the realm of expertise of most English faculty members, but as members of the larger institutional community they will probably be called upon to help craft policy in these arenas. Of concern is that few students seem to understand clearly the practices for refereeing papers for publication or determining the authorship order on co-authored papers. Perhaps the relative rarity of co-authorship in English studies explains this finding.

Chemistry

There were responses from 574 chemists, 200 (34.8 percent) of whom were interested in faculty careers. Of the "faculty-oriented" chemistry students, 35.9 percent were female (nearly the opposite composition of the English respondents), 46.4 percent reported that they were partnered, and 9.3 percent had children. The survey was overrepresentative of U.S. citizens relative to the overall population of chemistry Ph.D. recipients (Hoffer et al., 2002); 81.8 percent of the chemists were domestic students. Again, at somewhat higher proportions than the overall chemistry doctoral population, of the U.S. citizens, 91.8 percent described themselves as White. The mean age of the students was 28.4 years (somewhat younger than their English counterparts), the mean duration of enrollment was 4.3 years (one year shorter than the English students), and 80.0 percent had advanced to candidacy.

Nature of Doctoral Study in Chemistry

Chemistry is widely considered a central science, bridging the gap between the physical and biological sciences, and doctoral study in chemistry is geared toward the preparation of laboratory scientists. Although 190 departments in the United States grant the doctorate, the thirty largest programs produce about half the graduates. The average size of chemistry departments is eighty-four students and twenty-two faculty. There are about two thousand Ph.D.'s conferred each year, and about half of the graduates take postdoctoral positions following graduation. Most Ph.D. chemists work in industry, not academia: nearly 60 percent in industry, a third in academia, and about 5 percent in government (American Chemical Society [ACS], 2002a).

Graduate work in chemistry takes an average of 6.29 years in the highest-ranked departments (Goldberger et al., 1995). Students generally complete coursework in their first year or two of study by taking survey courses (ACS, 1997). An ACS survey of students showed that many believe that they would have benefited from additional coursework, especially outside their areas of specialization or outside their departments (ACS, 1999). Principally, doctoral students spend most of their time working in laboratories under the direction of their research advisors. (In our survey, 96.2 percent of chemists reported that they did their dissertation research in labs.) After the first year, students continue to learn in more informal settings: seminars, journal clubs, lab meetings, and during proposal writing. Their studies are usually funded in the first year by teaching assistantships and in the remaining years by research assistantships that come from their advisors' research grants or a program's training grant. Some select students are able to obtain fellowships from government agencies (National Science Foundation, National Institutes of Health, and so on) or private foundations.

Life in the laboratory defines the experience of graduate students in chemistry—they spend most of their time there working on research experiments. It is impossible to distinguish between the research conducted by the student as a research assistant and her own research; they are one and the same. (Again, the contrast with English is illustrative: 43.2 percent of the chemistry students agreed or strongly agreed that their dissertation topics were of their own choosing, compared with 95.6 percent of those in English.) The dissertation is usually composed of a collection of related research projects conducted by the student and written as a series of papers already in the publication pipeline with a synthesizing chapter. (In our survey, 70.5 percent of students reported that the dissertation would include work from several projects.) Students often felt dependent on the advisor, who was frequently the sole determiner of when a student had completed sufficient experimental work to graduate.[3]

Interest in Faculty Careers

When asked if they were considering a faculty job at any point in the future, 36.3 percent of the chemistry students in our survey answered in the affirmative, which represents the lowest level of interest in the eleven disciplines we studied (see Table 2.1). Interestingly, a slightly higher percentage (40.4 percent) believed that a faculty career was realistic, yet 41.7 percent reported that their interest in a faculty career declined while in graduate school. An even smaller number (19.8 percent) of respondents indicated that they had a definite interest in a faculty position as a next step. The low level of interest in a faculty career compared with other disciplines is probably attributable to the wide range of research careers available to chemists in industry and government. Indeed, 57.1 percent of Ph.D. chemists under the age of forty work in industry, while 34.7 percent and 5.4 percent work in academia and government, respectively (ACS, 2002a). The nonacademic career track seemed to be supported; two-thirds of students believed that their advisors would support any career path they chose.

Despite popular wisdom, survey respondents in chemistry who were considering a faculty career were not primarily interested in a faculty position at a research university. Fully 58.5 percent had a very strong preference for teaching at a four-year liberal arts college; 34.5 percent and 34.2 percent indicated a strong preference for working at a research university and at a comprehensive university, respectively. Although the distribution of preferences for working at research and comprehensive universities mirrors the distribution of tenure-track faculty (37 percent and 35 percent, respectively), only 14 percent of faculty are at bachelor's granting colleges, so this aspiration is unrealistic (National Center for Education Statistics, 1999). Although the data revealed no statistical gender difference in considering a faculty career, of those who were considering a faculty career, women were less likely to be interested in positions at large research universities than their male counterparts.

Preparation for Research

Doctoral students in chemistry usually work on research projects as part of a team with a common, broad research goal. The team is composed of other graduate students, postdoctoral associates, technicians, and faculty members at the same or other departments and institutions. (In our survey, 35.0 percent of the chemists said their research was conducted as part of a group of more than twelve people, and another 44.4 percent as part of a smaller group. By contrast, only 1.4 percent of the English students said they were part of a small research group, and none were part of a large one.) Overall, 70.9 percent of the chemistry students felt their programs were preparing them to conduct research; 83.1 percent of the respondents had the opportunity to present their research at conferences; and 75.4 percent were encouraged to do so. A good research program should place increasingly more responsible roles on the student over time, yet only 55.1 percent reported that this was the case for them. Other aspects of research appear to be shortchanged as well; 56.8 percent felt prepared to publish, and 43.7 percent believed their programs prepared them to collaborate in interdisciplinary research (see Table 2.2). Considering how much influence chemistry has on other disciplines and the prevailing sentiment that the most interesting research problems are found at the interface between disciplines, we find the low level of preparation to conduct interdisciplinary research disappointing.

Preparation for Teaching

Teaching requirements are more common in science fields, chemistry in particular (83.8 percent reported that a teaching assistantship was required; see Table 2.3), than in other disciplines. Ideally, students who aspire to become faculty should take progressively more responsible roles in teaching (much as many do in research), yet only 38.4 percent of the survey respondents reported that this was the case. Further, 45.7 percent reported that a workshop on teaching in chemistry was available to them, but only 28.4 percent said that they could take a teaching assistant training course, lasting at least one term. So although chemistry students serve as teaching assistants, usually in introductory lab courses, most of them do not have access to the broad scope of teaching-related training and experiences available to students in fields such as English.

Chemistry students believed themselves to be best prepared to teach discussion sections (50 percent reported being "very prepared"; see Table 2.3) and laboratory sections (about 60 percent). Nevertheless, the lack of pedagogical preparation is borne out in the low levels of perceived preparation for various activities, such as teaching lecture courses (36.2 percent reported being "very prepared"), creating inclusive classroom environments (21.6 percent), developing teaching philosophies (20.1 percent), teaching graduate students (22.7 percent), and incorporating instructional technology in the classroom (21.7 percent). Respondents also reported low levels of preparation to advise undergraduates (32.7 percent reported being "very prepared") and graduate students (23.9 percent).

Preparation for Other Professional Responsibilities

In chemistry, students had a clear understanding of the issues that confront graduate students regularly or that were codified in written policy (see Table 2.4). Respondents reported that they had a clear understanding of what constitutes an appropriate relationship with undergraduates (71.1 percent indicated a "very clear" understanding). However, they were less certain about some issues that chemistry graduate students will face at some point in their programs: the appropriate use of copyrighted materials (47.8 percent indicated a "very clear" understanding), generating and using research data (54.5 percent), grading student work fairly (51.4 percent), and care of resources, including biosafety and human subjects (40.1 percent). The low level of reported preparation in the area of resource care might be due to the fact that it is relatively unusual for chemists to work with human subjects during the course of their dissertation research. Nevertheless, the rising influence of chemistry in the biological disciplines makes understanding biosafety issues a matter of some importance. Issues more likely to face them after they have received the doctorate were quite unclear to most of the sample: determining authorship on papers (only 30.5 percent of the respondents in chemistry indicated a "very clear" understanding), appropriate use of research funds (33.5 percent felt "very clear"), refereeing papers (23.6 percent), and patent policies (11.7 percent). This last finding is of some concern because as many universities elect to license technology developed by faculty members, it is increasingly important for faculty to understand the ethical issues surrounding the interface between the academic and commercial research enterprises.

Comparisons Between English and Chemistry

Doctoral education is a highly individualized enterprise; no two students have the same goals and experiences. Looking at our data aggregated by discipline masks the range of experiences among students in the same program and hides important institutional variations. Nevertheless, comparisons between English and chemistry reveal some overall differences in the preparation of graduate students for faculty careers. Although we cannot make definitive claims, here we highlight some of those differences and speculate about the sources of those differences, which we believe are rooted in the different histories and norms for doctoral education embodied in these two fields of study.

A faculty career is the normative and desired career path for English graduate students, but it is not for chemistry students. A very high proportion of English students desire and expect such a career, and many English departments are (students say) geared to help them find academic careers. Multiple career paths are open to chemists, and we attribute this pattern to the historically strong connections between the chemical sciences industry and doctorate production, the likes of which are not apparent in English. Data from the disciplinary societies make this evident: only a third of Ph.D.-holding chemists work in academia (ACS, 2002a) and there is detailed information available about the work done by industrial chemists (ACS, 2001b), whereas 80 percent of new Ph.D. recipients in English find permanent or temporary college-level teaching positions in the first year (MLA, 2003).

Of those chemistry and English students interested in faculty careers, far greater proportions of English students said that they were interested in and believed that it is realistic to work at every type of college than their counterparts in chemistry. In some measure, this finding is likely a simple reflection that students in English desperately want to work as faculty members and are clearly willing to work in any setting to do so. Chemistry students, in contrast, are most interested in liberal arts college settings. Both chemistry and English students recognize that, if they are interested in faculty careers, the community college setting is a fruitful one—more students in each field see work in a community college as a realistic outcome than perceive it as desirable. This perception is, we believe, a fairly accurate read of the academic job market. One-third of faculty positions are at research universities; many more are in comprehensive and community colleges (National Center for Education Statistics, 1999). Another, not necessarily competing, explanation for the higher levels of interest in nonresearch institutions is that the socialization of doctoral students into the climate of research and scholarship in the discipline—socialization that is carried out at research universities—may have failed.

The survey did not focus as much attention on the component skills of research as it did on teaching. Nevertheless, we see that, at least in the terms that we set forth, chemistry students as a group, when compared with English doctoral students, perceive that they are better prepared to conduct and share research and scholarly findings. The nature of the research and scholarly enterprise is different in the two fields. In chemistry, knowledge is advanced incrementally by experiment and quickly published in scientific journals, whereas scholarship in English is about acts of interpretation and analytic application, more than discovery, and it is more frequently published in books rather than in time-sensitive journal articles (Donald, 2002; Greenblatt, 2002). Moreover, the research enterprise is funded by research grants from federal and industry sources in chemistry, but is often not funded at all in English. In turn, chemists are trained in labs, working on an advisor's research, whereas English students rarely have the opportunity to support a faculty member's scholarship or work collaboratively on a project (see Donald, 2002, Chapters Four and Eight; and the Carnegie essays by Kwiram, 2003, and Lunsford, 2003). These differences in disciplinary work help explain why so few English student survey respondents, compared with their chemistry counterparts, reported having the opportunity to take progressively more responsible roles in research, and likewise, why so few had any experience with interdisciplinary collaboration.

Although the survey data do not initially suggest this, we know from the program descriptions we have reviewed that students in English teach more than their counterparts in chemistry. In fact, we suspect that the higher prevalence of teaching assistantship requirements in chemistry reflects an effort on the part of educators to provide a small sample of teaching to graduate students who might never have such an opportunity otherwise. It might also reflect a need to ensure a flow of lab assistants for undergraduate chemistry courses. By all other measures in the survey, English students are able to participate in much more in-depth pedagogical preparation than students in chemistry. And as the students reflected in assessing their level of preparation, more English students felt better prepared in more teaching-related tasks than the chemists. However, we caution that, overall, both groups of students seemed unprepared in many areas.

Finally, when we look at the professional responsibility dimensions of faculty work, we see that students in chemistry had more often reached some clear understanding of how to comport themselves and how to proceed in the face of ethical dilemmas. We have two possible explanations for this finding. On the one hand, it is possible that the questions we posed were more salient for science students and that chemists have simply had to confront more of these issues. On the other hand, it is possible that, through forms of apprentice-master learning, more students in chemistry have had conversations about these issues in their programs and with their advisors. The tremendous difference in levels of contact between students and advisors in chemistry compared with English might yield, in this case, the positive outcome of conversations about faculty life.

Implications and Recommendations

These data show that there are strong connections between the nature of the research enterprise, the normative forms of doctoral education in each discipline, and the strengths and weaknesses of faculty preparation in each discipline. When it comes to recruiting talented students into faculty careers, more active recruitment into the professoriate may be needed in chemistry (women and ethnic minorities are underrepresented in both graduate programs and the professoriate [ACS, 2000, 2001a]). In English, the nonacademic vistas need to come into sharper focus. The centrality of research in chemistry students' lives, without competition from other activities, combined with the close working relationships between students and advisors, means that chemists feel better prepared for the activities of research and publication than English students do. Conversely, the importance that teaching plays for students in English, reflected in the broad range of courses taken and the amount of teaching done by students, results in stronger preparation for teaching activities, particularly in such areas as developing a teaching philosophy and creating an inclusive classroom environment. These findings reinforce for us the importance of thinking in discipline-specific ways in all matters related to doctoral education—in this case, the preparation of new faculty. The nature of doctoral education differs among disciplines, and not surprisingly, the preparation of new faculty also differs among disciplines.

Recognizing the need for making changes in the preparation of future faculty is, of course, only the first step. The responsibility for changing current practices—to prepare future faculty better and to improve doctoral education more broadly—lies with all the parties engaged in doctoral education. Suggestions are as follows:

- *Students can initiate and argue for change.* They should not hesitate to advocate for themselves. They must take responsibility for educating themselves about the academic profession and seek out experiences that provide them with mentored learning opportunities.
- *Faculty members can reflect on how they conduct themselves and what they communicate to students about the academic profession.* They have a responsibility to discuss openly and explicitly the choices they have made in their careers, as well as the daily professional decisions that they make.
- *Department chairs and directors of graduate study can ensure that realistic career outcomes are presented at all stages of the process* and that opportunities to prepare for faculty careers at all kinds of institutions are available and valued.

- *Graduate deans can create policy, advocate with conviction, and provide resources aimed to catalyze change and support others.* Indeed, many have supported Preparing Future Faculty programs and helped them gain an institutional foothold.
- *Professional associations can help shift the norms of practice in the discipline* by raising questions about how future faculty are prepared, collecting data on job placement and job requirements, and showcasing promising practices in the preparation of future faculty for the discipline.

Conclusion

We must emphasize again that compensatory strategies—both preparing future faculty and new faculty orientation programs—need to take disciplinary differences into account. For example, teaching development programs may be more important for chemists, whereas help navigating the publication process may be more pressing for English scholars. Cookie-cutter, one-size-fits-all policy responses are unlikely to be as effective as tailored efforts. Many programs, as described elsewhere in this volume, have taken this insight to heart. Current Preparing Future Faculty efforts, for example, are often centered in departments and emphasize aspects of faculty roles that have not traditionally been addressed. We offer the data from this survey, including the data from the disciplines we were unable to discuss in this chapter, as evidence for the need to craft interventions that are sensitive to the disciplinary contexts at which they are aimed.

Acknowledgments
This research was supported by a grant from The Pew Charitable Trusts. We thank Amita Chudgar and Jenifer Viencek, graduate research assistants who contributed to this effort, and Alexander C. McCormick and Mary T. Huber for their help with background data.

Notes
1.   For more on disciplinary cultures see Becher & Trowler (2001), Clark (1997), Donald (2002), and Huber & Morreale (2002).
2.   Additional information about doctoral studies in English and data about job placement are available in *The Future of Doctoral Studies in English* (Lunsford, Moglen, & Slevin, 1989), *Refiguring the Ph.D. in*

English Studies (North et al., 2000), the *Conference on the Future of Doctoral Education* (Conference on the Future of Doctoral Education, 1999), the Carnegie Essays on the Doctorate in English (Graff, 2003; Lunsford, 2003), and the *ADE Bulletin* from the Association of Departments of English, part of the MLA (2003).

3. Additional information about doctoral studies in chemistry and the job market for chemists can be found in the Carnegie Essays on the Doctorate in Chemistry (Breslow, 2003; Kwiram, 2003; Stacy, 2003), and the surveys and reports of the American Chemical Society, particularly a compilation of several studies entitled *Graduate Education in Chemistry. The ACS Committee on Professional Training: Surveys of Programs and Participants* (ACS, 2002b).

References

American Chemical Society. (1997). *Survey of Ph.D. programs in chemistry.* Washington, DC: American Chemical Society, Committee on Professional Training.

American Chemical Society. (1999). *Survey of Ph.D. recipients in chemistry: Part 1. Statistical analysis.* Washington, DC: American Chemical Society, Committee on Professional Training.

American Chemical Society. (2000). *Women chemists 2000.* Washington, DC: American Chemical Society.

American Chemical Society. (2001a). *Academic chemists 2000. A decade of change: 1990–2000.* Washington, DC: American Chemical Society.

American Chemical Society. (2001b). *ChemCensus 2000.* Washington, DC: American Chemical Society.

American Chemical Society. (2002a). *Early careers of chemists.* Washington, DC: American Chemical Society.

American Chemical Society. (2002b). *Graduate education in chemistry. The ACS committee on professional training: Surveys of programs and participants.* Washington, DC: American Chemical Society, Committee on Professional Training.

Association of American Universities. (1998). *Committee on graduate education: Report and recommendations.* Washington, DC: Association of American Universities.

Becher, T., & Trowler, P. R. (2001). *Academic tribes and territories: Intellectual enquiry and the culture of disciplines* (2nd ed.). Buckingham, United Kingdom: The Society for Research into Higher Education & Open University Press.

Bowen, W. G., & Rudenstine, N. L. (1992). *In pursuit of the Ph.D.* Princeton, NJ: Princeton University Press.

Breslow, R. (2003). *The doctorate in chemistry.* Menlo Park, CA: The Carnegie Foundation for the Advancement of Teaching.

Clark, B. R. (1997). Small worlds, different worlds: The uniquenesses and troubles of American academic professionals. *Daedelus, 126*(4), 21–42.

Committee on Science, Engineering, and Public Policy (COSEPUP) of the National Academy of Sciences, The National Academy of Engineering, and the Institute of Medicine. (1995). *Reshaping the graduate education of scientists and engineers.* Washington, DC: National Academy Press.

Conference on the Future of Doctoral Education. (1999). *PMLA, 115*(5), 1137–1278.

Donald, J. G. (2002). *Learning to think: Disciplinary perspectives.* San Francisco: Jossey-Bass.

Goldberger, M., Maher, B. A., & Flattau, P. E. (Eds.). (1995). *Research-doctorate programs in the United States: Continuity and change.* Washington, DC: National Academy Press.

Golde, C. M., & Dore, T. M. (2001). *At cross purposes: What the experiences of doctoral students reveal about doctoral education.* Philadelphia: A Report for The Pew Charitable Trusts. [www.phd-survey.org]

Graff, G. (2003). *The Ph.D. in English: Toward a new consensus.* Menlo Park, CA: The Carnegie Foundation for the Advancement of Teaching.

Greenblatt, S. (2002). *Letter circulated on behalf of the MLA executive council.* New York: Modern Language Association of America.

Higher Education Research Institute. (1999). *The American college teacher: National norms for the 1998–99 HERI faculty survey.* Los Angeles: University of California, Los Angeles.

Hoffer, T. B., Dugoni, B. L., Sanderson, A. R., Sederstrom, S., Welch, V., Guzman-Barron, I., et al. (2002). *Doctorate recipients from United States universities: Summary report 2001.* Chicago: National Opinion Research Center.

Huber, B. (1989). A report on the 1986 survey of English doctoral programs in writing and literature. In A. Lunsford, H. Moglen, & J. F. Slevin (Eds.), *The future of doctoral studies in English* (pp. 121–175). New York: Modern Language Association.

Huber, M. T., & Morreale, S. P. (Eds.). (2002). *Disciplinary styles in the scholarship of teaching and learning: Exploring common ground.* Washington, DC: American Association for Higher Education and The Carnegie Foundation for the Advancement of Teaching.

Kennedy, D. (1997). *Academic duty.* Cambridge, MA: Harvard University Press.

Kwiram, A. L. (2003). *Reflections on doctoral education in chemistry.* Menlo Park, CA: The Carnegie Foundation for the Advancement of Teaching.

Laurence, D. (2001). The 1999 MLA survey of staffing in English and foreign language departments. *Profession 2001,* pp. 211–224.

Laurence, D. (2002, Spring). Count of listings in the October 2001 MLA job information list. *ADE Bulletin, 131,* 3–11.

Leatherman, C., & Wilson, R. (1998, December 18). Embittered by a bleak job market, graduate students take on the MLA. *Chronicle of Higher Education,* p. A10.

Lunsford, A. A. (2003). *Rethinking the Ph.D. in English.* Menlo Park, CA: The Carnegie Foundation for the Advancement of Teaching.

Lunsford, A., Moglen, H., & Slevin, J. F. (Eds.). (1989). *The future of doctoral studies in English.* New York: Modern Language Association of America.

May, W. W. (Ed.). (1990). *Ethics and higher education.* New York: Macmillan.

MLA Ad Hoc Committee on the Professionalization of PhDs. (2002). Professionalization in perspective. *Profession 2002,* pp. 187–210.

Modern Language Association. (2003). 2000–01 survey of Ph.D. placement. *ADE Bulletin.*

National Center for Education Statistics. (1999). *1999 national study of postsecondary faculty, data analysis system.* Washington, DC: U.S. Department of Education.

National Science Board. (1997). *The federal role in science and engineering graduate and postdoctoral education.* Washington, DC: National Science Foundation.

Nerad, M., & Cerny, J. (2000, Winter). From rumors to facts: Career outcomes of English PhDs: Results from the *PhDs—Ten years later* study. *ADE Bulletin, 124,* 43–55

North, S., Chepaitis, B. A., Coogan, D., Davidson, L., MacLean, R., Parrish, C. L., et al. (Eds.). (2000). *Refiguring the Ph.D. in English studies. Writing, doctoral education, and the fusion-based curriculum.* Urbana, IL: National Council of Teachers of English.

Scholes, R. (1998, Winter). The Ph.D. situation. *ADE Bulletin, 121,* 9–15.

Stacy, A. M. (2003). *Training future leaders.* Menlo Park, CA: The Carnegie Foundation for the Advancement of Teaching.

Chapter Three

The Development of Graduate Students as Teaching Scholars
A Four-Year Longitudinal Study

Donald H. Wulff, Ann E. Austin, Jody D. Nyquist, Jo Sprague

Since the mid-1980s, institutions of higher education have engaged in renewed public dialogue about preparing graduate students for their instructional roles, both as teaching assistants (TAs) during their graduate study and as future college or university instructors. Although individual departments and a few disciplinary association meetings focused on this topic before, the issue was not the subject of sustained interinstitutional attention until the first national conference on the training and employment of TAs at The Ohio State University in 1986. Since then, the issues have been very much a part of the discussions across institutions in higher education. The 1986 conference and subsequent conferences every two or three years for the next decade—along with meetings, initiatives, and publications supported by faculty and TA developers, campus administrators, professional associations, and funding agencies— brought increased attention to the preparation of future faculty.

During the conferences and other activities, conceptualization of the issues became increasingly sophisticated, focusing on the complex interplay of organizational, economic, teaching, and developmental factors that characterized the transition from graduate student to junior faculty member. However, there was little systematic research to help us understand how the graduate TA experience contributes to the emergence of professors, especially over time, as students proceed through their graduate programs. We conceived the four-year Longitudinal Study of the Development of Graduate Students as Teaching Scholars to address this need.

Background and Purpose

The study was a qualitative research project spanning four years of the participating graduate students' experiences. We based it on the premise that in order to prepare professors, we need insights about the changes that graduate students aspiring to the professoriate undergo during their graduate years, the ways their experiences contribute to their development as teaching scholars, and the kinds of training that can best prepare them for their careers as knowledgeable, competent instructors.

Our initial interest in the study was prompted partially by the many calls for reform in the quality of college and university teaching—from the critical reports of the early 1980s[1] to harsh criticism in the popular press[2] and the public dissatisfaction that led to legislative intervention in some states. Among the forces driving concerns for the quality of college teaching were economic retrenchment; a student population whose life experiences, ways of knowing and learning, and prior preparation for college required different modes of teaching; the availability of new technology to support instruction; an array of societal expectations of what educated citizens should be able to do; the information explosion that resulted in an increasing fragmentation of knowledge; and strong efforts to redefine the work of faculty. The concerns were about not only the quality of college instruction but also the way that college instructors were prepared.

We further grounded our study in the need for a more complete understanding of faculty careers. Research had acknowledged developmental stages of faculty during their careers, the special demands on faculty members, and the stresses during their pretenure years. In addition, there was literature on tenure-year and midcareer issues of faculty and senior faculty, including literature on strategies for development and renewal (Finkelstein

& LaCelle-Peterson, 1993; Schuster & Wheeler, 1990). Despite these bodies of work, limited attention had been paid to what has been called a period of "anticipatory socialization," a time when graduate students begin the process of acquiring the values, norms, attitudes, and beliefs associated with a particular discipline and with being a professor (Anderson & Seashore Louis, 1991; Bess, 1978; Tierney & Rhoads, 1994) and to the period directly before arrival at a first position in academia (McHenry, 1977; Tierney & Rhoads, 1994; Waggaman, 1983; Wanous, 1992). Although there had been research on satisfaction, concerns, development, and stresses of new and junior faculty (Olsen, 1993; Sorcinelli, 1988, 1992; Sorcinelli & Austin, 1992), the graduate student experience was still being viewed as primarily separate from progression through the faculty career.

An additional reason for conducting this research was the need for further understanding of developmental stages of "aspiring faculty." We were particularly interested in understanding more about the Nyquist and Sprague conceptualization of graduate student development (Nyquist & Sprague, 1992, 1998; Sprague & Nyquist, 1989, 1991). These two researchers had posited that TAs move through developmental stages during their years as TAs and that by understanding these stages, faculty and TA directors could provide appropriate training. They suggested also that one can tell where TAs are in the developmental process by examining their concerns, the ways they talk about their disciplines, the ways they interact with students, and the ways they perceive the authority relationship with their supervisors. In addition to the literature on faculty careers, these two scholars drew on other relevant literature including that on professional development (Fuller, 1962; Schön, 1987; Staton-Spicer & Bassett, 1979; Stoltenberg, 1981), developmental frameworks of personal competence (Belenky, Clinchy, Goldberger, & Tarule, 1986; Gilligan, 1982; Pearce & Cronin, 1980), and teaching assistant development (Abbott, Wulff, & Szego, 1989; Book & Eisenberg, 1979; Darling & Dewey, 1989) and the literature focused on how people become members of organizations or learn new roles (Staton & Darling, 1989; Zeichner, 1980). Despite those bodies of literature and the earlier work of Nyquist and Sprague (Nyquist and Sprague, 1992; Sprague and Nyquist,

1989, 1991), we still lacked understanding of the development of TAs as learners and the phases of development that might be specifically experienced by TAs. As a result, we set out to explore such developmental patterns during the aspiring faculty period, focusing particularly on the TA experience.

Methods

To gain a more comprehensive view of graduate student development, we designed the qualitative study to follow a group of graduate students over a four-year period at three geographically diverse institutions: two research universities with multiyear graduate programs and a comprehensive university with a two-year graduate program. Master's granting institutions with two-year TA programs had suggested that the needs of their TAs were not being adequately addressed in the national conversations about TA preparation. We therefore wanted not only to follow TAs over the course of their experiences (longitudinally) but also to seek answers for programs at both doctoral and master's granting institutions. We designed the research to provide insights about ways both to ensure the quality of TAs and to employ the TA experiences as a significant part of the preparation of the future professoriate.

Working as a team consisting of four co-principal investigators and several graduate research assistants, we designed the research around four broadly conceived, guiding questions:

1. How do aspiring professors who are TAs understand the teaching process and their teaching roles, and how does this understanding change during the graduate school experience?
2. What factors in the graduate school experience contribute to aspiring professors' understanding of the teaching process and the teaching role?
3. Are there discernible patterns or stages in the development of aspiring professors' understanding of the teaching process and their teaching roles?
4. What findings from the study can inform those involved in the preparation of graduate students (aspiring professors) for the teaching aspects of their scholarly lives?

We used as our primary source of data regularly scheduled interviews with graduate students who had indicated when they started their graduate programs that teaching in academia was a career goal. We wanted to hear the student voices about how their perspectives on their career goals, their understandings about teaching, and their experiences as graduate students changed over time during the graduate student experience. We planned to follow a total of fifty-five of the students in a variety of disciplines who had roles as they began their graduate study as TAs in a variety of disciplines, including a group of twenty doctoral students at each of the two research-intensive universities and one group of fifteen master's level students at the comprehensive university. To ensure an adequate cushion to produce a critical mass, given typical attrition rates in graduate education, we started with a pool of ninety-nine graduate students. Along the way, some remained in graduate school but discontinued their participation in the study; others took some time away from graduate school or left graduate education and took jobs or changed careers; a couple simply disappeared. In the end we had substantial data from fifty-one participants in the two research universities and fifteen in the master's granting institution, providing sixty-six cases on which to base our findings. See Table 3.1 for participant demographics.

We had the graduate students complete a survey during their first year and then interviewed them twice a year throughout the four years of the study. Interviews were taped and transcribed. Then, using respected qualitative methods (Creswell, 1994; Glesne & Peshkin, 1992; Lincoln & Guba, 1985; Miles & Huberman, 1984, 1994; Strauss & Corbin, 1990), we engaged in ongoing data analysis that included categorizing, synthesizing, finding patterns, and developing interpretations throughout the study. We also applied the constant comparative method (Lincoln & Guba, 1985) to identify broad themes and patterns in the data. We discussed emerging interpretations with some respondents (member checks) as well as with colleagues, and openly discussed with the participants and among team members the ways in which our own subjectivity seemed to relate to emerging interpretations.

Table 3.1. Demographic Profile of Graduate Student Participants, in Number and Percent

Disciplinary Cluster	Number of Participants	Gender Distribution M = Male F = Female	Age Range	Ethnicity/Nationality ANGL = Anglo American HA = Hispanic American AFR = African American AS = Asian American FN = Foreign National	Institution Type RU = Research Universities CU = Comprehensive Universities
Natural Sciences: Biology Chemistry Fish and Wildlife Physics Zoology	19	M: 10 F: 9	20s: 14 30s: 3 40s: 2	ANGL: 18 HA: 1	RU: 14 CU: 5
Math and Engineering: Math Computer Science	14	M: 10 F: 4	20s: 12 30s: 1 40s: 1	ANGL: 8 AFR: 1 AS: 1 FN: 4	RU: 12 CU: 2
Arts and Humanities: English History Music	16	M: 6 F: 10	20s: 12 30s: 1 40s: 3	ANGL: 15 AFR: 1	RU: 12 CU: 4

Table 3.1. (Continued)

Disciplinary Cluster	Number of Participants	Gender Distribution M = Male F = Female	Age Range	Ethnicity/Nationality ANGL = Anglo American HA = Hispanic American AFR = African American AS = Asian American FN = Foreign National	Institution Type RU = Research Universities CU = Comprehensive Universities
Social Sciences:	11	M: 4 F: 7	20s: 9 30s: 1 40s: 1	ANGL: 10 FN: 1	RU: 7 CU: 4
Communication Studies					
Criminal Justice					
Food Sciences					
Human Ecology					
Human Performance					
Psychology					
MQM/CEPSE*					
Professional Schools:	6	M: 2 F: 4	20s: 3 30s: 2 40s: 1	ANGL: 4 FN: 2	RU: 6
Business Administration					
Education					
Educational Psychology					
Mass Media					
Telecommunications					
TOTALS:	66	M: 32 (49%) F: 34 (51%)	20s: 50 (76%) 30s: 8 (12%) 40s: 8 (12%)	ANGL: 55 (84%) AFR: 2 (3%) AS: 1 (1.5%) FN: 7 (10%) HA: 1 (1.5%)	RU: 51 (77%) CU: 15 (23%)

*MQM/CEPSE = measurement and quantitative methods/counseling, educational psychology, and special education.

Note: Foreign national participants come from the following countries or regions: Germany, India, Wales, Taiwan,

Key Findings

In previous publications (Austin, 2002; Nyquist et al., 1999) we identified some of the themes emerging from this study. Here, we have organized the findings around the four general questions identified for the longitudinal project.

Question 1: How Do Aspiring Professors Who Are TAs Understand the Teaching Process and Their Teaching Roles, and How Does This Understanding Change During Graduate School?

Some TAs in the sample grappled with questions related to their teaching, and over time, some developed more complex and nuanced understandings of teaching-related issues. For example, in response to interview questions, they deliberated in increasingly complex ways about such issues as the role of the teacher; the appropriate relationships between teacher and student, including issues of power and authority; how students learn and how teachers can facilitate this learning; and teaching methods appropriate for their content. For some of the participants in our study, we observed over time what appeared to be an integration or coming together of their understandings about teaching—as well as their other roles. As they described their development, some indicated that through their experiences they had moved as teachers from standing in front of the room to lecture to guiding students to gain new understandings. For some TAs, specific incidents contributed to such integration, whereas for others growth occurred more slowly over time.

Not all reached such levels of integration, however. There was a subgroup that moved through the TA experience with less developed understandings or awareness of such issues as the dimensions of their roles, how students learn, and the development of a teaching philosophy. Within this subgroup were some graduate students who never really moved beyond a conception of teaching as full responsibility for a course. Thus, those in this subgroup who held advising roles or instructional roles in laboratories or sections often responded to questions about development by saying, "I am not teaching this quarter; I am just advising" or "I am not teaching; I am just doing the lab for a large class."

When we asked TAs questions about their development as teachers and researchers, they tended to assess themselves along the dimensions of "comfort" and "confidence." In addition, they reported the greatest increase in confidence and comfort in the area of teaching, with much less confidence in their ability to do the necessary research. Often, they would say, "I am much more confident about my teaching than I was last year when I talked to you." Interestingly, even those who were not teaching and had assumed research assistantships or fellowships still perceived themselves as increasingly confident in their teaching abilities. Those in this group tended to equate confidence in teaching with increased content knowledge. Thus, they reported achievements such as taking a course in a specific content area, passing their comprehensive exams, making a successful presentation at a conference, or selecting a dissertation topic as the events that boosted their confidence in teaching.

Question 2: What Factors in the Graduate School Experience Contribute to Aspiring Professors' Understanding of the Teaching Process and the Teaching Role?

Throughout the study, we identified both human influences and elements of academia that contributed to the graduate students' understanding of the teaching process and their roles. Most of the students had varied assignments and experiences during the study. By analyzing these individual experiences, we were able to understand students' journeys more fully and to identify the phases and turning points most significant to their development as professionals generally and as teaching scholars specifically. Beginning with the influence of prior experience and background, we briefly highlight nine of those major factors in this section of the chapter.

Background and Experience

Numerous factors in the backgrounds and experiences of the graduate students contributed to their understanding of teaching and ultimately influenced their development. Among the factors were age, educational background (for example, whether they had attended a liberal arts college or not), family situation (whether there were teachers in their families, or whether they were married or partnered, or had children), and previous employment (whether, for example, they had prior teaching experience). Some talked of the importance of family support, while several participants explained that they had been influenced strongly by their observations of other teachers. In some cases, elementary and high school teachers or professors that the participants had when they were undergraduates were cited as exemplars of teaching excellence and commitment that influenced the students to pursue graduate study. Some also mentioned their professors in undergraduate and graduate courses as examples of what they intended to avoid doing in the classroom.

Roles and Assignments

The roles they assumed in graduate school also influenced the students' development. Some served as TAs for a number of semesters, whereas others had some TA experience but worked more often as research assistants. For example, in some disciplines, such as English, graduate students often hold teaching assistantships for most of their time in graduate school, either assisting a professor or as sole instructional authority for a course. In contrast, in many of the sciences, graduate students frequently work in laboratories and teach less often—and when they do, they are less likely to teach courses alone and more likely to assist in labs or lead sections of larger courses. We found that the participants' overall understanding of teaching was linked to the nature and ordering of these assignments and other components of the entire graduate student experience. In addition, activities involved in their formal assignments as teaching assistants contributed to the graduate students' growth. For example, grading papers, developing course syllabi, and instructing classes provided situations that, for many TAs, required deeper and more complex thinking about teaching and learning. TAs who experienced progressively challenging assignments, involving new and additional responsibilities over time, appeared to benefit the most from their formal assignments, particularly when those responsibilities were accompanied by helpful mentoring or supervision.

Informal Connections

TAs also learned about teaching through their informal connections with TA peers and sometimes with faculty members or friends, spouses, and relatives. Both in their surveys and in their interviews, however, the graduate students indicated that conversations in TA offices among peers were the most prevalent sources of influence. Most often, peer interactions occurred inside departments but could extend to include students from a range of departments. For most of the graduate students, dialogue with TA supervisors or other faculty on substantive teaching issues occurred far less frequently than such conversations with peers. Although many TAs indicated they would appreciate more interactions with faculty regarding teaching, they also recognized mitigating factors. For instance, some students reported that physical space was a factor, because they were situated in offices with groups of TAs where peers were readily accessible for conversation. They pointed out that offices for graduate teaching assistants, particularly at the research institutions, were often separated from faculty offices, making chance encounters or spontaneous conversations with faculty less likely.

Messages

At a time in their lives when many of them felt extremely vulnerable, graduate students were confronted with multiple explicit and implicit messages that influenced their perceptions of their teaching and their roles as teachers. There were a variety of messages, frequently contradictory or ambiguous, about the relative value of various dimensions of academic and faculty life, especially teaching. The graduate students received such messages not only through official institutional documents and statements but also from administrators, faculty, and supervisors. In addition, they constructed meaning out of their experiences, including observations, listening, and interactions with faculty, peers, and friends and family.

They also cited examples of conflicting and negative messages about what constituted success, balance, and the values of the academy. Certainly, at the research universities the most contradictory or ambiguous messages concerned the relative value of the teaching and research dimensions of academic life. However, even at the explicitly teaching-oriented master's granting comprehensive institution, some participants reported internalizing this ambivalence about the value of teaching in faculty life. For example, the official discourse of university representatives embraced teaching as central to the missions of the universities. In addition, graduate students acknowledged less explicit messages that suggested that teaching was an important activity in the academy and for their own development, including TA awards, faculty members' expressions of interest in TAs' teaching, and conversations that indicated faculty interest and commitment to teaching. Yet students simultaneously noted that some faculty members urged them to confine their teaching activities in order to ensure that they could emphasize their research and that, in many departments, there was little formal observation and feedback to TAs about their teaching. Even when the various explicit messages graduate students heard coalesced meaningfully, implicit academic structures, policies, and practices tended to undermine, confuse, or obscure those messages.

Personal Events

During the four years of the study, a number of the graduate students experienced life-changing events, including marriage, parenthood, divorce, and illness. In some of the cases, faculty and other advisors were aware of these situations and addressed them as part of the inevitable challenges of graduate school life. In other instances, however, students kept such personal events to themselves and struggled to maintain the appearance of normalcy in their development as teaching scholars. For some, handling such events interfered with their involvement in their graduate study. Also, such events led some participants to recognize that it was impossible to separate the personal dimensions of their lives from their development as scholar-teachers.

Disciplines

In several ways, we observed the impact of the disciplines on the students' teaching development. When asked why they chose to pursue graduate school, many of the students, particularly at the research institutions, focused on "love of the content." They were often eloquent in describing what attracted them to the content of their disciplines, and many were able to identify the specific life incidents that solidified their interests in and determination to pursue careers in their chosen disciplines. As previously discussed, their increasing immersion in areas they "loved" gave them greater confidence in their ability to teach. Paradoxically, at the same time that they became increasingly focused on specific areas of interest in their disciplines, many were given additional teaching responsibilities in broader areas or in disciplinary topics unrelated to their specific areas of research. Such expectations for teaching beyond their specialties presented distinct challenges. We observed, for example, that some were less able to make the broader connections across various parts of the disciplines, and especially, to link parts of their disciplines to other fields. Another way in which the disciplines affected some students, particularly at the research universities, occurred when disciplinary conventions required research time away from campus in the field or at archival sites. Such absences limited the variety of teaching experiences and the levels of teaching responsibility that graduate students could have.

Career Paths

How students viewed possible career paths also affected their development as teachers. Although some were thoughtful and systematic in their thinking about careers, others seemed less informed about career options.

We characterized four groups of graduate students at the research institutions based on the professional goals they indicated at the start and at the close of the study. First, some students began graduate school aspiring to enter traditional, assistant professor tenure-track jobs at top-tier research universities and held onto that goal. A second group identified that traditional avenue as "ideal" but showed over time a more flexible attitude toward career options than they did when the study began. For example, in addition to aspiring to be full-time university faculty members, this group also found appeal in visions of teaching in a liberal arts or community college or applying their instructional knowledge for consulting in business, research, or policy. For some of these students, especially those at the research universities, the "ideal" visions of intellectual stimulation and academic entrepreneurship that attracted them to graduate school had been tempered by less appealing perceptions of scholarly life, such as isolation, economic bottom lines, and overworked faculty. A third group of students, who attended small liberal arts colleges as undergraduates or private institutions as master's students, entered graduate school expressing a strong desire to return to that environment as professors. They continued to retain that goal as their ideal teaching scholar job, despite four years of exposure to academic life in a research university, and in some cases, because of it. A fourth group concluded, after observing academic life, that their interests and personal goals would be better met if they pursued work outside academia.

Institutions

There were some institutional differences that influenced students' understanding of teaching and teaching roles. Here we focus briefly on the differences between the comprehensive university and the two research universities. One area of difference was in students' reasons for pursuing graduate education. Students in the comprehensive university knew that their careers were likely to emphasize teaching more than research. Indeed, only one student of fifteen continued on for doctoral studies; of the rest, most entered academic life in the form of community college teaching while some took their teaching aspirations into positions in industry. As a result, most approached their teaching roles with a different sense of purpose than their counterparts studying in the research universities. In addition, the master's degree students in the comprehensive university saw different kinds of faculty work lives than those observed by the doctoral students. Faculty in the research universities were balancing heavy demands for grant writing, research, teaching, and service, whereas faculty at the comprehensive university, although certainly involved in some of those same activities, tended to be far more immersed in activities related to their heavy loads in teaching, advising, and service.

Reflection

At all the institutions, one of the themes that emerged from the interviews with the graduate students was the importance of having time to reflect about their experiences in graduate school, including their teaching experiences. The theme was especially strong at the two research institutions where we spent four years interviewing the students. In their responses to a question about what had been most useful about their involvement in the study, thirty-three of fifty-six respondents (59 percent) from the research universities mentioned that participation in the interviews provided opportunities for thinking about their teaching, their graduate experiences, and their careers. Eighteen of those fifty-six respondents explicitly used the words "reflect" or "reflection" in describing the usefulness of the study. They volunteered that such opportunities to reflect on a regular, periodic basis with "neutral" listeners would be a very useful addition to the graduate experience. As they expressed interest in such possibilities, many students also indicated they would value more opportunities for such discussions with their own disciplinary faculty. In instances when those opportunities with faculty did occur, students attested to their significance as part of the developmental process in their teaching.

Question 3: Are There Discernible Patterns or Stages in the Development of Aspiring Professors' Understanding of the Teaching Process and Their Teaching Roles?

Based on the group of graduate students studied, we concluded that the development of graduate students is neither linear nor entirely predictable. As the work of Sprague and Nyquist has suggested (Nyquist & Sprague, 1992, 1998; Sprague & Nyquist, 1989, 1991), changes did, indeed, occur over time as graduate students developed as professionals, but those changes were neither straightforward nor the same for everyone. The students started at different points, and, as indicated in responses to the previous question about influences, a variety of factors affected their development to differing extents along the way.

Furthermore, through the students' changes, we came to understand more fully that the development of graduate students as teachers is embedded in other important issues, including development as a researcher, as a member of the discipline, as an institutional citizen, and as a person. Although the study from its inception focused especially on how graduate students develop in their teaching roles and identities, our analyses of the data helped us understand that development as a teaching scholar can be examined successfully only in the broader context of development across the several dimensions. Furthermore, as they developed and grew in their understanding of what it means to be faculty members, members of disciplines, and for some, professionals outside academia, the students also grappled with the kinds of lives to which they aspired. The process of development in any one of these domains was interrelated with development in the others, and, overall, the rate of students' development in the domains varied.

Given the holistic process and the variety of factors that affected it, we did not find support for systematic movement from one stage to another. This is not to say that each student's progression was completely idiosyncratic. Rather, each student's developmental path was best understood in the context of other interrelated factors, all of which ultimately affected development. Thus, our study confirmed, as we suspected from the outset, that prior developmental models do not capture the complexity of the stages through which graduate students move.

Question 4: What Study Findings Can Inform Those Involved in Preparing Graduate Students (Aspiring Professors) for the Teaching Aspects of Their Scholarly Lives?

We can use each of the previous results, of course, to inform faculty members and others involved in preparing aspiring professors. However, in addition to the results in response to the specific research questions about teaching, we also identified some more global key findings about graduate education. In this section of the chapter we highlight four of the overall findings from our research that can help inform those involved in the preparation of graduate students for their scholarly lives.

Too Much of Graduate Education Is Characterized by a Lack of Systematic, Developmental Preparation

Often the graduate programs for these students did not purposely plan systematic opportunities for their developmental progression as teachers, researchers, institutional citizens, and scholars engaged in their communities. During the first year, many of the students were unclear about what graduate education entailed and what the path to a graduate degree would require. In addition, throughout the study, they reported that they were not particularly knowledgeable about what a faculty career involved, and even less knowledgeable about careers in other kinds of academic institutions. Most of the students knew little about professional service and had little opportunity to talk with faculty about service components of their work. Even at the end of their time in the study, the students reported virtually no knowledge of faculty or institutional governance.

Possibly, some might assert, these issues might be more appropriately addressed during the latter part of a graduate student's experiences. Nevertheless, we observed that opportunities for exploration of these and many of the other facets of a faculty career rarely occurred in ways that fostered systematic development with the intent of helping the aspiring faculty develop appropriate skills across the range of faculty responsibilities.

Graduate Education Too Often Does Not Provide for Systematic Feedback and Mentoring That Could Help Eliminate Unnecessary Barriers to Success

In using metaphors to describe their experiences, many of the students spoke of uncertainties and challenges—chasms, mountains, dilapidated bridges to be crossed, or rocks being thrown down on them as they proceeded to climb—that were significant barriers to their progress. In explaining a picture that he drew to represent his graduate experience, one fairly successful doctoral student portrayed himself running a marathon. His path was punctuated with some signposts, but, he explained, they were not accurate. At various intersections, without good directions, he was uncertain how to proceed. Geraniums on a window ledge were falling on him, logs obstructed his path, and a car nearly hit him. He explained, "You know, I've been pretty successful despite these things," but continued by pointing out that too many unexpected barriers occur in the graduate experience. Graduate students often must find their way through the obstacles of graduate education with minimal guidance from faculty. Through such examples, the students demonstrated that the departments represented in our study did not systematically or frequently pay attention to providing preparation, orientation, and feedback to graduate students in their work and development as teachers. Much of the assessment of which students were aware occurred in annual reviews (when these did take place), when faculty met privately with students to discuss their programmatic progress. Formative feedback provided for students to assess their progress or make changes in what they were doing occurred far less frequently. Although some of the graduate students reported receiving some feedback from supervisors about their teaching, it often was not thorough or carefully designed to help them grow as teachers. In the absence of thorough input, they relied on feedback from their own students (both formal evaluations and informal comments or discussions) and their students' performance and grades to consider what constituted effective and ineffective student learning, what teaching strategies were most effective, and how teachers and students should relate.

As They Progress Through Graduate Education, Many Students Begin to Wonder If They Really Aspire to Academic Life

We observed too many students who had entered graduate school excited about particular driving passions and questions become increasingly disillusioned and disenchanted. When they began, most were not aware of the value system of the academy. Although ultimately some students explicitly discovered and internalized academic norms, many had a difficult time. As these students struggled to demystify the values of the academy and to make sense of expectations within what some perceived as daunting bureaucracies and difficult-to-decipher institutional cultures, they became concerned about how to align academic values and expectations with their own. Some reported that there seemed to be a "secret model" of graduate education that had implicit norms and rules. Some students also reported difficulty in interpreting various parties' expectations for what counts as "success." Other students experienced clashes of differing values and expectations with their advisors or faculty members. Authority and relationship issues—with students, and with advisors and supervisors—were significant.

Simultaneously, finding balance in their scholarly, professional, and personal lives emerged as an important issue for the students. They often commented in interviews that faculty members appeared to experience considerable pressure in lives characterized by lack of balance between professional and personal commitments and interests. Some of these students flatly reported that they could not lead the kinds of harried lives they observed in professors around them and thus leaned toward applying their knowledge in what they thought would be less stressful environments.

Ultimately, some students who entered graduate school with aspirations to become professors perceived that the academic life might leave little room for their own passions, values, and commitments. Some only maintained a sense of empowerment when they felt they could explore alternative approaches or careers and discuss these options with their faculty advisors or supervisors. Some of the students who felt disempowered and disenchanted progressed in silent resignation. For others, however, this sense of their own diminishing priorities and aspirations left them wondering about the desirability of an academic life. In some instances, students prolonged completion of their studies, discontinued their graduate education, or in a couple of the very worst scenarios, simply dropped out of their programs without any word about where they were going.

Current Graduate Education Does Not Match the Needs and Demands of the Changing Academy and Broader Society

Looking across the study findings, we conclude that there are problems in the ways that universities prepare graduate students for the future. Many academics seem to be hanging onto an idealized and traditional model that heavily emphasizes research preparation with little attention to the other roles of faculty members. This model does not adequately take into account changes in faculty roles, in student characteristics and needs, in modes of education delivery, and in societal expectations of the academy. As illustrated by the experiences of many of the students in this study, faculty members sometimes try to "clone" themselves—training graduate students only for the tasks and roles for which they themselves were prepared. Although many elements of traditional academic training remain very important, faculty members should not ignore the demands of the changing academy and the broader society as they prepare future faculty. Otherwise, the academy will be producing highly specialized graduates who are not sufficiently prepared to make connections between their own work and the needs of their students, the academy, and the broader society.

Implications and Recommendations

Based on the key findings of our longitudinal study of the development of graduate students as prospective teaching scholars, we have identified overall recommendations in eight areas. The recommendations are relevant to anyone involved in preparing graduate students for their future academic roles. They relate to graduate student development, the definition of *teaching*, the balance between students' needs and institutional expectations, students' perceptions of academic life, feedback and assessment, reflection, the changing needs of the academy and society, and the role of longitudinal research. So, what can we do in each of these areas?

- *Provide systematic preparation that acknowledges the holism of graduate student development.* Department chairs, advisors, and supervisors should understand the multiple dimensions on which graduate students must develop and how development occurs. Advisors and supervisors should work with graduate students to identify and monitor progressively more challenging preparation opportunities along the multiple professional dimensions of teaching, research, institutional service, and scholarly citizenship. Although we recognize that graduate students fill important roles in institutional teaching and research, we encourage senior campus administrators to ensure that organizational needs for employing graduate students do not restrict their developmental opportunities. Advisors and supervisors also should recognize the impact of personal issues on graduate students' lives, including their retention, success, and completion. Furthermore, faculty members should ensure that graduate students are aware of resources for addressing personal issues.
- *Work from a broad definition of teaching.* For too long we have defined teaching primarily in terms of stand-up lecturing: if you are not lecturing, then you are not teaching. What this narrow definition overlooks is the wide array of activities involved in effective teaching, including, for example, responding to papers, designing courses and lessons, grading exams, and holding individual meetings and office hours with students. The use of a broader definition of teaching opens the way for preparing aspiring faculty in explicit ways to handle the multiple elements of teaching. Such preparation should help graduate students understand the different kinds of faculty-student interactions required in diverse learning environments (classes versus laboratories, for example) and at different levels of student expertise (introductory courses versus advanced courses).

- *Help students balance their passions, idealism, and identities with disciplinary, university, and academic expectations.* Faculty members should encourage graduate students to talk about their passions, identities, and goals, and help them explore how those goals relate to both the opportunities and the expectations of their programs, institutions, and disciplines. A particular challenge is to encourage students to nurture the interests and passions that brought them into the field, while also helping them to identify and address unrealistic or unclear expectations. To begin this process, advisors and supervisors should meet with students early on in their doctoral programs to discuss goals and ambitions, to make explicit the departmental expectations for developmental progress as well as for work assignments, and to clarify paths through graduate education. Then, faculty advisors and supervisors should schedule regular meetings to talk with graduate students about their career goals and aspirations, their progress in graduate school, and the values, issues, and challenges associated with being a scholar in the particular discipline or field.

- *Prepare to address ambiguous and contradictory messages that students receive about life in academia.* Since graduate students are constantly observing, experiencing, and hearing comments about academic life, faculty advisors and supervisors can do much to help these aspiring faculty interpret the array of messages so that they retain their appreciation for and commitment to pursuing academic careers. Specifically, when promising graduate students express interest in the faculty career, faculty advisors and supervisors can explain the commitments, interests, and rewards that led them to enter and remain in the academy. They also can model and discuss how they successfully handle the pressures of their work. They can ensure that graduate students have opportunities to ask questions about academic life and how it is changing, explore the implications of the choice to enter academia, and consider those observations that concern them. In addition, faculty and institutional leaders should make sure students have opportunities to learn about different institutional types in higher education and the kinds of academic communities and faculty appointments characterizing each. Finally, institutional leaders and faculty should review institutional documents, communications, and symbols, such as awards, to analyze where and how unintended messages about graduate school and academic life might be conveyed. In the process, it is important to be attentive to what is said and done as well as what is not said and not done. Silence and omissions convey messages as powerfully as the most clearly articulated public statements. Faculty members should be alert to myths and misunderstandings that develop among graduate students and prepare to clarify inaccuracies.

- *Provide systematic feedback and assessment on an ongoing basis.* Those who work with graduate students should engage in assessment that provides ongoing feedback and mentoring. Such efforts should monitor student progress along the multiple dimensions of academic work—including teaching, research, service, and institutional citizenship. Structured conversations, inventories and surveys, and self-assessments, individually and in group discussion with other students, can be useful strategies for identifying such areas as prior teaching and research-related experiences, skills and understandings acquired from those experiences, career aspirations, and understandings and assumptions about faculty work. A significant part of the process should be formative—designed to help students determine how they are doing and make adjustments as they proceed. Then, to build on the assessment data, supervisors and advisors should help graduate students link data about their experiences and growth with plans for future activities.

- *Make opportunities for reflection a significant part of the assessment process.* In contrast to formal advising conversations, reflection requires a safe environment for exploratory, complex thinking. Faculty members can encourage students to engage in informal reflective conversations during visits with faculty members, in peer group discussions, and through such self-assessment practices as developing teaching portfolios. Department leaders also can encourage more formal venues for reflection—during graduate courses, as part of the responsibilities expected of teaching and research assistants, and as a component of formal annual review of graduate students' progress.

- *Prepare graduate students to contribute to an academic workplace and a society that are both changing rapidly and dramatically.* Faculty members, teaching assistant supervisors, and institutional leaders should view the graduate experience for aspiring faculty as a significant stage in the faculty career. Based on this perspective, they should prepare students for the full range of skills and the diverse ways of thinking that are needed in the rapidly changing workplace. They should provide occasions for graduate students to explore the dramatic changes facing the academy, including new approaches to teaching and learning; the increasing diversity of students; the uses of new technologies, including distance learning opportunities; changing societal expectations of how the academy should respond to critical problems; and new kinds of faculty employment arrangements, including term and part-time appointments. Similarly, faculty members, advisors, and institutional leaders must acknowledge that across all parts of the knowledge economy, future professors will have to demonstrate an array of abilities, including flexibility and nimbleness in applying knowledge and skills to demanding and changing problems, ability to connect and integrate diverse bodies of knowledge, skill in collaborating with colleagues across disciplines and national lines, ability to work both individually and in teams, and skill in using technology to facilitate teaching and knowledge production.

  It is particularly important, as students become more specialized in their fields and disciplines and progress in their graduate studies, to help them develop a sense of "connectedness." Connectedness implies an appreciation of the ways in which one's area of expertise fits into the larger field or discipline, the relationships and the increasingly blurring lines between disciplines, and the responsibilities that a scholar has as a member of the broader society. Balancing the specialized expertise that is achieved through long and thorough disciplinary study with an understanding of and commitment to participating in the broader institutional and societal community is a talent that will be especially needed in the next generation of faculty. Helping graduate students develop this ability is a daunting challenge for current faculty members.

- *Recognize the importance of longitudinal data in efforts to improve graduate education.* The design of our study greatly enhanced our understanding of the complexity of the graduate experience. The qualitative, longitudinal approach helped us recognize that recommendations for change have to balance complex tensions between student needs and institutional, departmental, and societal needs, and therefore cannot simply reflect the preferences of individual graduate students, faculty, administrators, or institutions. The longitudinal study also reinforced for us that decision makers need to be extremely cautious about basing actions only on data from reports of graduate students' perceptions at a single point in time. During the four years of our study, the students went through dramatic changes in their goals, needs, and priorities. For example, what was salient to a student immersed in a first teaching assignment was dramatically different from what consumed him or her when the dissertation proposal was being created or when the job search was under way. This variability reminded us to approach with caution many of the generalizations based on studies at one point in the graduate experience, even while appreciating the information and insights such studies provide.

Conclusion

After several years of ongoing conversations with the graduate students in this study, we continue to be intrigued by the journeys of these young scholars, many of whom have now assumed positions in higher education. The study has revealed rich and fascinating stories that highlight aspects of graduate education from the perspectives of the students and offer insights into the socialization process and professional development provided by the American academy. The findings from the qualitative data in our study gain even greater impact when juxtaposed with the results from other studies (some using different methods) discussed in this volume. Among the array of recent studies on graduate education, this study is a strong reminder of the richness of student voices and the importance of understanding graduate students' perspectives as we prepare aspiring faculty to succeed in the rapidly changing world of academia and society.

Acknowledgments

This chapter draws from the final report for the project: *The Development of Graduate Students as Teaching Scholars: A four-year longitudinal study* (Final Report, Grant #199600142) (Nyquist, Austin, Sprague, & Wulff, 2001). The research was generously supported by The Pew Charitable Trusts and the Spencer Foundation. The opinions expressed in this chapter are our own and do not necessarily reflect the views of the funding agencies. We are indebted to the five then–graduate students who served on the research team at various times and contributed greatly to the data collection, analysis, and interpretation: Claire Calcagno, San Jose State University; Julie Chiapelone, University of Washington; Patricia Kenney, Michigan State University; Laura Manning, University of Washington; and Bettina J. Woodford, University of Washington.

Notes

1.   A number of national studies have been critical. See, for example: *To Reclaim a Legacy: A Report on the Humanities in Higher Education* (Bennett, 1984); *Involvement in Learning: Realizing the Potential of American Higher Education* (National Institute of Education, 1984); and *A Nation at Risk* (National Commission on Excellence in Education, 1983).

2.   The following books have been read widely outside the academic community: *Impostors in the Temple* (Anderson, 1992); *The Closing of the American Mind* (Bloom, 1987); *Killing the Spirit: Higher Education in America* (Smith, 1990); *ProfScam: Professors and the Demise of Higher Education* (Sykes, 1988); and *The Hollow Men: Politics and Corruption in Higher Education* (Sykes, 1990).

References

Abbott, R. D., Wulff, D. H., & Szego, C. K. (1989). Review of research on TA training. In J. D. Nyquist, R. D. Abbott, & D. H. Wulff (Eds.), *Teaching assistant training in the 1990s*. New Directions for Teaching and Learning, No. 39 (pp. 111–123). San Francisco: Jossey-Bass.

Anderson, M. (1992). *Impostors in the temple*. New York: Simon & Schuster.

Anderson, M. S., & Seashore Louis, K. (1991). The changing locus of control over faculty research: From self-regulation to dispersed influence. In J. C. Smart (Ed.), *Higher education: Handbook of theory and research* (Vol. VII.) (pp. 57–101). New York: Agathon.

Austin, A. E. (2002). Preparing the next generation of faculty: Graduate school as socialization to the academic career. *Journal of Higher Education, 73*(1), 94–122.

Belenkey, M. F., Clinchy, B. M., Goldberger, N. R., & Tarule, J. M. (1986). *Women's ways of knowing: The development of self, voice, and mind.* New York: Academic Press.

Bennett, W. J. (1984). *To reclaim a legacy: A report on the humanities in higher education.* Washington, DC: National Endowment for the Humanities.

Bess, J. L. (1978). Anticipatory socialization of graduate students. *Research in Higher Education, 8,* 289–317.

Bloom, A. (1987). *The closing of the American mind.* New York: Simon & Schuster.

Book, C., & Eisenberg, E. M. (1979, November). *Communication concerns of graduate and undergraduate teaching assistants.* Paper presented at the convention of the Speech Communication Association, San Antonio, TX.

Creswell, J. W. (1994). *Research design: Qualitative and quantitative approaches.* Thousand Oaks, CA: Sage.

Darling, A., & Dewey, M. (1989, November). *Becoming a teaching assistant: An examination of communication experiences with peer leaders.* Paper presented at the annual convention of the Speech Communication Association, San Francisco.

Finkelstein, M. J., & LaCelle-Peterson, M. W. (Eds.). (1993). *Developing senior faculty as teachers.* New Directions for Teaching and Learning, No. 55. San Francisco: Jossey-Bass.

Fuller, F. F. (1962). Concerns of teachers: A developmental perspective. *American Educational Research Journal, 2,* 207–226.

Gilligan, C. (1982). *In a different voice: Psychological theory and women's development.* Cambridge, MA: Harvard University Press.

Glesne, C., & Peshkin, A. (1992). *Becoming qualitative researchers: An introduction.* White Plains, NY: Longman.

Lincoln, Y. S., & Guba, E. G. (1985). *Naturalistic inquiry.* Thousand Oaks, CA: Sage.

McHenry, D. E. (1977). *Academic departments.* San Francisco: Jossey-Bass.

Miles, M. B., & Huberman, A. M. (1984). *Qualitative data analysis: A sourcebook of new methods.* Thousand Oaks, CA: Sage.

Miles, M. B., & Huberman, A. M. (1994). *Qualitative data analysis: An expanded sourcebook* (2nd ed.). Thousand Oaks, CA: Sage.

National Commission on Excellence in Education. (1983). *A nation at risk.* Washington, DC: U.S. Government Printing Office.

National Institute of Education. (1984). *Involvement in learning: Realizing the potential of American higher education.* Washington, DC: U.S. Government Printing Office.

Nyquist, J. D., Austin, A. E., Sprague, J., & Wulff, D. H. (2001). *The development of graduate students as teaching scholars: A four-year longitudinal study* (Final Report, Grant #199600142). Seattle: University of Washington, Center for Instructional Development and Research.

Nyquist, J. D., Manning, L., Wulff, D. H., Austin, A. E., Sprague, J., Fraser, P. K., Calcagno, C., & Woodford, B. (1999). On the road to becoming a professor: The graduate student experience. *Change, 31*(3), 18–27.

Nyquist, J. D., & Sprague, J. (1992). Developmental stages of TAs. In J. D. Nyquist & D. H. Wulff (Eds.), *Preparing teaching assistants for instructional roles: Supervising TAs in communication* (pp. 100–113). Annandale, VA: Speech Communication Association.

Nyquist, J. D., & Sprague, J. (1998). Thinking developmentally about TAs. In M. Marincovich, J. Prostko, & F. Stout (Eds.), *The professional development of graduate teaching assistants* (pp. 61–88). Boston: Anker.

Olsen, D. (1993). Work satisfaction and stress in the first and third year of academic appointment. *Journal of Higher Education, 64*(4), 453–471.

Pearce, W. B., & Cronin, V. F. (1980). *Communication, action, and meaning: The creation of social reality.* New York: Praeger.

Schön, D. A. (1987). *Educating the reflective practitioner: Toward a new design for teaching and learning in the professions.* San Francisco: Jossey-Bass.

Schuster, J. H., & Wheeler, D. W. (Eds.). (1990). *Enhancing faculty careers: Strategies for development and renewal.* San Francisco: Jossey-Bass.

Smith, P. (1990). *Killing the spirit: Higher education in America.* New York: Viking.

Sorcinelli, M. D. (1988). Satisfactions and concerns of new university teachers. *To Improve the Academy, 7,* 121–133.

Sorcinelli. M. D. (1992). New and junior faculty stress: Research and responses. In M. D. Sorcinelli & A. E. Austin (Eds.), *Developing new and junior faculty.* New Directions for Teaching and Learning, No. 50 (pp. 27–37). San Francisco: Jossey-Bass.

Sorcinelli, M. D., & Austin, A. E. (Eds.). (1992). *Developing new and junior faculty.* New Directions for Teaching and Learning, No. 50. San Francisco: Jossey-Bass.

Sprague, J., & Nyquist, J. D. (1989). TA supervision. In J. D. Nyquist, R. D. Abbott, & D. H. Wulff (Eds.), *Teaching assistant training in the 1990s.* New Directions for Teaching and Learning, No. 39 (pp. 37–53). San Francisco: Jossey-Bass.

Sprague, J., & Nyquist, J. D. (1991). A developmental perspective on the TA role. In J. D. Nyquist, R. D. Abbott, D. H. Wulff, & J. Sprague (Eds.), *Preparing the professoriate of tomorrow to teach: Selected readings in TA training* (pp. 295–312). Dubuque, IA: Kendall/Hunt.

Staton, A. Q., & Darling, A. L. (1989). Socialization of teaching assistants. In J. D. Nyquist, R. D. Abbott, & D. H. Wulff (Eds.), *Teaching assistant training in the 1990s.* New Directions for Teaching and Learning, No. 39 (pp. 15–22). San Francisco: Jossey-Bass.

Staton-Spicer, A. Q., & Bassett, R. E. (1979). Communication concerns of preservice and inservice elementary school teachers. *Human Communication Research, 5,* 138–146.

Stoltenberg, C. (1981). Approaching supervision from a developmental perspective: The counselor complexity model. *Journal of Counseling Psychology, 28,* 59–65.

Strauss, A. L., & Corbin, J. M. (1990). *Basics of qualitative research: Grounded theory procedures and techniques.* Thousand Oaks, CA: Sage.

Sykes, C. J. (1988). *ProfScam: Professors and the demise of higher education.* Washington, DC: Regnery.

Sykes, C. J. (1990). *The hollow men: Politics and corruption in higher education.* Washington, DC: Regnery.

Tierney, W. G., & Rhoads, R. A. (1994). *Faculty socialization as a cultural process: A mirror of institutional commitment* (ASHE-ERIC Higher Education Report No. 93–6). Washington, DC: The George Washington University, School of Education and Human Development.

Waggaman, J. S. (1983). *Faculty recruitment, retention, and fair employment: Obligations and opportunities* (ASHE-ERIC Higher Education Report No. 2). Washington, DC: Association for the Study of Higher Education. (ED 227 806)

Wanous, J. P. (1992). *Organizational entry: Recruitment, selection, orientation and socialization of newcomers* (2nd ed.). Reading, MA: Addison-Wesley.

Zeichner, K. M. (1980, April). *Key processes in the socialization of student teachers: Limitations and consequences of oversocialized conceptions of teacher socialization.* Paper presented at the annual convention of the American Educational Research Association, Boston.

Chapter Four

The 2000 National Doctoral Program Survey

An On-Line Study of Students' Voices

Adam P. Fagen, Kimberly M. Suedkamp Wells

The National Doctoral Program Survey, an on-line study of students' perspectives on educational practices in doctoral programs in the United States and Canada, was conducted as part of the work of the National Association of Graduate-Professional Students (NAGPS) in the spring and summer of 2000. Funded by a grant from the Alfred P. Sloan Foundation, the survey was a follow-up to a pilot effort, the PhDs.Org Graduate School Survey, which was conducted in 1999 by Geoff Davis and Peter Fiske. The 2000 National Doctoral Program Survey is an important contribution to research on graduate education because it was created, implemented, and completed by graduate students themselves. It represents a grassroots attempt by a national organization to make positive and constructive improvements in the process of doctoral education.

Background and Purpose

The study was designed to obtain a broad cross section of graduate student perceptions. Through the study, current and recent doctoral student participants reported on their experiences in graduate school and assessed their programs' implementation of educational practices recommended by the National Academy of

Science Committee on Science, Engineering, and Public Policy (COSEPUP, 1995), the National Research Council (1998), the Association of American Universities (1998), and others.

The results were compiled in overall responses; responses by broad discipline type (education, engineering, humanities, life sciences, physical sciences, social sciences, professional, and other programs); and responses by participant demographics, such as gender, enrollment status, ethnicity, and citizenship. Program-level responses are currently available for approximately thirteen hundred U.S. programs from which ten or more responses were received. In addition, program-level results for programs receiving between five and nine responses are available to participants, their chairs, and their deans, but not to the general public. A Web-based tool allows users to create a customized ranking of doctoral programs based on a user-selected weighting of recommended educational practices, and each doctoral program has an associated discussion board to facilitate conversations among students, faculty, and administrators. A detailed compilation of the survey results can be accessed online at http://survey.nagps.org/.

In this chapter, we describe the 2000 National Doctoral Program Survey and its unique student perspective on doctoral education. By highlighting a few of the key findings and recommendations based on the results, we show that the survey, and student voices in general, can provide important insights for evaluating student experiences, processes, and outcomes in graduate programs.

Methods

The 2000 National Doctoral Program Survey consisted of forty-eight questions in nine areas relevant to doctoral education: information for prospective students, curricular breadth and flexibility, teaching, professional development, career guidance and placement services, time to degree, faculty mentoring, program climate, and overall satisfaction. Each section contained a set of multiple choice questions with the following possible responses: strongly agree, agree, disagree, strongly disagree, don't know, and not applicable. Each section also contained a free-response box to allow respondents to expand on their responses.

Procedures

The survey was administered on-line from March 30 to August 15, 2000. NAGPS and the volunteer survey team publicized the survey widely. They were assisted by other stakeholders in doctoral education who were invited to become supporters of the survey by advertising it to students. Members of the survey team requested that major disciplinary societies and professional associations in each academic field help to publicize the survey among their memberships. Automatically, program chairs, graduate deans, and university presidents were informed about the survey as soon as someone from their program or university completed it and provided the administrator's e-mail address. Survey volunteers also contacted graduate deans, graduate student associations, and program chairs to encourage them to invite participation from their students.

As the survey progressed, graduate deans, program chairs, graduate student leaders, and professional associations were contacted again and provided with statistics on their students' participation along with a request to publicize the availability of the survey again. At least 60 universities, 115 doctoral programs, 60 graduate student associations, 80 professional societies, and 19 additional associations notified the survey team about their efforts to publicize the survey through newsletters, e-mail lists, flyers, and Web sites and are listed as "Supporters" on the survey Web site (http://survey.nagps.org/).

After completing the survey, respondents were directed to a confirmation screen that included an invitation to send an e-mail message about the survey to other graduate students by completing an on-line form. This grassroots, viral publicity mechanism was one of the most effective means of survey promotion, along with announcements from institutions, doctoral programs, and graduate student associations. Ultimately, over 32,000 students completed the survey, representing nearly 5,000 doctoral programs at almost 400 graduate institutions across the United States and Canada.

Several measures were employed to certify the validity of responses. First, participants were asked to make an explicit affirmation that their responses were truthful. Responses without such an affirmation were discarded. Second, participants were prompted for their e-mail addresses, and codes were sent to those addresses. Each participant was prompted for the code at the end of the survey to verify that the participant had provided a correct e-mail address. Open response comments were reported only for participants who verified their addresses.

Respondent Demographics

The 2000 National Doctoral Program Survey was an observational study, not a controlled experiment. Participants self-selected, and as a result, their responses may not have fully reflected the opinions of the entire doctoral student population. Despite the self-selection, however, there is good evidence that the concerns expressed in their responses represent widely held student opinions rather than a small but outspoken set of negative voices:

- Most of the students expressed satisfaction with their programs and with their advisors overall.
- Comparisons with a survey conducted using more traditional methods showed very similar findings. The 1999 PhDs.Org Graduate School Survey, on which the 2000 National Doctoral Program Survey was based, shared a number of questions with a previous national study entitled the Survey on Doctoral Education and Career Preparation, which was conducted at the University of Wisconsin-Madison, funded by The Pew Charitable Trusts (see Chapter Two of this volume; see also Golde & Dore, 2001 and http://www.phd-survey.org/). The latter survey had a response rate of 42.3 percent for the students surveyed; it included doctoral students in their third year or beyond in eleven disciplines at twenty-seven leading research universities. Student assessments of their educational experiences as measured in that study were similar to those in the PhDs.Org and National Doctoral Program surveys. In fact, comparison suggests that our results, if anything, may be positively biased, because the responses in the Golde and Dore study were nearly uniformly more negative than in the PhDs.Org study (see http://survey.nagps.org/about/sample.php for more detailed comparisons).

- Our survey reached a broad cross section of the graduate student population. The demographics of the survey participants, after controlling for discipline, were similar to the demographics of graduate students and recent cohorts of Ph.D.'s. Selection bias appeared to have had little effect on participant demographics. In particular, we could compare the demographics of our sample to those of the survey population using data from the National Science Foundation (NSF, 2001). Although the comparisons are imprecise, because the NSF data do not disaggregate doctoral students from master's students, they serve as a useful first approximation.

The use of the viral publicity mechanism introduced a source of significant variability into the sampling process. Small actions by individuals could have had large effects on the sample. For example, suppose a respondent sent an announcement to a friend in another department. The friend then completed a survey and provided the e-mail address for the department chair. An announcement was then sent to the dean, who then forwarded it to all students at the institution. Thus, a single announcement sent by a participant could have triggered hundreds or thousands of new responses. The result was dense sampling in some programs or disciplines, and sparse or no sampling in others.

The first two rows of Table 4.1 illustrate this variability. Although the proportions of responses from the various disciplines approximate the fractions of students in each discipline, we see that, for example, our response rate in engineering was significantly lower than in other disciplines. The viral variability did not appear to have had a large effect on other characteristics of the respondents, however. We see comparable sample and population demographic characteristics in the remaining sets of rows. The discrepancy in U.S. citizens in the physical sciences was largely due to the lower rate of participation by computer science students, a field with a higher than average fraction of non–U.S. citizen students. The smaller percentages of underrepresented minority students in our sample were likely due in part to differences in the data: the numbers from the NSF were for U.S. citizens and permanent residents, whereas ours were for U.S. citizens only.

Key Findings

As suggested earlier, an overwhelming majority of survey participants reported positive educational experiences:

- Eighty-one percent of respondents said they were satisfied with their doctoral programs.
- Eighty-six percent of respondents said they were satisfied with their advisors.
- Eighty percent said they would recommend their programs to prospective students.

One student reflected on her program by saying, "The faculty are committed to having a strong program with successful and happy graduate students. . . . " Although common, this positive view was not universal. For instance, another student reported, "If I had it to do over again, I would have never gone to my graduate program knowing what I know now. I have been extremely disappointed in the way I was treated, in the lack of support I received, and in the overall learning climate."

Students reported the greatest satisfaction with programs that had curricula that prepared them for a variety of careers, provided them with comprehensive information before enrollment, and treated them with respect. The common thread was that satisfaction was strongly linked to choice: students wanted curricula broad enough to give them a choice of careers; they wanted information to ensure informed choices; and they wanted the choices they made to be respected.

Despite overall satisfaction with their doctoral programs, survey participants expressed concerns in areas previously identified as important in recent reports from the Association of American Universities (1998), the National Science Board (1997), the National Academies of Science Committee on Science, Engineering, and Public Policy (COSEPUP, 1995), the National Research Council (NRC, 1998), and others. Among the areas in which the greatest concerns were expressed were mentoring, career guidance and placement services, teaching, professional training, program climate, and information for prospective students.

Table 4.1. Demographic Characteristics of National Program Survey Respondents Compared with Those Enrolled in Graduate School or Postdoctoral Programs in Science and Engineering, 1999

Population and Sample	Engineering (%)	Life Sciences (%)	Physical Sciences (%)	Social Sciences (%)
Population: Relative fraction of full-time graduate students in each field, U.S. doctorate-granting institutions, 1999	21	32	22	25
Sample: Relative fraction of survey respondents in each field (current students at U.S. institutions only)	13	35	25	28
Population: Percentage of male full-time graduate students in each field, doctorate-granting institutions, 1999	80	41	69	43
Sample: Percentage of male survey respondents in each field (current students at U.S. institutions only)	74	44	65	41

Population and Sample	Engineering (%)	Life Sciences (%)	Physical Sciences (%)	Social Sciences (%)
Population: Percentage of U.S. citizen and permanent resident graduate students in each field, all institutions, 1999	59	87	65	87
Sample: Percentage of U.S. citizen and permanent resident survey respondents in each field (current students at U.S. institutions only)	63	85	74	88
Population: Percentage of under-represented minority graduate students in each field, U.S. citizens and permanent residents only, all institutions, 1999	16	16	16	24
Sample: Percentage of underrepresented minority survey respondents in each field (current U.S. citizen students at U.S. institutions only)	12	12	10	16

Source: Adapted from the National Science Foundation (2001). Available at http://www.nsf.gov/home/pubinfo/reuse.htm

Mentoring

There is no more central aspect to doctoral training than the relationship between doctoral student and faculty advisor. If this relationships is not amicable and supportive, the graduate school experience is diminished. As one student recommended, "Graduate students need to be very careful about their choice of advisor. . . . This is so often a matter of personality fit, and requires that the graduate student do his or her homework before he or she agrees to work with a particular person." One student who reported a negative mentoring relationship said, "My advisor does very little to aid in my education. He is extremely negative, and offers absolutely no positive feedback. He has stripped me of my confidence and feelings of self."

Encouragingly, more than 80 percent of students in all fields reported positive mentoring experiences, including continuous and constructive feedback on their progress toward their degree. As one student put it, "The mentoring I have received in my program, both from my advisor and from several other faculty members, has been by far the most positive aspect of my graduate experience." Recommendations for best practices have stressed the need for students to receive frequent and thoughtful assessments of their progress, and about two-thirds of respondents were satisfied with the availability of annual assessments.

According to the students, the quality of advising depended not only on the individual student and advisor but also on a student's chosen career path: "Faculty mentoring is more than sufficient if one is interested in an academic position. Faculty mentoring is utterly nonexistent otherwise. I cannot put it any more concisely." Thus, it is essential that consideration of advising takes the individual student's needs and career goals into account.

What happens if a disagreement occurs in mentoring or if a student observes misconduct by a faculty or staff member? The majority of respondents, ranging from 77 percent to 84 percent across all disciplines, felt there was a person or office they would turn to if they perceived misconduct or abuse in their program, by an advisor, or by a committee member. However, these percentages leave a significant number of students who did *not* feel that they had any place to turn. One such student argued that "advisors operate as rogues in a vacuum. There is no accountability. There is no one to turn to in cases of conflict or questions. I feel that I am at the mercy of my advisors—there is absolutely no recourse for their actions and neither is there any accountability for their actions." Another said, "I had nowhere to turn because my advisor had sole responsibility for assessing my performance."

Even on campuses where an ombudsperson's office or grievance procedure existed, students often did not feel that they could use such resources without fearing retribution. Respondents made a distinction between a resource they *could* turn to and one that they *would* turn to. As one student said, "There is an ombudsman's office on campus, but this faculty is notorious for ignoring all efforts by that office to attend to or resolve student-initiated academic concerns. This office will admit that professors may do as they like." Another claimed that "committees rarely act to protect students from abusive or neglectful advisors, and the department rarely acknowledges when there is a significant problem between a student and advisor. When such problems reach crisis there is no one in the department with either the responsibility or the desire to champion the student. Consequently, there really is no safety net for students when there is conflict with the advisor." Still another reported, "In cases I have observed where problems arise between faculty and students, students have most often found someone to turn to, but without successful resolution of the problems. That is, most students with such problems leave the program."

Career Guidance and Placement Services

One of the most common concerns expressed by respondents to the survey related to career guidance and placement services. As one student related, "The overall attitude was 'Oh, don't worry about job prospects, you'll be fine.'" Sixty-two percent of the respondents reported insufficient guidance to prepare them for nonacademic careers, and 30 percent indicated they needed more guidance for academic careers. Placement services were also lacking, with 64 percent of the respondents citing inadequate placement services for nonacademic careers and 36 percent citing the same lack for academic careers. According to one student, "I can only say that I felt completely abandoned by my department in my job search. Had I known what I was facing when I received a letter of acceptance, I would have declined it."

Many respondents felt that graduate students who expressed an interest in pursuing nonresearch careers lost favor and became "black sheep" in their programs. Individuals expressing this concern included those interested in both nonacademic positions and academic positions at teaching colleges. For instance, one respondent said, "Preparation to even *think* about a career outside the role of a research university professor, let alone outside academe, was nonexistent. Even a teaching position at a small, nonstatus liberal arts college was viewed as a failure." Another reported, "I had an exceptional advisor for an academic career. My advisor could not have been more helpful. However, I think my advisor would have turned me out on the street if I had even mentioned a career outside of academia." Although 65 to 75 percent of respondents in all fields reported satisfaction with preparation for academic careers, the ratings for satisfaction with preparation for nonacademic careers ranged widely, from a high of over 65 percent satisfied in engineering to 21 percent in the humanities.

Teaching

Most doctoral students teach as part of their graduate training, and many undergraduates are taught by graduate teaching assistants. Nevertheless, 45 percent of our survey respondents reported that they had not received appropriate preparation and training before they entered the classroom and 49 percent indicated that they lacked appropriate supervision to help improve their teaching skills. Further, 39 percent did not feel that their needs and interests were given appropriate consideration in determining which courses they were assigned to teach. In a typical comment, one respondent explained, "Teaching assistants are thrown into teaching environments in a sink-or-swim manner. No advice, preparation, or supervision is given."

Some students, especially those in the sciences, questioned whether the teaching opportunities they received were sufficient, particularly for academic careers. Only 43 percent of students in the life sciences believed that the teaching experience available to students in their program was adequate preparation for an academic-teaching career. One student reported, "I don't feel that the typical role of a TA (that is, holding office hours and grading papers) at all prepares a student for, or gives a student exposure to, the teaching responsibilities of a professor." One who was satisfied with the training highlighted teaching: "The best thing about my program is that Ph.D. students teach their own classes (independently). This is why I came here and why I would recommend it to others." Preparation for teaching careers differed significantly by field; in contrast to the life sciences, 72 percent of respondents indicated satisfaction in the humanities, where teaching opportunities for graduate students more closely resemble those of faculty members.

Professional Training

Nearly all recommendations for excellence in doctoral education call for students to have the opportunity to broaden their educational experiences outside their own departments. Only by providing a broad multidisciplinary educational experience will Ph.D.'s have the appropriate preparation for the wide range of careers they are likely to pursue. Few of the recommendations in this area were actually put into practice, however; only about half of the respondents said that they were encouraged to gain additional skills through internships and coursework outside their programs. One student said, "Students are not treated as individuals with individualized goals, but rather as units with the singular desire to succeed in exactly the same way the present faculty have." Another explained, "I still think the expectation of single-mindedness amounting almost to blinded vision is a bad idea, because well-rounded individuals not only make better consultants, they make much better university teachers!" Just raising the issue of broad training was eye-opening for some: "I'm finding the questions themselves very thought-provoking because I'm realizing as I respond to them that my program has essentially prepared me for nothing."

Despite increasing attention to ethics in academic fields, few students reported training in this area. One student offered that "learning about professional ethics is more by faculty example—mostly by negative examples that confirm ways that I never want to act." Another said, "I would have loved to receive training in ethics, responsibilities, public speaking, grant writing, etc., but I didn't even know I *should* have been asking for such things." The disciplines with the largest fraction of students reporting such training were education (71 percent), life sciences (70 percent), and social sciences (62 percent), while engineering (44 percent), the humanities (43 percent), and physical sciences (35 percent) had the smallest fractions. Students further reported that the ethics training that did exist, especially in life sciences, was often instituted only as a way to satisfy the conditions of training grants awarded to the department.

Program Climate

Although 62 percent of respondents said that their programs actively recruited students from underrepresented groups, there was evidence that program environments were not always supportive of these students once they arrived. One reported, "I am a member of an underrepresented group, and I have been discriminated against by all levels (faculty and administration) and made to feel very uncomfortable and unwelcome by their comments and actions." Another said, "The program is gradually beginning to accept more women and students of color but both groups remain underrepresented, and women, in particular, feel uncomfortable in certain settings and unsupported." The percentage of women indicating that they were satisfied with program environment was 11 percent lower than their male counterparts (69 percent versus 80 percent). In addition, whereas 74 percent of Caucasians and Asian Americans felt comfortable and supported, only 60 percent of African Americans, Latinos, and Native Americans reported the same degree of comfort and support. Female and minority students' responses to all questions were consistently more negative than those of their male and majority counterparts. Overall, however, more than 80 percent of students in all fields indicated the presence of a supportive student community in their program, and with percentages ranging from 69 to 76 percent, the respondents in the various fields reported involvement in decisions relevant to their education.

Information for Prospective Students

According to our survey findings, most programs provided accurate information about expectations and costs. However, few programs addressed some of the other common recommendations for excellence in doctoral education. For example, only 35 percent of the respondents reported receiving information on the career placement outcomes of recent program graduates and only 30 percent received information on completion rates. In some cases, there were concerns that students were not given sufficient information about their fields of study to make educated decisions about whether to pursue the Ph.D. degree at all. In fact, some students were even unaware of the issues to consider: "At the time of my application to graduate school, I was not very savvy about what it meant to get a Ph.D. In retrospect, the department didn't really address the above questions, and we didn't ask."

Implications and Recommendations

As a result of our experience with the survey, we have had ample opportunity to examine both what students have said and what role their perspectives can play in the important national conversation about enriching graduate education. The following recommendations emerge from what we have heard graduate students say as they have identified their most pressing concerns:

- *Doctoral programs, graduate schools, institutions, and disciplinary societies should involve students as equal participants at all stages of discussions related to graduate education.* This recommendation includes research studies, relevant committees in disciplinary societies, departmental committees, and institutional discussions, among other forums. Because graduate students have the most to gain—or lose—from discussions of graduate education, they should be the most vital and integral participants in any conversation on the subject. Student stakeholder groups can and should play an instrumental role in soliciting this participation and in encouraging dialogue among students to identify the most pressing issues and concerns. These student groups include program-specific committees and organizations, graduate student governments and representative associations, graduate student delegates to institutional committees and oversight bodies, and graduate student committees and members of disciplinary societies.

- *Instead of brainstorming about what should happen, those involved in enriching graduate education should take well-considered suggestions that have already been made and turn those ideas into reality.* Although most students in the study were positive about their graduate school experiences, they also highlighted a number of areas in which recommendations for best practices in doctoral education have not been universally and successfully implemented. Students indicated that problems in graduate education are not the result of a shortage of good ideas but rather of the difficulty in and resistance to putting existing recommendations into practice. It is increasingly useful to concentrate on implementation of specific ideas, look for models of successful adoption, and learn from them in order to implement them effectively elsewhere.

- *Graduate programs should provide greater transparency in what students can expect from their graduate experience.* In other words, they should provide not only accurate and complete information about program requirements, expectations, costs, and financial support but also data on completion rates, time to degree, and career outcomes of recent students. Providing these data requires programs and institutions to enhance collection of this type of information and communicate more fully with program graduates. Finally, transparency means educating students and the undergraduate faculty and administrators advising them about graduate school. Students need to know what to expect from graduate school even before they enroll, so that they can make more informed decisions about whether they should pursue graduate degrees and in which programs they would be most successful.

- *Graduate education should include closer supervision of mentors and consistent standards for advising.* One of the suggestions from respondents in the study was to use regular progress reports. Most important, though, the reports require the participation of both students and faculty advisors, especially with multiple mentors and committees so students are not solely dependent on individual faculty members. Further, support mechanisms should be readily available to provide students with clear options if they are not satisfied with the advising they receive. Although several of these ideas have already been implemented in many settings, they are by no means universally available to all students.

- *Graduate programs should provide greater opportunities for students to develop teaching and other professional skills.* The study found that students were concerned about not being adequately prepared and trained to fulfill their roles as teachers. This lack of preparation does not simply affect graduate students' experiences and the opportunities they have for professional development; it also greatly affects the quality of undergraduate education provided by many universities. Teaching centers can help prepare students for situations they will face in the classroom and provide practical and useful recommendations for responding to those scenarios. Doctoral programs and graduate schools should also seek to offer training in other professional skills that will be valuable in any career, such as public speaking, grant writing, working in teams, and academic ethics.

- *Graduate programs should increase the availability of career guidance targeted to the graduate student population.* Student respondents in the study mentioned that many career centers provide only minimal services to graduate students. Where graduate career services exist, respondents particularly noted the absence of support for those interested in pursuing nonacademic careers. Graduate programs and campus career centers may have different specialties in the kind of resources they are able to provide, but both should support students for the full range of careers they may pursue. Such support requires curricula broad enough to prepare students for a variety of career paths, ways to introduce individuals to career prospects and opportunities in different fields, and proactive programming to encourage students to think about future careers from the beginnings of their graduate school experiences.

- *Students' graduate experiences need to be examined at the level of individual doctoral programs and on a continual basis.* The study data made it clear that there can be significant differences between programs at a single institution and between programs in a discipline. Further, students are most influenced by the policies and practices of their individual graduate programs, even more so than by their institution as a whole. Thus, it is essential, as we did in this study, to seek ways to identify concerns in specific programs while also making it possible to detect disciplinary or institutional trends by examining the data in aggregate.

Conclusion

As these recommendations suggest, then, the 2000 National Doctoral Program Survey provides a unique perspective on doctoral education in North America: that of doctoral students themselves. Ironically, it is the voice of the students that is often least represented in discussions of graduate education. The survey highlights the importance of involving current and recent students—both graduates and noncompleters—in any consideration of graduate education. Finally, it provides a significant overview of the kind of thoughtful consideration that most students give to their own graduate experience and to the experiences of their fellow students.

Acknowledgments

We would like to acknowledge the critical role played by all members of the NAGPS survey team, which, in addition to ourselves, included Malaina L. Brown, Geoff Davis, and Susan Mahan Niebur. We also thank the NAGPS executive board and membership for their continuing support. The National Doctoral Program Survey Advisory Committee—Geoff Davis, Chris Golde, Charlotte Kuh, Maresi Nerad, Peter Syverson, Michael Teitelbaum, and Ric Weibl—offered invaluable advice and guidance. Funding for Web hosting of the results has been generously provided by the University of Missouri-Columbia, with particular support from Graduate School Dean Suzanne Ortega and Assistant Dean Jim Groccia.

The research in this chapter reflects a recent effort of the National Association of Graduate-Professional Students (NAGPS). Founded in 1986 as a 501(c)(3) nonprofit organization, NAGPS is dedicated to improving the quality of graduate and professional student life in the United States. To this end, it actively works to promote the interests and welfare of graduate- and professional-degree-seeking students in public and private universities as well as in the public and private agencies at the local, state, and national levels. In addition, through its national office and regional networks, NAGPS acts as a clearinghouse for information on graduate and professional student groups at all stages of development. NAGPS represents about nine hundred thousand graduate and professional students at more than 130 universities throughout the United States. More information can be found at the NAGPS Web site: http://www.nagps.org/.

References

Association of American Universities. (1998). *Committee on graduate education: Report and recommendations.* Washington, DC: Association of American Universities. [http://www.aau.edu/reports/GradEdRpt.html]

Committee on Science, Engineering, and Public Policy (COSEPUP) of the National Academy of Sciences, the National Academy of Engineering, and the Institute of Medicine. (1995). *Reshaping the graduate education of scientists and engineers.* Washington, DC: National Academy Press. [http://www.nap.edu/readingroom/books/grad/summary.html]

Golde, C. M., & Dore, T. M. (2001). *At cross purposes: What the experiences of doctoral students reveal about doctoral education.* Philadelphia: A Report for The Pew Charitable Trusts. [http://www.phd-survey.org]

National Research Council. (1998). *Trends in the early careers of life scientists.* Washington, DC: National Academy Press. [http://www.nap.edu/readingroom/books/trends/]

National Science Board. (1997). *The federal role in science and engineering graduate and postdoctoral education* (NSB 97–235). Washington, DC: National Science Foundation. [http://www.nsf.gov/cgi-bin/getpub?nsb97235]

National Science Foundation. (2001). *Graduate students and postdoctorates in science and engineering: Fall 1999* (NSF 01–315). Washington, DC: National Science Foundation, Division of Science Resources Studies. [http://www.nsf.gov/sbe/srs/nsf01315/]

Chapter Five

Theories and Strategies of Academic Career Socialization

Improving Paths to the Professoriate for Black Graduate Students

James Soto Antony, Edward Taylor

Over the last several years we have examined the manner in which Black doctoral students' ambitions to enter an academic career are shaped during the graduate school years. This research (Antony & Taylor, 2001; Taylor & Antony, 2001) has provided useful observations of how Black doctoral students experience graduate school and has confirmed several disturbing facts about the challenges confronting those aspiring to academic careers. Examining the status of Black graduate students shows, for example, that even in fields where they are most likely to pursue and successfully complete doctoral training (such as education and other fields in the social sciences), these students pursue, and ultimately attain, academic careers less often than their White counterparts. Our research indicates that even among the most academically prepared Black students in the field of education (those who earn prestigious national fellowships and research-training grants to study in the top schools and colleges of education with the very best faculty), an alarmingly high rate change their initial academic career aspirations.

In previous research, we thoroughly explored the theoretical ideas underlying socialization and used our data to describe how

Black graduate students develop anxiety and self-doubt in response to the expectations placed on them by traditional congruence and assimilation socialization practices (Antony, 2002; Antony & Taylor, 2001; Taylor & Antony, 2001). Yet we stopped short of confirming the extent to which such anxiety was responsible for changes in students' academic career aspirations, and if so, how this process occurred.

Social psychologists have long been discussing the connection between context-derived anxiety and its deleterious impact on achievement. However, no one has specifically applied these theoretical insights to the situation we were observing in the field—that is, large numbers of intelligent and confident Black doctoral students abandoning their aspirations of pursuing academic careers. We believe that the theoretical model of stereotype threat, first advanced by Claude Steele (1997), is the mechanism connecting the context-derived anxiety observed in graduate students of color and their ultimate decisions to pursue or abandon their academic career aspirations. In this chapter, we draw on empirical data to consider a set of important questions about the socialization of Black graduate students.

Background and Purpose

We begin this chapter by offering a theoretical description of how minority doctoral students experience graduate school socialization and professional development. We argue that the traditional modes of socialization often force Black students to adjust to expectations of congruence and assimilation. Then, drawing on data from a larger study on Black graduate student socialization, we discuss how the need to adjust to these expectations serves as a profound trigger of stereotype threat, and as a result, attenuates the efficacy of traditional socialization practices to advance the academic career aspirations of Black graduate students. We then review what we have previously argued to be the tenets of effective minority socialization and professional development and offer specific strategies, derived from our findings in this chapter, for improving the academic career socialization of these students.

Socialization is generally viewed as a process of active social engagement in which an individual (or organization) directly influences the perceptions, behavior, and skill acquisition of another individual. In educational settings, this socialization occurs as a function of direct communications between teachers and students, and also occurs indirectly—or at least in a more latent fashion—through interactions between peers and the perceptions students develop of how to engage the curriculum and earn positive evaluations.

In a helpful text that summarizes socialization theories relevant to graduate education, Weidman, Twale, and Stein (2001) wrote metaphorically about the socialization process, indicating that graduate students undergo a spiral-like developmental process, or a gradual "metamorphosis," during the graduate school years. Thinking about socialization as a developmental process essentially ascribes a serial nature to the development of identity, commitment, and role acquisition. This serial development takes the neophyte from the earliest thinking about what it might be like to play a particular role, and, through interactions with the training or professional preparation process, that individual is socialized to become an accepted member of that profession or role. Throughout that socialization process, the neophyte's conceptions of self and role are challenged. Classical stage theories of socialization see the ultimate end of socialization as one in which the neophyte has adopted not only the identity of the role but also the values and norms of the profession (for more details, see Antony, 2002; Wiedman et al., 2001).

As indicated in other literature (Antony, 2002), traditional socialization theory assumes that in order for an individual to be successfully socialized, two conditions must be satisfied. First, the individual must develop characteristics that are congruent with those of others in the field of choice. Second, the individual must assimilate his or her values to be congruent with the norms of the profession. Researchers have long been dissatisfied with the linear nature of traditional socialization theories. Linear models of socialization assume that all individuals progress through the socialization process in a single way. That is, all individuals progress through each of the stages and core elements of socialization in a step-by-step, incremental fashion. The normative congruence and assimilation expectations common to most traditional socialization theories are, by definition, a primary feature of linear models of socialization theory.

This linear perspective has been criticized by researchers (for example, Fordham, 1988; Taylor & Antony, 2001; Tierney, 1997; Turner & Thompson, 1993) for four main reasons. First, critics of this traditional linear view of socialization claim that it ignores the effects of graduate students' perceptions (Wentworth, 1980) and gender on the way those students perform a professional role (Gilligan, 1978). Second, critics (for example, Thornton & Nardi, 1975) believe that linear approaches to socialization fail to account for change in normative role expectations over extended periods of time. Third, researchers (for example, Feldman, 1974; Gilligan, 1978) charge that linear socialization theories assume that students are all the same. Fourth, the homogeneity assumption and the normative consensus orientation required by traditional socialization perspectives have been shown to limit women's opportunities for equal access to professional roles and networks (McClelland, 1990; Weidman et al., 2001).

Recognizing many of the problems associated with traditional linear approaches to conceptualizing socialization, Stein and Weidman (1989, 1990) developed a modified conceptual view of socialization that affords an alternative way to think about, and hence, shape, graduate student socialization. This modified view maintains that socialization is a complex, developmental process in which the relationship between student background characteristics, university experiences, socialization outcomes, and mediating elements—such as personal and professional communities prior to and during the graduate school experience—comes into play (Weidman et al., 2001). Contrary to the linear relationship among socialization elements in traditional models, the elements in Stein and Weidman's (1989, 1990) framework are assumed to be linked in a bi-directional fashion (Weidman et al., 2001). This approach recognizes "a reciprocity of influences on the student so that the context and processes of the educational experience influence one another and the socialization outcomes affect the normative context of the higher education environment experienced by students" (Kerchoff, 1976, as cited in Weidman et al., 2001, p. 48). In sum, the socialization process is conceived as developmental, involving interaction between and among the various constituent elements rather than being a strictly linear, causal phenomenon.

That theorists no longer see the socialization process as strictly linear indicates a fundamental shift in theory that has not yet been appreciated in practice. Specifically, most academic programs still socialize students in ways that assume socialization to be a linear process. We have shown in other studies (Antony & Taylor, 2001;

Taylor & Antony, 2001) that the result of this type of socialization is increased anxiety among Black graduate students. Anxiety, in and of itself, is not a bad thing. In fact, at times, increased anxiety can lead to improvements in performance. But the manner in which a person responds to anxiety is largely a function of the amount of anxiety that person feels, and the context from which that anxiety is derived. Said simply, not all anxiety is the same. In fact, according to Steele (1997), the kind of anxiety minorities experience in certain social situations is predictably deleterious on achievement and performance. Steele referred to these conditions as *stereotype threat conditions.*

Stereotype threat is the sense of social and psychological peril that negative racial stereotypes induce, bringing about a climate of intimidation that can hamper academic achievement. The fear comes not from internal doubts about one's ability but from situations such as testing, class presentations, or token status, where concerns about being stereotyped can cause anxiety and self-consciousness. Steele (1997) described this "threat in the air" as follows: "It is the social-psychological threat that arises when one is in a situation or doing something for which a negative stereotype about one's group applies. This predicament threatens one with being negatively stereotyped, with being judged or treated stereotypically, or with the prospect of conforming to the stereotype" (p. 614).

Furthermore, stereotype threat is a situational pressure that affects a specific subgroup of the stereotyped group—the bright, capable, and confident students who are recognized as having good prospects in the domain. Thus, stereotype threat has the greatest impact on students who represent the academic vanguard of their group. Such students—few in number—are cast in a "spotlight" (Cross, 1991) from which they are judged against a racial stereotype. In order for the stereotype to be forbidding, it must be deemed self-relevant and must threaten the students so that they feel they must conform to, or be judged by, the stereotype.

Given that graduate students of color report high levels of anxiety in academic departments that practice traditional congruence and assimilation forms of socialization, we must ask if their anxiety results from their perceptions of stereotype threat. If so, can this anxiety be directly linked to these students' abandonment of academic career aspirations? The research reported in this chapter addresses these questions.

In the remaining sections of this chapter, we describe a study designed to answer three key questions:

- Do traditional congruence and assimilation socialization practices create stereotype threat conditions for Black graduate students?
- If so, can the resultant anxiety that Black graduate students feel be linked to their abandonment of academic career aspirations?
- And, finally, if so, are there ways to inoculate students against these deleterious effects?

Methods

What follows is a detailed description of the study methods: the participants and the procedures.

Participants

Data were derived from ongoing conversations with twelve Black doctoral students (including eight women; average age of all participants was 30.2 years) in the field of education. The interviews occurred as part of a larger research agenda to study graduate students' socialization experiences in a variety of fields.

Six schools and colleges of education that consistently rank in the top fifteen nationally were chosen as sites for the study. The names and contact information of Black doctoral students who had completed two or more years of graduate school were obtained from student personnel offices and key contacts at those institutions. Students who had academic career aspirations were invited to participate in a study of their graduate school experiences. The final sample of twelve Black students who agreed to participate constituted roughly 65 percent of the eligible Black doctoral student pool in the six schools and colleges of education contacted. Eight participants were attending West Coast universities, two were in East Coast programs, and two were from universities located in the southern part of the United States. Ten of the participants were pursuing Ph.D.'s and two were pursuing Ed.D.'s. The sample was moderately skewed toward more advanced years in the graduate program: three were in the second year of their programs, three were in the third year, five were in the fourth year, and one was in the fifth year. One man was married with three small children; two women were married without children. Three women were single parents, with one having a teenage son and the other two having daughters under the age of ten. The remaining six participants were single with no dependents.

All twelve students received funding and attended school full-time. Academic preparation among the participants was high, including not only undergraduate and master's degrees from prestigious universities, but lifelong experiences of being at or near the top of their classes. Many had parents with advanced degrees or siblings who had completed doctoral work.

Procedures

Traditional research methodologies, such as surveys and graduation rate data, although important, may limit understanding of the dynamics of relationships among students, faculty, and institutions. Malaney (1988) suggested that qualitative, ethnographic studies, especially ongoing and longitudinal investigations, have been overlooked in the field of graduate education research. Nettles (1987) and Stanfield (1994), noting that the quality of life for minority students has been underexamined, also called for more qualitative research. Because oral interviews represent the most comprehensive way for people of color to articulate holistic explanations of how they construct their experiences and realities (Stage & Maple, 1996; Stanfield, 1994), researchers conducted one- to two-hour, in-depth, face-to-face interviews. The interviews were conducted with students at the site of their graduate study in order to allow ample time for the interviews and to build relationships that would elicit trustworthy data.

Research questions were asked using a semistructured interview protocol developed by the researchers and pilot-tested on Black graduate students. Each interview continued until interviewer and student mutually agreed that the information was comprehensive. The interviewers sought to gather data that went beyond the mere reporting of experiences and that provided "thick description" of students' intentions, motives, circumstances, and choices. The two interviewers took notes, tape-recorded, and transcribed the interviews.

Each interview began with demographic questions, including age, marital status, number of dependents, full-time or part-time status, the year in program, department affiliation, and intent to pursue an academic career. Students then were asked to describe their educational history, how they had made the decision to apply to graduate school, and how they had chosen their particular institution. Their experiences in the doctoral program were explored, including their interactions with colleagues and faculty. In addition, students were asked to discuss the manner in which their professional and career aspirations were encouraged or hampered. Finally, they were asked to assess their ultimate career aspirations, whether or not they considered the professoriate as a goal and why, what they knew about faculty careers, and where they had gained this information. Data were coded to permit systematic analyses of students' responses to the questions about graduate school and about the process of acculturating to academic life. The analysis of the students' narratives took an interpretive approach that allowed the rich, substantive content to suggest emergent themes.

Key Findings

Key findings are as follows.

Stereotype Threat Conditions Exist in Graduate School

The perception of negative stereotyping toward Black doctoral students was universal among the students. Respondents experienced this stereotyping in a variety of ways, including tokenism, marginalization, and labeling, and in a variety of situations, including campus life, classrooms, faculty interactions, and exposure to education's body of knowledge. Students felt that most mainstream journals, textbooks, discussions, and lectures depicted Black parents and their children in problematic ways. In myriad subtle (and not so subtle) ways, students were reminded of the negative connotations of their group membership. Stereotyping pervaded virtually every aspect of their lives—in how issues affecting Blacks in society were framed and researched, in their professional and social interactions on campus, and in how they were received by faculty members in their departments. The remarks of some of the respondents provide examples:

> *Michelle:* There is a faculty member who's studying aggression in Black males from a psychological perspective. We wouldn't do that. We wouldn't do that. It buys into the idea that something's *wrong* with these kids. And then people hold her up as this great scholar, but to me, it's doing some damage, you know? She makes compromises that we wouldn't make.
>
> *Kim:* Well, I'm very aware of some of the politics in the sense that a lot of my research, in particular, may not be valued, because Black students have been called marginal, deviant, unwanted, unwelcome by several scholars. So we know that my research may not be valued by traditional journals, which is a *big* issue in talking about tenure.

The research interests identified by the graduate students were linked to their experiences with racial stereotyping as well. Concern for Black children as a group was ubiquitous and served as a primary motivator:

> *Melissa:* Research is an opportunity to generate theory, which can impact how people think about Black students and communities of color. And that was one of the reasons that we became more and more interested in theory. And research is exciting; we like it.
>
> *Kim:* Faculty [life] is for me because I love students and I love teaching. It also gives me flexibility to do research—to start to challenge the myths [formulated by Whites] that exist, in particular about Black students, and also begin to look at their success as opposed to failure. It gives me the power of the pen, the power of the voice.

Despite the absence of *overt* racial hostility on campus for most of the participants, all felt pressures to prove themselves academically and to overcome negative stereotyping about Black doctoral students' intellectual inferiority. There was a widespread sense of being watched, of not quite fitting in, or of being admitted because of race and not because of credentials. Given the academic backgrounds of the respondents, such scrutiny was not welcome. One National Merit Scholar reacted to an incident when flyers were posted around campus denigrating minority students as affirmative action admits:

> *Cheryl:*   I graduated summa cum laude from [Ivy League university]. I'm currently like a 3.8 and this is a hard damn school. I know that people look at me as quota and not doing very well, you know, just getting over or something. Meantime, I'm working really hard.

Cheryl also reported widespread anti-Black student racism on her campus, which is located in the South. Besides having a professor who explicitly endorsed the book *The Bell Curve* and other faculty who openly questioned Cheryl's intellect and writing abilities (although she had already published two articles), the university had a fraternity that held a "slave auction." The only two Black professors previously at the school had chosen to leave.

Another participant, while doing her practicum in a local school, had found Ku Klux Klan literature slipped under the door of her office. Close scrutiny of these brochures revealed that they were not aimed at her personally but rather were intended for recruitment. The local Ku Klux Klan members knew the location of graduate student offices, and they routinely left informational recruitment materials.

The three students in the sample who abandoned their academic career aspirations all reported that having to attend to the stereotypes in the department led to an aversion to the idea of pursuing an academic career, a reaction Steele (1997) called *disidentification*. Disidentification is the result of sustained pressure that causes "a reconceptualization of the self and of one's values so as to remove the domain as a self-identity" (p. 614). One is then protected from further injury—a chilling side effect is the loss of a once-promising career.

Observations and data from the study clearly indicated that the anxiety and pressure of attending to stereotype threat conditions in academic environments had the potential to promote disidentification with academic career aspirations. All students in the sample reported sensing stereotype threats throughout their graduate school experiences. The data showed that traditional congruence and assimilation socialization practices created an environment that was likely to foster stereotypical thinking about, and interactions with, Black graduate students (see Antony & Taylor, 2001). Clearly, this is bad news.

Of note, most students in the sample, despite having experienced the side effects of stereotype threat fostered by traditional socialization practices, continued to pursue their academic career aspirations. What was different about these students that inoculated them from eventually disidentifying with an academic career? It is to this important issue that we now turn.

Wise Schooling Practices Inoculate Against Stereotype Threat

In adapted form, Steele's theory provides the basis for a conceptually strong and pragmatically useful framework. Steele noted that school success depends on *domain identification*. In contrast to disidentification, domain identification is the degree to which students incorporate not only a sense of themselves as having appropriate interests and skills to achieve but also a sense of being accepted and valued by their educational institutions. Using undergraduates as the unit of analysis, he suggested that "sustained school achievement depends, most centrally, on identifying with school—that is, forming a relationship between oneself and the domains of schooling so that one's self-regard significantly depends on achievement in those domains" (Steele, 1997, p. 616).

Steele proposed that schooling can be improved through institutional strategies that reduce stereotype threat. He argued that there are ways in which programs can be designed to assure students that they will not be cast in the shadow of negative stereotypes and that individual characteristics can surmount perceptions associated with group membership. "Wise schooling" practices include strategies designed to reduce the threat of negative racial stereotyping that can undermine student performance (Steele, 1997, p. 624). In early results, such practices have been shown to improve academic performance for groups negatively affected by stereotyping, such as Black students and women in math and science (Steele, 1992; Steele & Aronson, 1995). Examples include these: optimistic teacher-student relationships, where teachers make their confidence in students explicit; challenging, rather than remedial, expectations and academic work, which build on promise and potential, not failure; stress on the expandability of intelligence and the idea that skills can be learned and extended through education and experience; affirmation of a sense of intellectual belonging; emphasis on the value of multiple perspectives; and the presence of role models who have successfully overcome stereotype threat conditions.

The empirical question at hand is clear: To what extent did the students who successfully continued to pursue their academic career aspirations experience wise schooling practices that inoculated them against the stereotype threat conditions universally reported by all the study's respondents? For purposes of the study, four of the six categories of wise schooling practices mentioned here warranted investigation; two of the practices did not. That is, because challenging (not remedial) work was the universal experience for this group, remediation was not an issue. The programs studied gave students work at a level that conveyed respect and high expectations. Thus, stereotype threat in this area was not observed. In addition, these departments presumed the expandability of intelligence through experience and training (rather than intelligence as genetically limited). This presumption is generally deep-seated in the field of education, where traditional paradigms about the inheritability of intelligence, for example, are challenged and may account in no small part for enhanced domain identification among Black doctoral students in education. We did study, however, how the respondents who continued to pursue their academic career aspirations experienced the other four wise schooling practices: optimistic student-teacher relationships, affirmation of a sense of intellectual belonging, emphasis on the value of multiple perspectives, and the presence of role models who successfully overcame stereotype threat.

Optimistic Teacher-Student Relationships

Optimistic teacher-student relationships were defined in order to make a distinction between advisors and other faculty. Although all members of a department are "teachers" in graduate school, the influential role of advisors merits separating this category into two subgroups.

Advisor. Widely known to be of vital importance for all graduate students, the relationship with advisors for Black doctoral students has proven to be as important as it is complex. Although the data indicated generally good outcomes when there was a match by race and gender, they also suggested that it is unreasonable to expect that every Black woman, for example, is going to bond with the sole Black female faculty member. However, those students who chose departments based on the work being done by Black faculty reported particularly supportive relationships, primarily because of matched research interests.

Seven participant-advisor dyads were matched for both race and gender, with the remaining dyads being an assortment (some were gender- but not race-matched; some were race- but not gender-matched; and some were neither race- nor gender-matched). Despite this mixture of dyadic composition, eleven out of twelve participants enjoyed what they described as satisfactory and positive relationships with their advisors. Comments from several respondents illustrate this point:

> *Kim:*   We [Black students in this department] are in a very unique situation. We have extreme support. We have one Black female in our department who carries *all* of us on her shoulders, literally. The picture of Hercules holding the world basically is my advisor [Black female advisor].
>
> *Michelle:*   My advisor's wonderful. Our interests really click well so that we're interested in a lot of the same things. But I bring some issues to the table that he never even really considered. But I think it's he being so interested in my work, and me being interested in his work that has fostered a good

relationship between us. So we have really good
mentorship. [White male advisor]

Melissa: She's been my savior. [White female advisor]

Other Faculty. The support and encouragement of other faculty
members also has an effect on student success. The data suggested
that a number of departments and their faculty members, despite
good intentions, were unprepared to share that responsibility. Five
students spoke about their sense of not being welcomed or valued
by White faculty. Some faculty were described as "having no background for understanding my work," being patronizing, or being
genuinely surprised at the academic success of Black students. Students also reported endemic departmental insensitivity and racial
stereotyping, such as faculty members looking at new (minority)
admits and asking if the department was lowering its standards or
showing no interest in students' research ideas if they related to
issues affecting Blacks in American society.

Despite the presence of some faculty members perceived as
obstructive, many respondents described faculty relationships outside of the advisor's support as professional and helpful. When these
relationships affirmed students, the students reported feeling valued
and secure and reported a sense of safety from stereotype threat:

Carol: Individuals here have been able to really respond
to my needs, learning style, and interest areas. It's
just like . . . wonderful. That's what I am totally
grateful for.

Kim: My senior faculty, who all happen to be White male
professors, have been extremely supportive of my
initiative. My colleague established a graduate-
mentoring program for people of color at our
institution. By participating in that program, we
have been able to become close to a White male
junior faculty member and we have cultivated a
very positive and professional relationship. And
through that relationship, we've been able to
meet national scholars in my area. So it's been
very positive, very beneficial.

Affirmation of a Sense of Intellectual Belonging

One of the many important ways that departments foster a sense of belonging is through adequate financial support. Freedom from undue financial stress is critical for all students, and Black doctoral students are no exception. Moreover, the receipt of fellowships, grants, research assistantships, and teaching assistantships are often a preamble to successful academic careers. The respondents all enjoyed adequate financial support through teaching-research assistantships and grants, but many reported benefits extending far beyond relief from financial stress. Spencer Foundation grants to support doctoral work were particularly beneficial. Spencer travel grants allowed presentations at conferences and created opportunities for respondents to meet other students with similar research interests. Research groups were formed, multicampus collaborative studies were started, and peer support networks across the country were established. Such networks help neutralize negative effects from other areas, as described by two students:

Tonya: I don't think anything has been done actually to shape me into a professor at all. If anything, I feel like it's been more obstacles. Well, actually, I take that back. I have a fellowship—a Spencer Research Training Fellowship—where we meet with a group, a cohort of us. And we discuss publications, proposal writing, grant writing, how to do presentations, things like that.

Roger: I think my experience is somewhat unique. I don't know, I guess I've just been somewhat fortunate to be given opportunities. I rarely talk to other Black students around the country who have been given these opportunities. I think if you don't get those experiences, you can oftentimes take a lot of your own perceptions of what being a faculty member is like and kind of run with them and never have them challenged by any other, um, position, because you never get that opportunity.

Other student respondents described experiencing a sense of intellectual belonging stemming from invitations by their faculty members to participate on departmental committees and search committees, and to be part of other governance conversations:

> *Tony:* You know, presenting, being a participant in classes, and doing some other key things. One of those key things would have been, I sat on a faculty committee. I also sat on a committee that was interviewing candidates for faculty positions. I saw myself—I said, "I could see myself sitting here, you know, talking about my areas of interest, what I've done, why I've done it, how I think it is important." Ah, it just seemed like something that I would enjoy. . . . There are certain parts of it that don't fit in terms of the way I see myself. But just the [hiring] process . . . seeing that let me know this is something I could do.

Overall, students felt these opportunities allowed them to see themselves as academics and to be able to play out in their own minds how they would respond to various situations. Such opportunities to experience a sense of intellectual belonging also gave them common ground from which they could relate to a variety of faculty members.

Emphasis on Multiple Perspectives

Students who connected with a diverse group of faculty mentors, or whose programs encouraged the exploration of alternative views about academic careers, were likely to filter out negative information about graduate school and academia. They tended to have a positive outlook on faculty work, even in the face of evidence suggesting it would be difficult at times. These students' comments illustrate how they developed positive perspectives:

> *Roger:* Coming in, my whole perception was that I kept hearing a lot that the politics involved in the academy are too difficult for people of color to survive

as academics. If you want tenure, you have to put up with a lot of things. And it was a lot of hearsay that was affecting my decision to not want to go the faculty route. Um, but just being here, talking with my advisor. . . . I think my whole position in this now is the work kind of rises above any politics that may take place. . . . I guess I was realizing that my contribution would make a difference.

Sheila: In a faculty position, I would not only be able to influence people in the institution, but also outside. I worked in another sector for many years, on and off, and I really didn't feel I could affect people directly. Usually you are marginalized in that sector. True, that can still happen with faculty. However, my advisor says there are other meetings, other journals. You may not get published in the mainstream, traditional, functionalist journals. But hopefully, the different humanist and subjective and qualitative journals will appreciate the work that I'll do.

As these examples illustrate, these students gained much information from faculty mentors that helped them process their observations and the discussions they had with fellow students. In particular, students were quick to acknowledge that the faculty route would present unique challenges to them as Black scholars. However, they were able to draw upon the experience and advice of their faculty mentors to see viable ways of reconciling the tensions present in the faculty career so that they could pursue that career.

Presence of Successful Role Models

Successful role models included not only students' faculty members (as discussed in the preceding section) but also successful Black student peers at other institutions. According to the respondents, like-minded peers helped mitigate the social and intellectual isolation resulting from stereotype threat. Eleven of twelve participants discussed the value of peer relationships that were largely very positive despite the competitive nature of academic work. Many of these peers were not on the same campus, but relationships were formed at conferences and maintained through e-mail. A sense of solidarity with, rather than competition among, Black students was common, as illustrated by these respondents' comments:

> *Michelle:* You go to these conferences and people are just sitting around loving their work and talking about it. When you see people that are excited about what they are doing, and you share your stuff and they're excited about that. *That's* what we like.
>
> *Kim:* All of us realize what is at stake now. The stakes are higher for Blacks in educational institutions—with affirmative action under the gun, with federal monies being cut—there's no time to play. There's no time for competition [against one another] in that sense.

Analysis of these data offers some support for Steele's framework for higher education and the successful socialization of Black graduate students in education. This study found a link between wise schooling strategies and the desire to pursue academic careers. Fortunately, successful socialization did not appear to depend on optimal conditions in all four of the wise schooling areas that we assessed. Table 5.1 summarizes the experiences of the respondents in terms of these wise schooling practices and indicates the students' academic career aspirations. Just one deficiency—such as a less-than-ideal advisor or a nonsupportive department—did not result in loss of academic ambitions, but two problematic areas put the student's future into serious question. The decision to avoid the academic career track was resounding for the one student with "No" answers in three areas.

The data also suggest that the effects of departmental deficits in one area may be neutralized by strategies that increase success in others. For example, financial support, which traditionally has

Table 5.1. Wise Schooling Practices Correlated to Academic Career Plans

							Participant					
Type of Wise Schooling Practice	1	2	3	4	5	6	7	8	9	10	11	12
Optimistic relationship with advisor	Y	N	Y	Y	Y	Y	Y	Y	Y	Y	Y	Y
Optimistic relationship with other faculty	Y	N	N	Y	N	N	Y	Y	Y	Y	N	Y
Affirmed sense of intellectual belonging	Y	Y	Y	Y	Y	Y	Y	Y	Y	Y	N	Y
Presence of academically successful role models	Y	Y	Y	Y	Y	Y	Y	Y	Y	Y	Y	Y
Maintained academic career aspirations*	Y	N	Y	Y	Y	Y	Y	Y	Y	Y	N	Y

*Determined upon completion of data collection at the end of the study period.

been important to most graduate students, had unexpected positive benefits for Black doctoral students. Spencer Foundation awards that provided travel grants, in particular, opened doors of opportunity and generated considerable excitement among respondents by promoting contact with other Black students and faculty on other campuses. These relationships promoted research projects, writing groups, and supportive friendships sustained over e-mail long after the conferences ended. Thus, well-being in this area was able to mitigate unfavorable circumstances in others.

Implications and Recommendations

Institutions of higher education should be encouraged by the presence of dynamic, enthusiastic, highly capable, motivated Black doctoral students. These students have the potential to reinvigorate both theory and practice in education, and specifically, the production of the culturally relevant pedagogy necessary for an increasingly diverse student body. What strategies can institutions employ to support more fully Black graduate students?

- *Departments that support Black graduate students are committed to strategies that reduce negative stereotyping and create academic environments in which students are valued, challenged, and supported.* However, departments also must confront some age-old tensions that are fueled by traditional congruence and assimilation socialization practices.
- *The first tension that must be confronted is the traditional distance between service and research.* Many faculty members model considerable separation between the two; the students in this study, however, operated in a value system that says research *must* be of service. The challenge is for faculty members to understand this mindset and begin to capitalize on the opportunity to bridge the gap between theory and practice and make their own work more relevant and exemplary.
- *A second tension that must be addressed is also embodied in traditional approaches to socialization—that is, whose responsibility is it to mentor graduate students?* There are long-standing issues in many departments over whether this responsibility is primarily individual (that is, the advisor) or collective (the faculty as a

whole). Data from this study suggest that Black doctoral students benefit from a collective approach. Students often realize that the sole Black faculty member must act as "Hercules" for all the minority students. They see such expectations as untenable, and in fact, this sort of treatment of Black faculty reinforces stereotypical ideas about whom Black faculty should mentor. No strong evidence exists to suggest that mentoring must come from relationships in which students and advisors are of the same gender and race. In fact, senior faculty members (usually White males) generally have more experience and resources than others; in this study, students supported by White male faculty appeared particularly well socialized. The potential of White male faculty members to contribute, however, must be weighed against the evidence that some (unknowingly or not) exacerbate stereotype threat for Black doctoral students. Often, this threat occurs as a function of these faculty members' insistence on employing a traditional congruence and assimilation approach to socializing their students.

- *A wise schooling model of successful socialization could serve departments and institutions that are attempting to reduce stereotype threats and other obstacles that have kept Black doctoral students from seeking academic careers.* Interested departments might engage in self-study and then develop strategies for improving or mitigating concerns. For example, institutions with very few Black students could compensate with a committed group of faculty members, a generous travel fund for conference attendance, and e-mail accounts. Those with very few (or even no) Black faculty could similarly counterbalance the situation by matching students to advisors by research interests, or by fostering interdepartmental relationships with faculty of color. The department could pursue potential mentoring relationships in a formal way without placing the burden on students to figure out how to create such relationships.

- *The wise schooling strategies that have been identified in this case study would profit from further research.* First, these findings need to be supported by large-scale studies, particularly of academic departments with fewer Black scholars and students than education departments usually have. Second, the experiences of more first- and second-year students should be examined; the sample for this study was skewed toward more advanced students and may have missed critical dynamics around the decision not to continue doctoral studies. Third, gender issues need to be addressed in a more direct fashion, particularly as they intersect with race.

Conclusion

Academic achievement for Black doctoral students in predominantly White settings has long been problematic. What prior research into causality has given us is a tower built of small bricks: stereotype threat is the mortar (theoretically speaking) that bonds these bricks into a cohesive whole. It is on this foundation that strategies for wise schooling are constructed and no longer based on anecdote or isolated studies. Steele's theories hold forth the promise of academic reform based on a comprehensive, evidence-based understanding of what threatens, what protects, what sustains, and what nurtures the intellectual lives of Black students.

References

Antony, J. S. (2002). Reexamining doctoral student socialization and professional development: Moving beyond the congruence and assimilation orientation. In J. C. Smart (Ed.), *Higher education: Handbook of theory and research* (Vol. 17, pp. 349–380). New York: Agathon Press.

Antony, J. S., & Taylor, E. (2001). Graduate student socialization and its implications for the recruitment of African American education faculty. In W. G. Tierney (Ed.), *Faculty work in schools of education: Rethinking roles and rewards for the 21st century* (pp. 189–209). Albany: State University of New York Press.

Cross, W. E. (1991). *Shades of Black: Diversity in African-American identity.* Philadelphia: Temple University Press.

Feldman, S. (1974). *Escape from the doll's house: Women in graduate and professional education.* New York: McGraw-Hill.

Fordham, S. (1988). Racelessness as a factor in Black students' school success: Pragmatic strategy or Pyrrhic victory? *Harvard Educational Review, 58,* 43–84.

Gilligan, C. (1978). *In a different voice: Psychological theory and women's development.* Cambridge, MA: Harvard University Press.

Kerchoff, S. (1976). The status attainment process: Socialization or allocation. *Social Forces, 55*(2), 368–481.

Malaney, G. D. (1988). Graduate education as an area of research in the field of higher education. In J. C. Smart (Ed.), *Higher education: Handbook of theory and research* (Vol. 4, pp. 397–454). New York: Agathon Press.

McClelland, K. (1990, April). Cumulative disadvantage among the highly ambitious. *Sociology of Education, 63,* 102–121.

Nettles, M. (1987). *Financial aid and minority student participation.* Princeton, NJ: Educational Testing Service.

Stage, F. K., & Maple, S. A. (1996). Incompatible goals: Narratives of graduate women in the mathematics pipeline. *American Educational Research Journal, 33*(1), 23–51.

Stanfield, J. H. (1994). Ethnic modeling in qualitative research. In N. K. Denzin & Y. S. Lincoln, (Eds.), *Handbook of qualitative research* (pp. 175–188). Thousand Oaks, CA: Sage.

Steele, C. M. (1992, April). Race and the schooling of Black Americans. *Atlantic Monthly,* 68–78.

Steele, C. M. (1997). A threat in the air: How stereotypes shape intellectual identity and performance. *American Psychologist, 52*(6), 613–629.

Steele, C. M., & Aronson, J. (1995). Stereotype threat and the intellectual test performance of African Americans. *Journal of Personality and Social Psychology, 69,* 797–811.

Stein, E. L., & Weidman, J. C. (1989). *Socialization in graduate school: A conceptual framework.* Paper presented at the annual meeting of the Association for the Study of Higher Education, Atlanta.

Stein, E. L., & Weidman, J. C. (1990, April). *The socialization of doctoral students to academic norms.* Paper presented at the annual meeting of the American Educational Research Association, Boston.

Taylor, E., & Antony, J. S. (2001). Stereotype threat reduction and wise schooling: Toward the successful socialization of Black doctoral students in education. *Journal of Negro Education 69*(3), 184–198.

Thornton, R., & Nardi, P. M. (1975). The dynamics of role acquisition. *American Journal of Sociology, 80*(4), 870–885.

Tierney, W. G. (1997). Organizational socialization in higher education. *Journal of Higher Education, 68*(1), 1–16.

Turner, C. S., & Thompson, J. (1993). Socializing women doctoral students: Minority and majority experiences. *Review of Higher Education, 16*(3), 355–370.

Weidman, J. C., Twale, D. J., & Stein, E. L. (2001). *Socialization of graduate and professional students in higher education: A perilous passage?* (ASHE-ERIC Higher Education Report, 28, No. 3). San Francisco: Jossey-Bass, in cooperation with the ERIC Clearinghouse on Higher Education, the Association for the Study of Higher Education, and The George Washington University.

Wentworth, W. M. (1980). *Context and understanding: An inquiry into socialization theory.* New York: Elsevier.

Chapter Six

Research on the Structure and Process of Graduate Education

Retaining Students

Barbara E. Lovitts

For almost fifty years, as long as there have been data on doctoral student attrition, the data have shown that close to 50 percent of people who start doctoral programs leave without completing the Ph.D. (See Benkin, 1984; Berelson, 1960; Bowen & Rudenstine, 1992; Katz & Hartnett, 1976; National Research Council, 1996; Nerad & Cerny, 1991; Office of Technology Assessment, 1988; Tucker, 1964.) This rate of attrition is costly to faculty, departments, and universities, but most importantly, it is costly to the students who leave.

During periods of economic austerity, low Ph.D. production rates—and by implication, high student attrition rates—can put the very existence of doctoral programs and the faculty who teach in them at risk for termination. During the 1970s, the early 1990s, and now in the post-dot-com, post-September-11 world, fiscal constraints have inspired state governments and universities to review their systems with the goal of eliminating programs, and sometimes even whole departments, judged to be unnecessary or ineffective.

Graduate student attrition also wastes scarce administrative and academic resources. Administrators know that it is cheaper to retain an undergraduate than to recruit a new one. Even though no research exists on the costs of recruitment versus retention at the graduate level, they are considered to be even greater than at the undergraduate level. Less tangible are the costs of attrition with respect to the time and effort faculty devote to educating and training graduate students who do not complete. These costs are greater when students depart in the later, as opposed to earlier, stages of their programs.

The financial, personal, and professional costs of attrition to the students who leave are also great. As will be discussed in the following section, because noncompleters are less likely than completers to have received teaching and research assistantships and more likely to have taken out loans, their level of debt at the time of attrition is often high. Few graduate students leave their programs because of lack of ability or academic failure, yet they often leave feeling like failures. When they leave, they have to give up an often deeply held image of themselves as individuals with Ph.D.'s, though some never do. And they have to construct a new professional self-image and pursue a career and a lifestyle that are often far different from the ones they had been envisioning.

From the standpoint of educating the next generation of faculty, the high rate of graduate student attrition reduces by roughly half the number of bright, ambitious people who desire faculty positions; it is also a huge waste of talent. Yet until recently, there has been very little research on the causes of graduate student attrition. Historically, the little research that has been done has focused primarily on individual characteristics. In essence, the previous research has asked: What is wrong with the student who leaves? How can we make better selection decisions? How can we fix the student? My research turns the issue around and asks what is wrong with the structure and process of graduate education.

Background and Purpose

In this chapter, I focus on the social-structural causes of attrition and present data in support of two themes:

- It is less the background characteristics students bring with them to the university than what happens to them after they enroll that affects decisions about completion.
- Graduate student attrition is a function of the differential distribution of resources for integration and cognitive map development.

Before providing the evidence in support of these arguments, I discuss the key theories underlying my research.

My approach is grounded in two theories—the theory of the cognitive map and the theory of integration—and their interaction (Howard, 1995; Morgan & Schwalbe, 1990; Spady, 1970, 1971; Tinto, 1975, 1987, 1993). Cognitive maps are mental models or mental representations. They help people make sense of their experiences and help them negotiate the environments in which they find themselves. I argue that graduate students need two kinds of cognitive maps: a global cognitive map and a series of local maps. The global map is analogous to a state map. It provides the major features of the terrain. In the case of graduate school this would include formal requirements such as coursework, qualifying exams, and a dissertation. The local maps are analogous to street maps. They provide the details for getting around in a locality. In the case of graduate school, this would be a map of informal or unwritten expectations, academic tasks, and social and political relationships.

The theory of integration is a theory of community membership. If someone is integrated into a community (for example, a religious, social, or political organization; a family; a workplace), that person has bonds and ties to members of that community that are difficult to break and as a result the person remains in or persists in that community. However, if someone is not integrated into a community, that person has no bonds or ties to others in that community. As a result, it is easy for that person to walk away or depart from that community.

Graduate school has two communities into which students must integrate: an academic community and a social community. The academic community is the primary community because participating in it is the primary reason for being in graduate school. Interactions and experiences that relate to the student's academic program and professional development lead to academic integration. The social community is incidental to the academic community. Integration into this community results from informal, casual interactions and experiences that often take place in academic settings.

I argue that the better students' cognitive maps of the academic and social communities of their graduate programs, the more likely they are to become integrated into their programs and persist. And the better integrated students are into their programs, the better their cognitive maps will be because they are in closer and more frequent contact with people who can help them develop the understanding necessary for degree completion.

Methods

My research is based on five sources of data. One, I conducted a survey of 816 students (511 completers, 305 noncompleters) who were members of the fall 1982 to fall 1984 entering cohort at two universities in nine departments. The universities, which are called Rural University and Urban University, are among the top forty Ph.D.-granting universities in the United States. The nine departments are traditional liberal arts disciplines and come from each of the three major domains of knowledge (*sciences:* mathematics, biology, chemistry; *social sciences:* sociology, economics, psychology; *humanities:* English, history, music). The attrition rates for each department at each university are as follows: mathematics (32 percent Rural, 47 percent Urban); biology (39 percent Rural, 65 percent Urban); chemistry (19 percent Rural, 42 percent Urban); sociology (28 percent Rural, 72 percent Urban); economics (22 percent Rural, 82 percent Urban); psychology (41 percent Rural, 23 percent Urban); English (34 percent Rural, 76 percent Urban); history (30 percent Rural, 61 percent Urban); and music (44 percent Rural, 65 percent Urban). Two, I conducted telephone interviews with thirty noncompleters, roughly two from each department from each university. Three, I conducted telephone interviews with eighteen directors of graduate study to gain background information on the participating departments' formal and informal structures and processes for educating graduate students. Four, I carried out face-to-face interviews with thirty-three faculty members, roughly two from each of the participating departments—one that had produced many Ph.D.'s and one that had produced few. These interviews were conducted in order to discern systematic differences in the attitudes, beliefs, and behaviors of those most responsible for educating and training graduate students. And, five, I made site visits to each department.

Data for this study were collected from 1994 to 1995. The 1982 to 1984 cohort was chosen in order to maximize the number of students who had either completed their degrees or made their attrition decisions, while at the same time minimizing the number of students who would have to be censored because they were still working on their degrees. The analysis and the continued relevance of data collected from this cohort are premised on the assumption that, barring major changes in the policies and procedures concerning the way graduate students are educated and trained, the forces acting on graduate students today resemble those acting on students in the early to mid-1980s. Interviews with directors of graduate study in 1995 about changes over the previous ten years in the structure and process of graduate education in their departments indicated that few significant changes had been made. Although a number of reform efforts have been instituted in departments around the country since the 1980s, many of the same structures and processes for educating graduate students still prevail. A casual perusal of graduate student listservs, Web sites, and other graduate student forums reveals little change in graduate students' often negative experiences with and concerns about their education.

Key Findings

I review key findings here related to predictors of success.

Students' Background Characteristics Do Not Predict Success

My study, like many others, finds no differences in undergraduate GPA between students who completed the Ph.D. and those who did not. The completers' undergraduate GPA was 3.53 and the noncompleters' was 3.55. In other words, the completers and noncompleters were equally academically able. More interesting, however, is the statistically significant finding that the female students reported higher undergraduate GPAs than the male students (3.59 versus 3.51), with females who did not complete reporting the highest undergraduate GPA (3.62). Furthermore, that women left their graduate programs in higher numbers than men suggests that something other than lack of academic ability influences their decisions to leave.

Noncompleters also had more of the background experiences that should predict success than did completers. The survey included nine items that asked about the students' academic integration as undergraduates and prior socialization to graduate school and the profession (that is, receiving mentoring, working as part of a team, publishing an article or chapter, presenting a paper outside the classroom, subscribing to a professional journal, attending professional meetings, belonging to a professional association, serving on department committees, and belonging to any campus organizations). Two of the nine items (attending professional meetings and serving on departmental committees) achieved significance and favored the noncompleters. A higher percentage of those who did not complete as compared with those who did responded positively to four of the remaining seven items (receiving mentoring, presenting a paper outside the classroom, subscribing to a professional journal, belonging to any campus organizations). When the nine items were collapsed into a single index and completers were compared with noncompleters, the result was significant and favored the noncompleters.

This counterintuitive finding is best explained by information gleaned from interviews with the noncompleters, those who had attended small liberal arts colleges in particular. These students had close collegial relationships with faculty and other students as undergraduates, went to graduate school expecting more of the same, and became disappointed and disillusioned when their experiences did not meet their expectations.

It Is What Happens After They Enroll

Cognitive map and integration issues are discussed in this section.

Cognitive Map Issues

Students' persistence outcomes were closely related to the quality of their cognitive maps of their departments' formal requirements and informal expectations. When I interviewed the directors of graduate study (DGSs), I asked them a series of questions about the information their departments gave students to help them develop cognitive maps about various aspects of their programs. Their responses to, and the students' perspectives on, several cognitive map issues, including those related to the advisor, are discussed briefly here.

Information After Arriving on Campus. Graduate students are provided with handbooks and other written materials that can often be an inch thick. Although graduate students are (and should be) responsible for reading the material, the directors of graduate study assumed that students understood everything contained in it. Unfortunately, this assumption can be fateful. Students who mentioned the materials indicated that a complete understanding of what was expected of them—the informal, unwritten aspects of graduate education—could only be obtained by interacting with an advisor or with more advanced graduate students. This observation underscores the importance of integration for cognitive map development. Indeed, one noncompleter told me he went through his whole first year not understanding what comprehensive exams were all about.

Orientation. I found that there was tremendous variability in the structure of orientations among departments, with orientations lasting anywhere from a half day to a week. The DGSs placed the greatest emphasis on their departments' teaching assistant (TA) orientations, indicating that students who entered with teaching assistantships underwent a longer and more in-depth orientation. In other words, students who enter with teaching assistantships have more opportunity to interact with and get to know faculty and more advanced graduate students than those who do not enter with teaching assistantships. Thus, these students are afforded the opportunity to start integrating into the graduate community and to develop better cognitive maps of their programs than the others.

Departments sometimes also send very negative messages to new students during the orientation, sometimes intentionally, sometimes unintentionally. One DGS told me that his department prided itself on having the toughest first-year program in the country: "I tell them, it's sort of like Quantico. You're going to Marine Boot Camp. This is it, gang." The militaristic, combative metaphor gives students the message that they are going to have to struggle and prove themselves. Another department unintentionally intimidated students by focusing on the prestige of the department and faculty. Emmie, a noncompleter from this department, said it thrilled her to think that she was becoming "a part of this very elite group," but "then it's kind of like, gee, can I do this?"

Program Planning. To construct a coherent program and get through it in a timely fashion, students must have some understanding of, and foresight in, selecting and sequencing courses.

Most departments have some structures in place to help students select courses during their first year. After that, the process becomes murky. In some departments, students are "left pretty free to take whatever advanced courses they might wish," but "what advanced courses are available in the given year depends very much on the whims and fancies of the faculty." Departments rely on student judgment of what courses will enhance their under-standings of their fields, but many students experienced a lack of departmental assistance.

Even when students consult with advisors it is not clear that they always get good advice. When asked about the kind of advis-ing he received, John, a noncompleter in history, replied, "They told me what was in the guidebook, but they didn't really give me any guidance as to what was a typical experience for a graduate stu-dent, I mean, as to how many courses I should take, which courses would be good to take this semester, which courses would go bet-ter if I waited a semester or two and that sort of thing." John took five courses each semester during his first and only year in gradu-ate school while holding a part-time job. He noted that some of his professors knew he was taking five courses, but "they never said, 'That's an unadvisable course of action.'"

Choosing an Advisor. Choosing an advisor is probably the single most important decision graduate students make during their graduate careers. Whom a student works with can often spell the difference between completion and noncompletion. This person influences the nature and quality of the student's graduate expe-rience, the student's socialization as a researcher and academic professional, and the student's subsequent job placement. Yet as with so many other aspects of graduate education, students are given very little formal advice about how to choose an appropriate advisor. By and large, the DGSs commented that graduate students frequently are attracted to particular faculty members when they take advanced-level courses with them; by talking to one another, students find out who has a good reputation, who seems to take care of students, and who does not. Susan's remarks about advisor selection supported those of the DGSs. Susan was a biology student who selected her advisor based on having taken classes with her and rotating through her laboratory. Yet Susan felt that it was not clear whose laboratory students should go into, that it was "pretty much up to you," and that selecting laboratories was done by word of mouth, "'Oh, he's a nice guy,' or 'She's a good person.'"

Although some students come in knowing the faculty member with whom they want to work, many do not, and consequently are either assigned to or must choose an advisor. In cases where students are assigned to an advisor, many do not know that the assignment is temporary or that they can change advisors without penalty. Noncompleters were six times as likely as completers to have been assigned to an advisor (44 percent versus 7 percent), and noncompleters who were assigned to advisors had shorter durations in their programs than noncompleters who were matched with their advisors through other means.

If the process of advisor selection is not clear to graduate students, it is apparently not clear to senior graduate faculty either. When asked about how they came to be a student's advisor, two faculty members used the term "mysterious" to describe the process. One noted, "It is probably something we need to do a little better than we do."

Information About Other Formal Requirements. The basic responses from the DGSs were that the information was in the student handbook, that students were provided with the information during orientation, or that students got the information from "scuttlebutt"—in other words, that it was contained in the graduate student subculture. Students who were not well integrated or were marginalized for other reasons, such as gender, race-ethnicity, or being part-time or commuter students, had less access to the "scuttlebutt" than full-time or well-integrated students, primarily because they often had less contact with the graduate student subculture that contained such information.

The DGSs also focused on the prerequisites for the requirements, not the standards of quality for meeting the requirements. By contrast, students who are approaching a requirement are less concerned about the timing and the prerequisites (because, presumably, they have fulfilled them) than about how they actually *do* the requirement—that is, what it means to fulfill the requirement successfully. Graduate students know that failure to fulfill the prerequisites and failure to hurdle the requirements in a timely fashion are likely to lead to termination from the program. They also know that fulfilling the prerequisites and meeting the requirements on time does not guarantee their retention in the program unless their *performance* meets a certain *standard of quality*. It is this standard of quality—how to prepare themselves to meet it and how they will be judged—about which they need more information.

The survey asked the students two two-part questions about their understanding of their departments' formal requirements and informal expectations. It also asked about their perceptions of other graduate students' understandings of these things. The results revealed that, when it came to their own understandings of their departments' formal requirements and informal expectations, completers felt they understood them far better than the noncompleters felt they did. There were no differences between completers and noncompleters in how well they thought other graduate students understood these things.

More interesting is what happened when the students' understandings of the formal requirements and informal expectations were compared with their perceptions of other students' understandings. The completers believed that they understood the formal requirements better than other students did and that they understood the informal expectations as well as other students. In contrast, the noncompleters believed that other students understood the formal requirements and informal expectations much better than they did. Such a belief can lead to a tremendous feeling of discomfort and unease, which is often resolved by leaving the program.

Integration Issues

The type of resources students are given for integration—or whether they are given such resources at all—also affects their fate. In this section, I focus on the roles that financial support, sharing an office, the advisor, and the learning environment play in integration and consequent persistence decisions.

Financial Support. Financial support is a factor in integration less for its monetary value than for the obligations inherent in the award. Some forms of support (teaching assistantships and research assistantships, in particular) require students to spend time on campus interacting with faculty and other students who have teaching and research assistantships. Students who receive full fellowships often do not have to come to the department to perform professional tasks; consequently, they may have less opportunity to interact. Students who receive no support at all have little reason to spend time in the department, and they may have to spend time off campus because of employment obligations. Therefore, students with teaching and research assistantships should be more academically integrated and more likely to persist than those without assistantships or with no support at all. The survey data supported this contention.

Completers were three times as likely as noncompleters to have received research assistantships (64 percent versus 21 percent). Completers were almost twice as likely as noncompleters to have received teaching assistantships (85 percent versus 45 percent). Students who received full fellowships (university or nonuniversity) were as likely to stay as to leave (university fellowships: completers, 16 percent versus noncompleters, 13 percent; nonuniversity fellowships: completers, 15 percent versus noncompleters, 16 percent). Noncompleters were six times more likely than completers to have received no support at all (25 percent versus 4 percent).

Office Space. Office space provides students with a place to work and to interact with other graduate students. As such, it is an important factor in integration and cognitive map development, and consequently, we should expect to see differences between completers and noncompleters with respect to their access to this resource. In fact, completers were almost twice as likely as noncompleters to have shared an office (85 percent versus 46 percent). Furthermore, completers who received teaching and research assistantships and university fellowships were significantly more likely to have shared an office than noncompleters who received the same forms of support (90 percent of the completers who had TAs shared an office, whereas only 81 percent of the noncompleters who had TAs shared an office; 67 percent of the completers who had RAs shared an office, whereas 36 percent of the noncompleters who had RAs did; 15 percent of the completers who had university fellowships shared an office, whereas only 8 percent of the noncompleters who had university fellowships did). However, there were no significant differences between the percentage of completers and noncompleters who shared an office among those students who received nonuniversity fellowships or did not receive any support (of the completers who received nonuniversity fellowships, 14 percent shared an office, and of the noncompleters who received nonuniversity fellowships, 9 percent shared an office; of the completers who did not receive any support, 3 percent shared an office, and similarly, of the noncompleters who did not receive any support, 3 percent shared an office). Completers were therefore more likely than noncompleters to have received the types of financial support that contribute to integration and persistence. They were further advantaged because they were also more likely to be given a desk in a group office, thus increasing their frequency of interaction with other graduate students and allowing them greater access to information contained in the graduate student subculture.

Advising. Students not only need good cognitive maps about choosing advisors and the advising process but also need to be well integrated with their advisors. The advisor is often the central and most powerful person on a graduate student's dissertation committee, as well as during the student's entire trajectory through graduate school. The advisor influences how the student comes to understand the discipline and the roles and responsibilities of academic professionals, his or her socialization as a teacher and researcher, the selection of a dissertation topic, the quality of the dissertation, and subsequent job placement. Consequently, integrative experiences with the advisor are critical both in helping students develop cognitive maps of the program, the discipline, and the profession and in helping them have a positive and fulfilling graduate school experience. As mentioned earlier, affiliation with the proper advisor can spell the difference between completion and noncompletion.

Completers were more likely than noncompleters to have had an advisor (97 percent versus 77 percent). They were twice as likely as noncompleters to have selected an advisor whose intellectual interests were closest to theirs (47 percent versus 23 percent). By contrast, as noted earlier, noncompleters were more than six times as likely as completers to have had an advisor who was assigned to them (44 percent versus 7 percent). Changing advisors did not account for why completers were less likely than noncompleters to have been assigned to their last advisor. There were no statistical differences in the percentage of completers and noncompleters who changed advisors (completers, 31 percent versus noncompleters, 26 percent). When interviewees who were assigned to their advisors were asked if they had ever considered changing advisors, most said that they had not. Some did not know that it was an option; others felt they would be putting their graduate careers in political jeopardy if they did.

The survey asked students to rate their level of satisfaction with their advisors and then to state in their own words the reason for their level of satisfaction. Completers were twice as likely as noncompleters to be *very satisfied* with their advisors (60 percent versus 31 percent). Completers and noncompleters were equally likely to be *somewhat satisfied* with their advisors (29 percent versus 29 percent), whereas higher percentages of noncompleters were *not too satisfied* (23 percent versus 7 percent) or *not satisfied at all* (18 percent versus 4 percent) with their advisors.

Analysis of the open-ended responses revealed six dominant types of reasons for satisfaction or dissatisfaction with an advisor. The categories, in declining order of frequency with which they were mentioned by the whole sample, are as follows: intellectual-professional development, interest in me, professionalism, personality, advising style, and accessibility. Table 6.1 summarizes the factors in each category by degree of satisfaction. It is important to note that students who were very satisfied were uniformly positive about their advisors, whereas students who were not too satisfied and not at all satisfied were uniformly negative. By contrast, those who were somewhat satisfied made both positive and negative comments, often in the same sentence. The interviews I conducted with high- and low-Ph.D.-producing faculty suggested that differences in students' level of satisfaction with their advisors might have stemmed, in part, from the type of advisor with whom they were working.

Table 6.1. Reasons for Satisfaction with Advisor, by Degree of Satisfaction

Reasons	Very Satisfied	Somewhat Satisfied	Not Too Satisfied	Not at All Satisfied
Intellectual-professional development	High degree of intellectual compatibility. Strong mentor. Helpful and supportive. Challenged thinking. Enthusiastic about student's work.	*Positive reasons:* Similar to "very satisfied" but less glowing. *Negative reasons:* Not helpful or encouraging. Not intellectually stimulating. Did not give enough direction. Not interested in student's work. Did not help student find a job.	Not helpful. Did not provide guidance or intellectual support. Showed little interest in student's work. Poor communication.	Uninformed about the program and discipline. Uninterested in advising. Uninterested in student.
Interest in student	Interested in student's ideas, research interests, academic progress, professional development. Dedicated and devoted to getting student through program and obtaining a good job.	*Positive reasons:* Interested in student and in student's work. *Negative reasons:* Not truly interested in student. Relationship was strained, formal, or declined over time. Relationship was not as personal as student desired.	Not particularly interested in student or in student's work.	Took *no* interest in student.

Reasons	Very Satisfied	Somewhat Satisfied	Not Too Satisfied	Not at All Satisfied
Professionalism	Excellent, brilliant, inspiring, dedicated teacher, researcher, scholar, advisor, mentor. Competent, knowledgeable, enthusiastic. Highly ranked and active researcher in the field. Excellent skills and integrity. Good role model.	*Positive reasons:* Similar to "very satisfied" but generally qualified with a negative reason. *Negative reasons:* Personality. Did not contribute to student's intellectual or professional development. Inaccessible.	Not on top of current research and methodological approaches. Out of touch. Generally incompetent.	—
Personality	Friendly, caring, kind, honest, moral, nurturing, easy to talk to.	*Positive reasons:* Same as "very satisfied." *Negative reasons:* Had rough edges. Was remote and hard to approach. Difficult to talk to and work with. Intimidating.	Same as "somewhat satisfied" for negative reasons.	Abrasive and abusive. Belittled student. Not honest.
Advising style	Flexible. Gave proper amounts of freedom and guidance.	*Positive reasons:* Same as "very satisfied." *Negative reasons:* Too controlling. Did not give student enough independence.	—	—
Accessibility	Always available. Generous with his or her time.	*Positive reasons:* Same as "very satisfied." *Negative reasons:* Too busy with his or her own work. Spent very little time interacting with the student.	Same as "somewhat satisfied" for negative reasons.	Same as "somewhat satisfied" for negative reasons.

Learning Environment. Students who pursue graduate education care deeply about their intellectual growth and development. Indeed, intellectual development is a component of academic integration and is the means to the end, the Ph.D. Consequently, the more satisfied students are with their level of intellectual development and the components of their education that contribute to it—their program of study, the faculty in their department, their fellow graduate students—the more likely they are to complete.

The central locus of intellectual development is a student's program of study, the individual courses, their content, and the materials and teaching styles used to impart knowledge. Overall, the survey data showed that noncompleters were less satisfied with their intellectual development and their programs of study than completers. Many interviewees were deeply disappointed with what transpired in the classroom. Many said that their classes were not of the caliber they had expected. They found many of their courses disorganized and poorly taught, with haphazard coverage of the material. Some remarked that classroom discussions were competitive, if not combative, and that they sometimes never got around to the topic of the course. Other students quickly discovered that their programs were designed to weed them out. Indeed, this message was often conveyed loudly and clearly during departmental orientations. Students in "sink-or-swim" programs felt that the system was trying to undermine them rather than support them and help them achieve their goals. If the interviewees' observations are correct about who among their fellow students left quickly, one unintended consequence of the "weed out" process is that graduate programs often lose some of the very students the practice intends to retain—the best and the brightest.

Although the ultimate goal of graduate education is to produce independent, creative scholars, several students felt that the experience had just the opposite effect—that is, they felt positively stifled. Indeed, several used the word *stifled* or such synonyms as *stultifying, constricted,* and *calcified* to characterize how they felt. Further, some students were particularly frustrated and disappointed by the perceived irrelevance of what they were learning to the world outside the academy. Thus, when the students realized that they were not getting the education they went to graduate school to get, many lost their interest, motivation, and desire to continue.

In their capacities as teachers, mentors, colleagues, and friends, faculty members play an important role in students' intellectual development and their integration into the departmental and larger disciplinary communities. They help students come to see how the fields are defined and how the roles of academic professionals are enacted.

Most of the interviewees reported that they had minimal interaction with faculty, and when they did interact, the interactions were limited. In addition, the responsibility for creating and sustaining a relationship was on them. Based on the little interaction they did have, the interviewees found the faculty to be cordial and civil, but not terribly open or warm. Some of the interviewees were bothered by what they perceived to be a wall between faculty members and students, and the faculty's lack of interest in developing any sort of personal relationship with them. These disappointments and this lack of connection with faculty caused some students to question their commitment to their programs.

As mentioned earlier, other graduate students make an important contribution to individual students' learning experiences. They are a significant source of intellectual stimulation and social support both inside and outside the classroom. Although most interviewees liked their fellow students and had good relationships with them, the survey data showed that noncompleters had fewer interactions and were much less satisfied with their relationships with other graduate students than were completers. The data also showed that the quantity of noncompleters' academic and social interactions with other graduate students decreased over time. This decrease was, in part, a function of their lack of access to formal social structures—research assistantships, teaching assistantships, and offices—that facilitate formal and chance interaction.

Their peers' single-mindedness and lack of interest in or involvement with activities outside the discipline disturbed a number of interviewees. They felt that some of their fellow graduate students were oblivious to the outside world, that nothing in life besides the discipline mattered to them, and that this lack of balance was not normal and not healthy. A number of interviewees talked about having or pursuing other interests and activities in addition to their graduate work. This made them feel different from other graduate students, and some felt sanctioned for it.

The interviewees' criticisms of their fellow students' single-mindedness and remarks interviewees made about their own broader interests and extracurricular involvement suggested that graduate programs may be losing, if not selecting against, some of their more well-rounded students. This raises important policy questions about the types of people graduate programs are producing as well as the nature of the research questions completers ask over the course of their professional careers compared with those the more well-rounded noncompleters might have asked had they gone on. This latter difference is particularly salient in light of noncompleters' complaints about the academic enterprise's lack of relevance to the world outside.

Implications and Recommendations

By studying the causes for graduate student attrition, we gain insight into ways to improve the education, training, and retention of graduate students, many of whom will soon assume the role of faculty, and in turn, educate and train graduate students themselves. As this chapter demonstrated, a key factor in attrition is the inequitable distribution of resources for action and interaction, which creates groups of haves and have-nots in a department. The inequitable distribution of resources has a differential effect on the ability of the haves and the have-nots to develop cognitive maps of the department's formal requirements and informal expectations, on their ability to become integrated into its academic and social systems, and on the quality of advising they receive, if they receive advising at all.

Another important factor in attrition is the department's culture—that is, the policies and practices it has in place for educating and training graduate students and also the taken-for-granted styles of interaction between and among faculty and graduate students. As we have seen, graduate students, who are their graduate instructors' future professional colleagues, desire closer, more personal and intellectual relationships with the faculty. Yet they soon perceive that the faculty members are not particularly interested in them and that the burden of creating and sustaining a relationship with faculty members is on them. Those who persist are socialized to this style of interaction, and unless things change, will likely reenact it when they become faculty themselves. Fortunately, some of the recent reforms in doctoral education have led to changes in the way faculty interact with graduate students. In programs like Preparing Future Faculty and the National Science Foundation's Graduate Fellowship in K–12 Education, graduate students have the opportunity to meet with one another and with faculty on a regular basis. Such interactions not only create a greater sense of community among graduate students and faculty but also provide graduate students with a greater sense of purpose and a better sense of where their education is leading.

Other entrenched practices and cultural norms in departments may be driving away many of the types of people who would make the best faculty. Departments that "weed out" students or send students the message to "sink or swim" may be losing the best and the brightest among those they admit. Such loss occurs because the best and the brightest have plenty of other options and are often unwilling to put up with the obstacles that are thrown in their paths. Further, department cultures that encourage and reinforce single-minded devotion to the discipline among their students often drive off students who have broader interests, who are more well-rounded, and who are interested in the real-world applications of the discipline. This is counterproductive for several reasons. First, single-minded devotion to the discipline can lead to burnout. Second, having broader interests can lead to the integration of fresh, new ideas into the discipline. Third, losing students who have an interest in real-world applications means that important, socially relevant questions are not getting asked, much less answered. Finally, many prospective faculty members want to see positive role models, professors who assure them that they can be both excellent scholars in their disciplines and people who lead "normal" lives; failing that, they opt to have "normal" lives (that is, they leave the academic profession).

These issues are of special concern because women and minorities often have a style of interaction and an interest in research questions that do not conform with prevailing norms, and they leave their graduate programs in higher numbers than men and members of majority groups. If we are to broaden the types of people who are faculty members, then the cultural norms that exist in today's universities and departments that drive away individuals in these groups must change. Norms and practices must become more inclusive of the ideas, perspectives, values, and intellectual styles that these groups bring to their graduate programs and will one day bring to the training of the next, more diverse, generation of faculty.

The best way for departments to retain more of the doctoral students they admit is to focus on the concept of community and seek ways to strengthen the department's communal life. This step requires making changes in both the structural organization and the organizational culture of the department.

- *Among the structural changes I recommend are those that can help students develop better cognitive maps of their programs.* Providing high-quality orientations for all new students is one important structural change. At these orientations, details on individual requirements and the standards for meeting them in terms of quality of performance should be discussed and supplemented with information about brochures or reference materials that students can access when they need them. New students should be introduced to one another, to faculty, and to advanced graduate students as well.
- *Other structural changes should focus on enhancing the integration of students into their departments.* Teaching assistantships, research assistantships, and other integrative forms of support should be distributed more equitably among graduate students. Indeed, departments should do as much as possible to engage all students, especially new students, in the professional tasks of the discipline (paid or unpaid), because working together on common projects appears to be the best means of achieving academic integration. Although office space is limited in most departments, graduate schools should seek ways to provide desks in multistudent offices for as many graduate students as possible. First-year students and students who do not have integrative forms of support should be given priority, because sharing an office helps integrate students into their departments and helps them access the informal information about their programs that is contained in the graduate student subculture. Departments should also increase the number and frequency of opportunities for faculty and students to interact both formally (for example, colloquia, brown bag lunches, departmental committee work) and informally (social hours, sports activities).

- *Departments should review and improve the quality of courses so that students receive the education and intellectual and professional development they hoped to receive in graduate school.* To this end, universities and departments need to develop more effective faculty, course, and program evaluation tools. Most attrition takes place in the first two years of graduate study. Therefore, the director of graduate study or a group of advanced graduate students should meet with first- and second-year students every term to determine whether the program is meeting their expectations and to explore ways in which their expectations and needs could be better satisfied.
- *Departments also should assess all aspects of their advising process to determine whether it is working in the best interests of their graduate students.* Among the steps departments could take to improve advising is to create a staff of faculty who are explicitly charged with helping predissertation students through their programs until such time as they have secured an advisor. Departments that assign students to advisors should do more to inform students that the assignment is temporary and that there are no penalties for changing advisors. Departments should also establish processes to help students select appropriate advisors and work with those advisors to establish mentoring and interaction styles that lead to higher levels of student (consumer) satisfaction.

Conclusion

Cultural change requires questioning the system. Faculty should ask what are the common underlying causes of attrition. Common negative experiences reported by those who depart are a good indicator that something is wrong with the system and that the system needs to change. Faculty can start the change process by examining what they take for granted about their departmental cultures and the structure and process of graduate education. One of those taken-for-granted assumptions is that new students must conform to the prevailing departmental culture. Faculty members need instead to consider how the organizational culture needs to change in order to ensure success for all students whom they thought worthy of admitting to their programs. Among these changes are valuing every student admitted to the program, respecting students' values, interests, and styles, and most importantly, viewing graduate students as an investment to be nurtured and mentored to completion and into the professoriate.

References

Benkin, E. M. (1984). Where have all the doctoral students gone? A study of doctoral student attrition at UCLA. *Dissertation Abstracts International, 45A,* 2770.

Berelson, B. (1960). *Graduate education in the United States.* New York: McGraw-Hill.

Bowen, W. G., & Rudenstine, N. L. (1992). *In pursuit of the Ph.D.* Princeton, NJ: Princeton University Press.

Howard, J. A. (1995). Social cognition. In K. Cook, G. A. Fine, & J. House (Eds.), *Sociological perspectives on social psychology* (pp. 90–117). Needham Heights, MA: Allyn & Bacon.

Katz, J., & Hartnett, R. T. (Eds.). (1976). *Scholars in the making: The development of graduate and professional students.* New York: Ballinger.

Morgan, D. L., & Schwalbe, M. L. (1990). Mind and self in society: Linking social structure and social cognition. *Social Psychology Quarterly, 53,* 148–164.

National Research Council. (1996). *The path to the Ph.D.: Measuring graduate attrition in the sciences and humanities.* Washington, DC: National Academy Press.

Nerad, M., & Cerny, J. (1991, May). From facts to action: Expanding the educational role of the graduate division. *Communicator.* Washington, DC: Council of Graduate Schools.

Office of Technology Assessment. (1988). *Educating scientists and engineers: Grade school to grad school.* Washington, DC: Office of Technology Assessment.

Spady, W. (1970). Dropouts from higher education: An interdisciplinary review and synthesis. *Interchange, 1,* 64–85.

Spady, W. (1971). Dropouts from higher education: Toward an empirical model. *Interchange, 2,* 38–62.

Tinto, V. (1975). Dropouts from higher education: A theoretical synthesis of recent research. *Review of Educational Research, 45,* 89–125.

Tinto, V. (1987). *Leaving college: Rethinking the causes and cures of student attrition.* Chicago: University of Chicago Press.

Tinto, V. (1993). *Leaving college: Rethinking the causes and cures of student attrition* (2nd ed.). Chicago: University of Chicago Press.

Tucker, A. (1964). *Factors related to attrition among doctoral students* (Cooperative Research Project No. 1146). Washington, DC: U.S. Office of Education.

Chapter Seven

"So You Want to Become a Professor!"

Lessons from the PhDs—Ten Years Later Study

Maresi Nerad, Rebecca Aanerud, Joseph Cerny

The U.S. Ph.D. is a much sought-after degree, both nationally and internationally. In fact, U.S. doctoral education serves as a model throughout much of the world. In the United States, however, the doctoral degree is not without its critics. During the past few years we have seen an increased focus on doctoral education, including the training of future faculty, researchers, and scholars. As this volume suggests, the attention has generated a number of studies and initiatives designed to improve doctoral education. We believe that both career path analysis of Ph.D. recipients and Ph.D. recipients' retrospective evaluations of their doctoral programs should inform recommendations for change. Guided by this belief, we undertook the PhDs—Ten Years Later Study described in this chapter as a way of bringing greater empirical understanding to Ph.D. education in the United States. In the information that follows, we begin by discussing our overall research and then highlight some of the key findings, implications, and recommendations that are most relevant to preparing future faculty.

Background and Purpose

PhDs—Ten Years Later is a national study of the career paths of doctorates and the feasibility of assessing doctoral programs based on the graduates' career outcomes. This survey contacted almost six thousand individuals in six selected disciplines. The study focused on individuals who completed their doctoral degrees at one of sixty-one doctoral granting institutions in the United States. The original interest in surveying Ph.D. outcomes on a national level arose out of ongoing research on current graduate students at the University of California, especially at Berkeley, and from the principal investigators' (PIs) participation on the 1993–1995 National Research Council (NRC) advisory board for the assessment of research doctorate programs in the United States. Research on recent Ph.D. recipients frequently lacks information on these individuals' career paths and on their perception of the usefulness of the education and training that they received for their subsequent professional careers and lives. The NRC debated the inclusion of educational outcomes, such as employment several years after degree completion and satisfaction with the Ph.D. experience. Because the NRC committee decided not to pursue this outcome analysis, however, the PhDs—Ten Years Later Study was in part piloted to evaluate the feasibility of assessing career outcomes several years after degree completion. In this chapter we address issues associated with preparing future faculty drawn from our study of the career paths of Ph.D. recipients in six disciplines and present their suggestions for current doctoral studies drawn from their years of employment and job satisfaction.

Methods

We focused our study on doctorates in six disciplines from five major fields of study: life sciences (biochemistry), engineering (computer science, electrical engineering), humanities (English), physical science (mathematics), and social science (political science). We studied doctorates in these fields at sixty-one universities selected on the basis of four major criteria. The first criterion was institutional participation in the 1982 National Research Council doctoral program assessment. The second criterion was their level of Ph.D. production; we only included programs that awarded a minimum of six

Ph.D.'s in three consecutive years. Third, we included only those institutions that had doctoral programs in at least three of the six disciplines. Finally, we sought balance in geographical and public-private distribution. Of the sixty-one participating institutions, thirty-two were members of the Association of American Universities (AAU). From these institutions we obtained the names of the doctoral graduates who ultimately participated in the study. Because we wanted to allow time for their careers to settle, we included only those doctoral recipients from the institutions who had received their Ph.D.'s ten to fourteen years prior to the study—that is, between July 1, 1982, and June 30, 1985. Once we selected an institution, we included all doctoral recipients of the relevant programs in the survey population. No subsampling occurred.

Using the selected disciplines, the institutional criteria, and the specified period for degree completion, we identified 5,859 Ph.D. recipients as the population for the study, including the international students, regardless of whether they remained in the United States after attaining their doctorates.[1] This survey population accounted for 57 percent of the total Ph.D.'s awarded in the United States in these six fields during the three years. Of the respondents in the survey population, 24 percent were women, and 23 percent were from other countries.

Once we had identified the population, we obtained our information primarily through a twenty-two-page survey that was mailed in late 1996 and early 1997. The questionnaire focused on the employment history of the participating doctoral recipients. It asked whether they took a postdoctoral position or positions, and if so, how many and for how long. It also inquired about their job-search process and the factors influencing their decisions to accept their first and current positions, asked for a retrospective evaluation of their doctoral programs and information on whether they had found the degree useful, and requested information on spouses and children. The survey also included five open-ended questions.

To ensure the highest possible response rate, we obtained addresses for these doctorate recipients in the selected fields and institutions from multiple sources, including participating institutions, professional association membership directories, a variety of national directories, commercial locator agencies, and on-line search engines. The response rate was 66 percent from domestic Ph.D. recipients (U.S. citizens and permanent residents) and 52 percent from international recipients (temporary visa holders at the time of their doctorate completion). Because of the large size of doctoral programs at AAU universities, 84 percent of the Ph.D.'s who participated in the study received their degrees from AAU institutions.

In addition to the survey, we used two other major sources of information in the study. The first was in-depth interviews with fifty-six people—about eight to ten from each discipline—to provide the context in which individuals make career decisions. In addition, with the cooperation of the graduate deans at all sixty-one universities, we were able to include as part of our database the responses to the Survey of Earned Doctorates, a national survey sponsored by the National Science Foundation (NSF) that is completed by doctoral students at the time their dissertations are filed. This NSF survey provided complete demographic information on our survey populations, such as parents' education level, and financial information, such as major fellowships.

Although our research included doctorates in all careers for the six disciplines, in the next section we highlight key findings that are most relevant to preparing future faculty. We define "faculty" broadly to include tenured, tenure-track, and non-tenure-track individuals who teach and are employed at institutions of higher education. Our study found that ten-plus years after Ph.D. completion (varying by field), between 3 percent and 18 percent of faculty were working in non-tenure-track positions as visiting, affiliate, or research professors, or lecturers. Indications are that the number of Ph.D. recipients who teach in non-tenure-track positions is growing (Baldwin & Chronister, 2001; Martin, 1998). We therefore have included both tenure and nontenure tracks when presenting results for future faculty.

Key Findings

An important goal of our study was to ensure that present Ph.D. students make informed career decisions. In this chapter we have selected those findings from the study that provide students and faculty with empirical evidence about the proportion of students who wanted to become professors or who actually became professors. We also want students to be informed about actual professorial career paths, including the job-search process. The reality that most Ph.D. recipients are married or live in committed relationships has consequences for their career paths. We therefore present findings associated with dual-career academic couples. We further present findings of the Ph.D. recipients' job satisfaction, with careers both inside academia and in the business, government, and nonprofit sectors. We believe that these research findings will allow current students to evaluate their career choices more realistically and accurately. Knowing what lies ahead will provide them with a clearer understanding of steps to take during graduate school in order to prepare for their chosen paths. The voices and recommendations of their peers of a few years back can help guide them in their preparation for the future.

As already noted, the key findings of our study presented here pertain specifically to preparing future faculty. The first set of key findings focuses on the career paths of the Ph.D. recipients in our study. The second set focuses on the retrospective evaluation of their Ph.D. education based on the career paths they have taken.[2]

Career Paths and Faculty Rank

This section focuses on the career paths of our study's respondents. Some key findings follow:

- About one-half (53 percent) of all respondents reported that they aspired to become professors at degree completion.
- Most English and political science Ph.D. recipients sought the professoriate (English, 81 percent, and political science, 72 percent).
- Less than one-third (28 percent) of *all* the surveyed Ph.D. recipients were employed in tenure-track positions as their *first jobs* after degree completion.
- Of the tenured faculty among the respondents, two-thirds began their paths to tenure in assistant professor positions immediately following degree completion. The remaining one-third began careers in various temporary positions, and on average, only after a period of four to five years moved into a tenure-track path.

The common faculty assumption in the non-engineering disciplines was that Ph.D. students are interested in a professorial career and follow a smooth career trajectory that starts with an assistant professorship, followed by promotion to a tenured faculty position. However, this assumption was not supported by our data. Ph.D. recipients in political science held the largest proportion (44 percent) of tenure-track faculty positions as their first job, followed by computer scientists (38 percent), English Ph.D. recipients (37 percent), and mathematicians (37 percent).[3] The proportion that joined the tenure-track and tenured ranks later varied by field. In biochemistry and mathematics, delayed entrance to tenure-track positions (32 percent in biochemistry and 27 percent in mathematics) was due to the convention of working as a postdoctoral fellow immediately after Ph.D. completion. In English and political science, the delayed entrance of Ph.D. recipients into faculty ranks (25 percent in English and 17 percent in political science) could be attributed to the limited academic job market in both fields. In English, increasing the number of publications while working in a non-tenure-track (or nonfaculty) job improved the academic job chances; however, the time spent in a non-tenure-track position translated into delayed job stability and earnings.

Ten to fourteen years after degree completion, 54 percent of our total survey respondents were working in faculty positions (42 percent were tenured, 7 percent were tenure-track, and 5 percent were non-tenure-track). (See Table 7.1.)

Looking only at the survey respondents who reported wanting to become a professor (53 percent), the percentages were somewhat higher: 67 percent were working in faculty positions (54 percent were tenured, 7 percent were tenure-track, and 6 percent were non-tenure-track). (See Table 7.2.)

In addition, the data suggested that:

- Mathematics had the highest percentage of tenured faculty (59 percent from the overall survey population and 64 percent from the subpopulation who wanted to be faculty).
- Biochemistry had the highest percentage of faculty still in assistant professor positions more than ten years after degree completion (14 percent from the overall survey respondents and 15 percent from the subpopulation who wanted to be faculty).
- English had the highest percentage of non-tenure-track faculty (10 percent from the overall respondents and 9 percent from the subgroup who wanted to be faculty).

Table 7.1. Employment in United States, Ten to Fourteen Years After Ph.D. Completion, by Field and Gender

Field of Education / Gender	Gender	Current Employment											
		Tenured		TT		NTT		All Faculty		All Other		Total	
		%	N	%	N	%	N	%	N	%	N	%	N
Biochemistry	Men	18.6	78	14.3	60	5.7	24	38.6	162	61.4	258	100	420
	Women	19.8	32	14.8	24	13.6	22	48.1	78	51.9	84	100	162
	Total	18.9	110	14.4	84	7.9	46	41.2	240	58.8	342	100	582
Computer science	Men	30.6	88	4.2	12	1.7	5	36.5	105	63.5	183	100	288
	Women	37.5	12	—	—	—	—	37.5	12	62.5	20	100	32
	Total	31.3	100	3.8	12	1.6	5	36.6	117	63.4	203	100	320
Electrical engineering	Men	21.5	88	2.2	9	0.5	2	24.2	99	75.8	310	100	409
	Women	56.3	9	6.3	1	—	—	62.5	10	37.5	6	100	16
	Total	22.8	97	2.4	10	0.5	2	25.6	109	74.4	316	100	425
English	Men	63.5	209	3.0	10	6.7	22	73.3	241	26.7	88	100	329
	Women	52.2	188	6.4	23	12.8	46	71.4	257	28.6	103	100	360
	Total	57.6	397	4.8	33	9.9	68	72.3	498	27.7	191	100	689
Mathematics	Men	61.4	290	5.3	25	3.8	18	70.6	333	29.4	139	100	472
	Women	49.1	54	5.5	6	3.6	4	58.2	64	41.8	46	100	110
	Total	59.1	344	5.3	31	3.8	22	68.2	397	31.8	185	100	582
Political science	Men	57.0	179	5.7	18	2.5	8	65.3	205	34.7	109	100	314
	Women	50.5	55	7.3	8	5.5	6	63.3	69	36.7	40	100	109
	Total	55.3	234	6.1	26	3.3	14	64.8	274	35.2	149	100	423
Total	Men	41.8	932	6.0	134	3.5	79	51.3	1145	48.7	1,087	100	2,232
	Women	44.4	350	7.9	62	9.9	78	62.1	490	37.9	299	100	789
	Total	42.4	1,282	6.5	196	5.2	157	54.1	1635	45.9	1,386	100	3,021

Note: Tenured = tenured faculty; TT = tenure-track faculty; NTT = non-tenure-track faculty; all faculty = T + TT + NTT; all other = employment in all sectors except the listed three categories.

Source: PhDs—Ten Years Later Study.

Table 7.2. Professorial Career Goal Realization in Employment, Ten to Fourteen Years After Ph.D. Completion, by Field

Become Professors	Current Employment											
	Tenured		TT		NTT		All Faculty		All Other		Total	
Field of Education	%	N	%	N	%	N	%	N	%	N	%	N
Biochemistry	24.4	40	15.2	25	7.3	12	47	77	53	87	100	164
Computer science	47.6	50	7.6	8	1.9	2	57.1	60	42.9	45	100	105
Electrical engineering	36.1	26	2.8	2	1.4	1	40.3	29	59.7	43	100	72
English	59.9	276	5	23	8.9	41	73.8	340	26.2	121	100	461
Mathematics	64.2	176	8.4	23	3.3	9	75.9	208	24.1	66	100	274
Political science	60.2	147	6.1	15	3.3	8	69.7	170	30.3	74	100	244
Total	54.2	715	7.3	96	5.5	73	67	884	33	436	100	1,320

Note: Tenured = tenured faculty; TT = tenure-track faculty; NTT = non-tenure-track faculty; all faculty = T + TT + NTT; all other = employment in all sectors except the listed three categories.

Source: PhDs—Ten Years Later Study.

- Political science, nationally the field with the highest proportion of African American and Latino faculty, had a proportionally low representation of African American and Latino faculty among their tenured faculty.
- Women in biochemistry, English, and political science made up a larger percentage of those in non-tenure-track faculty positions than men did.

Although the majority of Ph.D. recipients who had the goal of being a professor at the time of Ph.D. completion had indeed become professors, more than one-third had not yet realized this goal. The survey respondents who were tenure-track, as opposed to tenured, ten to fourteen years after degree completion, spent their first post-Ph.D. years in postdoctoral appointments rather than in tenure-track positions and therefore had a delayed tenure. There was also a gendered component to the postdoctoral years, particularly for dual-career academic couples. Given the difficulty in job searching for two tenure-track positions, women (more often than men) accepted postdoctoral appointments to remain in the same geographic locations as their partners. Our findings showed that although many postdoctoral appointments are followed by a tenure-track position, for the woman whose spouse is already in a tenure-track position, postdoctoral years can follow with a non-tenure-track position.

One of our women mathematicians, almost certainly married to a fellow mathematician, described the impact of postdocs on her career:

> My husband and I made the mistake that when I finished my Ph.D. we went to a temporary position for my husband—a great postdoc. This was a mistake. Our second move was much more difficult, and may have cost me any career. We should have moved to permanent positions when we could. The two-body problem is hard to solve. We did not get this advice. Academia is not responsive to the problems of women. In particular, there is little recognition of the problems of two careers, or of the conflicts of tenure and child-rearing. It is easier to find two assistant professor positions than two associate professor positions. Couples in two-body situations should solve their problem early. This does limit opportunities, and women are disproportionately affected.

After winning two extremely prestigious postdoctoral positions, this woman mathematician was working in a non-tenure-track position making $12,000 a year. Her husband earned more than $100,000 a year.[4]

Although our study showed a fairly small percentage of non-tenure-track faculty members, recent studies have pointed to a growing number of non-tenure-track positions (Baldwin & Chronister, 2001). And as previously suggested, gender differences for this population are notable. Comparing two fields with high representation of non-tenure-track positions (biochemistry and English), we found in biochemistry that 14 percent of the female faculty versus 6 percent of the male faculty were non-tenure-track. In English, 13 percent of the female faculty versus 7 percent of the male were non-tenure-track. These year-to-year, and even term-to-term, appointments constitute a secondary labor market in academia, which, according to our study, tends to be a feminized labor market.

Retrospective Job Placement Evaluations

Perhaps no information is more pertinent to current and future faculty and current students than the retrospective program evaluation that Ph.D. recipients provide a number of years after g raduating. They are in an ideal position to reflect on their doctoral education in the context of having worked for a number of years applying their education.

So what did the Ph.D. respondents—half of them now faculty—tell us? Table 7.3 presents the top three most cited topics by discipline and by question.[5]

The top suggestions for doctoral programs relate to the need for greater educational relevance to the changing world inside and outside academia and better labor market preparation, such as teaching and hands-on practice. In short, these survey respondents called for a curriculum of breadth that is interdisciplinary and that remains current so that students will have marketable skills. Comments such as this one were typical: "Keep curricula and program state of the art . . . constantly updating the programs to reflect changes, new needs, and demands in the workforce."

Table 7.3. Recommendations for Doctoral Programs,
Per Open-Ended Questions, Top Three Rankings

	Biochemistry	Computer Science	Electrical Engineering	English	Mathematics	Political Science
Provide breadth/interdisciplinary	—	2	3	3	1	1
Stay current/marketable	2	1	1	—	2	3
Teach how to teach	—	—	—	1	3	2
Downsize	1	—	—	2	—	—
Provide hands-on experience	—	3	2	—	—	—
Provide information on BGN	3	—	—	—	—	—

Note: BGN = business, industry, government, and nonprofit organizations.

Source: PhDs—Ten Years Later Study.

Respondents from fields with the highest proportion of doctorates in academia recommended that Ph.D. programs teach students how to teach. In addition, in both biochemistry and English, disciplines in which Ph.D. recipients faced the toughest academic job markets, respondents recommended "downsizing."[6] Biochemists said: "Take only as many students as can be realistically trained for the few [academic] jobs that are available. Also try to expose students to a multidisciplinary education to make them more well rounded and therefore more attractive hires." Biochemists suggested repeatedly that doctoral programs should provide information about employment in the business, government, and nonprofit sectors. Both engineering programs recommended offering hands-on, practical experience during graduate school through internships or exposure to people with professional industrial experience.

Their suggestions for current students' educational focus included the following points:

- Focus on interdisciplinarity; go for breadth.
- Get a broad acquaintance with the field before becoming entirely specialized.
- Define goals early on in graduate school.
- Love the field or leave it.

When it came to the job search, the many responses can be summed up as follows:

- Better assistance is needed with the practical aspects of the academic job search from the faculty.
- Better understanding of and guidance for jobs outside academia are needed.

Phrased in myriad ways, eighty-nine respondents mentioned the need for "practical advice on the mechanics of the job search, especially the packaging of oneself in a CV, letters, and interview techniques." Their responses suggest that they saw this kind of help as intimately connected to having supportive and positive relationships with their mentors. For example, a typical response asked for "more support from faculty and preparation for interviews once dossier requests came in. I received good prep for my oral and written qualifying exams, but little prep for what came after writing a vita in the job search."

In general, this cohort complained about the overall quality of relationships they had with their faculty. Even after more than a decade, resentments toward their advisors during the job search provoked strong comments, such as this one: "It would have helped if one of my referees had taken the time to write more than a four-line letter of recommendation!" Another suggested, "It would have been helpful if I received some support from my department and advisor. I had none—my advisor was a 'star' who had no interest in mundane matters like jobs."

Another expressed a desire for better, more compassionate guidance. This person said: "I can now see that the letters of recommendation I got were from lame people. Real mentoring from more savvy folks would have helped; but overall professors in my department saw graduate students as aliens—not as potential junior colleagues whose struggles they could relate to." In the midst of these voices, however, there were also some that acknowledged that they received "truly caring and skillful guidance."

Many respondents commented that they had only a dim understanding of the highly restricted and competitive academic job market they were entering. They expected their advisors and departmental faculty to provide them with better information. Some expressed the opinion that their advisors understood the nature of the academic job market but simply did not care enough to provide them with good information, whereas others perceived their advisors to be themselves ill-informed about the academic job-market situation. All in these groups felt that they would have been well-served by better information on the academic market in general, the expectations of potential employers, and a candid assessment of their own prospects in particular. For example, one respondent desired "a clear idea of the jobs people in the previous classes had obtained—we all naïvely thought [that] jobs at outstanding schools would just open up."

Regardless of discipline, respondents often felt that they graduated without having a good understanding of the "big picture" of employment possibilities. There was often a tendency for faculty to expect their students to become faculty also, or at least the students believed and acted as if this were the case. (See Table 7.4.)

**Table 7.4. Ph.D. Respondents' Views of Faculty Members'
Career Expectations for Their Students**

Major Field	Academic Careers (%)	Both Academic and BGN (%)	BGN Careers (%)	No Specific
Biochemistry	55	20	(3)	24
Computer Science	21	52	(4)	26
Electrical Engineering	8	53	5	34
English	73	8	(3)	19
Mathematics	54	24	(1)	22
Political Science	61	19	(1)	20

Note: BGN = business, industry, government, and nonprofit organizations.
When the number of respondents in a category was less than five, that number,
rather than a percentage, is shown in parentheses.

Source: PhDs—Ten Years Later Study.

A relatively narrow understanding of the ideal job often
worked against graduates, as they reflected later. Many felt that
more information was needed about the different types of academic institutions and jobs in business, industry, government, and
nonprofit organizations. One mathematician recommended more
advice and encouragement:

> Advice and encouragement about the different types of academic
> jobs—that is, university (research-oriented) versus small college
> (teaching-oriented). The nearly exclusive expectation of members
> of the department where I received my Ph.D. was that students
> would go to (hopefully good) research universities. It was felt that
> students who were interested in teaching at small colleges should
> keep quiet about it, lest the department lose interest in their
> progress. A few students were discouraged from continuing by their
> advisors when they made it known that they aspired to teaching at a
> small college instead of doing research at a university. Fortunately, I
> think this attitude has changed a lot in the last ten to twelve years,
> in my field generally, and in that graduate program in particular.[7]

A biochemist suggested, "My advisors could have spent more
time with me to discuss the job market and to prepare applications.

Their honest view on the general direction of the science (what's hot and what's not) and how my training and my accomplishments would fit in would have been very helpful." Another went so far as to say, "I never wanted an academic job, particularly, but it was all I knew about. I ended up as a tenured professor, but I probably would have been happier in industry."

We found that although Ph.D. students felt well educated in their particular fields, they did not feel particularly well educated in what being a faculty member actually entails. Most knew that they would teach, although not all of them gained teaching experience as graduate students. The majority, however, felt unprepared for the broader tasks of being a faculty member, such as being an advisor, being a good mentor, serving on committees, acquiring outside funding, managing a research group, organizing conferences, learning how to manage their time, or knowing about the ethics of their field. As one electrical engineering Ph.D. recipient in our study stated, "I would let engineering Ph.D. students who are planning an academic career know that they will spend much (or all) of their time trying to obtain research funding, and little (if any) time actually doing research." Thus, devoting attention to the multifaceted aspects of being a faculty member, indeed defining what it is to work in a faculty position, is key to preparing future faculty.

Implications

One implication of this study is that career path analysis and retrospective analysis can be employed effectively to benefit current and future student education. The better that graduate deans, faculty, and students understand career paths of Ph.D. recipients and the retrospective evaluations of their doctoral programs, the better prepared future faculty will be to assist their students in comprehensive and meaningful ways. For example, knowing that one-third of the tenured faculty in our study did not move directly from Ph.D. completion to assistant professor positions tells us that the first job after receiving the Ph.D. does not necessarily determine the career path. Having empirical information on career paths of tenured faculty can help faculty mentor and encourage their students.

The study also demonstrates that understanding discipline-based differences in career paths as tied to the job market can be useful. For example, some respondents in English and biochemistry called for downsizing Ph.D. programs on the basis of the difficulty in finding tenure-track faculty positions. Although such individual labor market–driven responses are understandable, adopting a pure short-term labor market outlook is vulnerable to constant labor-market fluctuations.[8] Any policy recommendation needs to address long-term labor-market trends in order to avoid being obsolete when doctoral students complete their studies. In the case of English, the academic market has been limited for thirty years and has not improved lately. Therefore, attention to the reality of a persistent limited academic labor market is well placed. The situation in biochemistry is more complicated. The rapid advancement in the area of molecular research and life sciences in general created more academic positions. However, the accumulated postdoctoral population waiting for academic jobs and the increase in Ph.D. recipients in the life sciences since 1995 has exceeded the available academic positions.[9]

The study also reinforces the notion that the doctoral degree itself is put to many different uses in a variety of employment sectors. Traditionally, faculty and students in fields such as English and political science have operated under the assumption that no employer outside the academy will hire Ph.D. recipients.[10] Also in these fields, there exists a general assumption—particularly by the faculty—that the successful Ph.D. student should become a professor. Numerous comments in the open-ended section of our survey reported the risk of appearing to be a less serious doctoral student if one does not aspire to the professoriate.

The fourth implication concerns gender and combination of family and career. The rise of dual-career academic couples puts specific burdens on a couple as they negotiate job searching, career advancement, and family. Marriage patterns of women Ph.D. holders have a significant impact on their career paths. Of the women in our survey, 61 percent were married to a spouse having a Ph.D., a J.D., or an M.D., but only 27 percent of the men in our survey had a spouse with such a degree. One consequence of this marriage pattern is that in order for couples to live in the same geographic area, one of them must often accept non-tenure-track employment. Although the pattern is not new, the percentages are increasing. Historically, women Ph.D. recipients either were barred from employment at the same institution as their husbands because of antinepotism laws or took administrative rather than research and teaching positions to remain in academia (Shoben, 1997; Stephan & Kassis, 1997). However, given the growing number of women earning Ph.D.'s, coupled with the changing economic structure of colleges and universities, the issue of an academic secondary labor market is especially acute. In fields where the postdoc is common, women are bridging the transition from Ph.D. education to post-Ph.D. work with more and longer stints in postdoctoral positions than men.[11]

There is a strong indication that after completing their Ph.D., women combine a committed relationship, family creation, and career with working in postdoctoral appointments that allow them to be in the same location as their partners. Our study found that women Ph.D. recipients in mathematics were especially affected by the dual-career academic couple phenomenon. In mathematics, prestigious postdoctoral fellowships are a key stepping-stone toward a faculty career in a research university. However, the kinds of postdoctoral appointments that married women in mathematics held appeared not to have that stepping-stone character. Among women mathematics Ph.D. recipients who wanted to become professors, their postdocs (sometimes organized around their husbands' postdocs) served to shunt them away from a tenure-track trajectory.

A particularly notable implication of this study concerns the feasibility of conducting a large survey of this sort, in terms of contacting people and interesting them in taking the time to fill out the survey. The success of this survey is a clear indication that former students can be located, and more importantly, are willing to participate. The study demonstrates that Ph.D. recipients value their education and recognize that their retrospective analysis of doctoral education and experiences can be utilized to benefit current and future students.

Recommendations

Our research findings lead to several recommendations:

- *Future faculty and those preparing them need to familiarize themselves with the general trends in Ph.D. production in the United States and particularly in their own fields, as well as the initial career plans of recent graduates.* They can do so by consulting the annual *Summary Report of Doctorate Recipients from U.S. Universities* or the *Survey of Earned Doctorates* (SED), published by the National Opinion Research Center (see National Opinion Research Center, 2001) and sponsored by five national agencies. However, as our findings indicate, Ph.D. advisors, department chairs, and graduate deans need to look beyond initial career plans as reported in the SED in order to give relevant placement information to their students. We therefore recommend that departments collect and make available placement information on their graduates at least up to five years after degree completion. Indeed, tracking Ph.D. recipients for ten years would be ideal because of the long entry period for a significant number of individuals.
- *Future faculty members need to receive broad career information so they are better informed that challenging and intellectually satisfying positions exist outside academia.* They also need institutional support to collaborate with other units (both inside and outside academia) to pass employment information on to their students. Finally, they need to work to create an environment that allows for career goals beyond the tenure track.
- *In preparing future faculty, departmental administrators and faculty need to have long-term (lifelong) educational goals and values in mind with a broad understanding of the various career paths open to their Ph.D. graduates.* They need to equip their doctoral students with the knowledge and skills required to meet changing academic and nonacademic employment conditions.

We end with specific recommendations for those who have the power to implement them in light of our key findings: the university central administration, graduate deans, department chairs, and faculty.

Graduate deans and the central administration should do the following:

- *Spend more time, money, and effort on career planning and placement activities for doctoral students.* This means establishing collaborations between career planning and placement centers and academic departments for career planning workshop activities to be offered starting in the third year of the doctoral program; working with faculty to broaden the acceptance of business, industry, government, and nonprofit (BGN) organization careers as legitimate and desirable Ph.D. outcomes; making student placement a collective departmental responsibility; providing incentives to ensure that key faculty participate in placement; looking for funding scenarios that create powerful incentives for turning the culture around; and recognizing departments that place a very high percentage of their Ph.D. recipients into meaningful first jobs, regardless of sector.
- *Develop creative solutions for dual-career couples in the university.* Also, heighten awareness to offer more spousal accommodation during the faculty hiring process and support the establishment of a more family-friendly university, especially for women in science and engineering.

Faculty and department chairs should do the following:

- *Broaden program emphasis to prepare students for jobs in academia and BGNs.* Enhance training in teamwork and collaboration, interdisciplinarity, managerial, and organizational skills. Provide internship opportunities (academia, administration, BGNs). Encourage contact with the BGN sector. Articulate skills that are applicable in a variety of situations.
- *Prepare students who aspire to the professoriate for a life of teaching, research, and service in different types of higher education institutions.* Offer workshops, seminars, and internships that allow students to familiarize themselves with other than research institutions. Reward mentoring by faculty, especially mentoring of students of color.

All groups should do the following:

* *Develop a process for program evaluations by current and former graduate students.* Conduct surveys at regular intervals during the doctoral program. Require a Ph.D. exit survey under the graduate dean's purview. And finally, survey Ph.D. graduates five (and ten) years after degree completion.

Conclusion

As our study demonstrates, understanding the road to the professoriate and faculty career paths is immeasurably enhanced by retrospective studies such as the PhDs—Ten Years Later survey.[12] These studies provide graduate deans, program heads, graduate faculty advisors, researchers, and students with a wealth of data from which to make informed decisions about doctoral education. In this conclusion we would like to emphasize the importance of the data provided by the "write ins." Although we were advised against including open-ended questions—because of the study's size and the coding and analysis work—we felt strongly that a survey that posits former Ph.D. student voices as integral to doctoral education assessment must give respondents an opportunity to use their own words. As researchers, we were richly rewarded. Not surprisingly, Ph.D. recipients are both thoughtful and articulate about their education and careers. They constitute an invaluable resource for those of us who seek to advise students wisely and continue to improve and advance doctoral education.

Acknowledgments

We especially want to thank Dr. Ta Liu for providing data runs and tables. This survey was funded by the Mellon Foundation, with selected analysis by the National Science Foundation. The survey principal investigators are two of the co-authors.

Notes

1. International Ph.D. students are concentrated in science and engineering fields. Roughly 50 percent of all international Ph.D. recipients remain in the United States.
2. Findings reported here are restricted to U.S. employment only.

3. Biochemistry was at only 1 percent because most took a postdoctoral appointment.
4. This case is a classic example of a more general finding: "For academic women, moves that advantaged their husbands' careers have certainly disadvantaged their own" (Miller-Loessi & Henderson, 1997, p. 37; see also Ferber & Huber, 1979; Marwell, Rosenfeld, & Spilerman, 1979; McElrath, 1992; Brooker-Gross & Maraffa, 1989).
5. The coding variables for the answers were established after reading over the majority of the responses. We then ranked the coded responses.
6. We assume the biochemists based this recommendation on their situation in 1985 *before* the increase of Ph.D.'s in biochemistry-molecular biology that occurred in 1987.
7. According to the Golde-Dore (2001) study conducted in 1999, this attitude had not changed.
8. See Zumeta and Raveling (2002), "Wither the Best and the Brightest?: Is There a Policy Problem Here?"
9. See National Research Council (1998), *Trends in the Early Careers of Life Scientists.*
10. See Nerad and Cerny (2000), "From Rumors to Facts: Career Outcomes of English Ph.D.'s."
11. See Nerad and Cerny (1999), "Postdoctoral Patterns, Career Advancement, and Problems."
12. See also Sadrozinski, R., Nerad, M., Cerny, J., with La, S. (March 2003), "PhDs in Art History—Over a Decade Later"; www.educ. washington.edu/COEWebSite/CIRGE/HTML/Getty.html.

References

Baldwin, R., & Chronister, J. (2001). *Teaching without tenure: Policies and practices for a new era.* Baltimore: Johns Hopkins University Press.

Brooker-Gross, S. R., & Maraffa, T. A. (1989). Faculty spouses: Their post-migration searches. *Initiatives, 52,* 37–43.

Ferber, M. A., & Huber, J. (1979). Husbands, wives, and careers. *Journal of Marriage and the Family, 41,* 315–325.

Golde, C. M., & Dore, T. M. (2001). *At cross purposes: What the experiences of today's doctoral students reveal about doctoral education.* Philadelphia: A Report for The Pew Charitable Trusts. [www.phd-survey.org]

Martin, R. (Ed.). (1998). *Chalk lines: The politics of work in the managed university.* Durham, NC: Duke University Press.

Marwell, G., Rosenfeld, R., & Spilerman, S. (1979). Geographic constraints on women's careers in academia. *Science, 205,* 1125–1131.

McElrath, K. (1992). Gender, career disruption, and academic rewards. *Journal of Higher Education, 63,* 269–281.

Miller-Loessi, K., & Henderson, D. (1997). Changes in American society: The context for academic couples. In M. A. Ferber & J. W. Loeb (Eds.), *Academic couples: Problems and promises* (pp. 25–43). Chicago: University of Illinois Press.

National Opinion Research Center. (2001). *Summary report of doctorate recipients from U.S. universities.* Chicago: National Opinion Research Center.

National Research Council. (1998). *Trends in the early careers of life scientists.* Washington, DC: National Academy Press.

Nerad, M., & Cerny, J. (1999). Postdoctoral patterns, career advancements, and problems. *Science, 285,* 1533–1535.

Nerad, M., & Cerny, J. (2000, Winter). From rumors to facts: Career outcomes of English Ph.D.'s: Results from the PhDs—Ten Years Later Study. *ADE Bulletin, 124,* 43–55.

Shoben, E. W. (1997). From antinepotism rules to programs for partners: Legal issues. In M. A. Ferber & J. W. Loeb (Eds.), *Academic couples: Problems and promises* (226–247). Chicago: University of Illinois Press.

Stephan, P. E., & Kassis, M. M. (1997). The history of women and couples in academe. In M. A. Ferber & J. W. Loeb (Eds.), *Academic couples: Problems and promises.* Chicago: University of Illinois Press.

Zumeta, W., & Raveling, J. (2002). Wither the best and the brightest?: Is there a policy problem here? In M. Feldman & A. N. Link (Eds.), *Innovation policy in the knowledge-based economy* (pp. 121–161). Norwell, MA: Kluwer.

Part Three

Strategies for Reform

In this part of the book we showcase some of the major national efforts—programs, projects, and movements—designed to address the issues identified in the research and the literature on graduate education and the preparation for future faculty. Some of these action projects have evolved in direct response to the research described in Part Two. Some were evolving simultaneously as parts of larger movements to enhance teaching and learning across institutions of higher education in this country. And some themselves contain elements of research that contributed to their evolution. Again, as in the previous section of the volume, although we wanted the authors to have full freedom in deciding what to highlight from their programs, for consistency across chapters we requested that they include specific information. Thus, all of the chapters describe the program, project, or movement and its purposes; explain primary themes and strategies that guide the work; identify any outcomes, given the current status of the project; and identify important implications or recommendations for others involved in graduate education.

Chapter Eight

The Scholarship of Teaching and Learning

Contributing to Reform in Graduate Education

Pat Hutchings, Susan E. Clarke

For most of the last century, the graduate school experience has been designed to prepare students as experts in their disciplines or their professional areas. Graduate students learn to frame questions that are significant to their chosen fields, investigate those questions systematically, and do so in ways that contribute to the thought and practice of others. Bringing these same scholarly skills, habits, and commitments to the work of teaching is what the scholarship of teaching and learning movement is all about—treating teaching and learning as matters of systematic scholarly investigation and discourse, subject to critical review, and generative of a body of knowledge that can be used and developed over time.

Efforts to promote the scholarship of teaching and learning are now under way on many fronts. Many of them have been undertaken in conjunction with the Carnegie Academy for the Scholarship of Teaching and Learning (CASTL), a major initiative of The Carnegie Foundation for the Advancement of Teaching that was launched in 1998. CASTL has three components. The Carnegie Scholars Program works with individual faculty in their capacity as scholars of their teaching and their students' learning. The CASTL Campus Program, coordinated by Carnegie's partner, the American Association for Higher Education, involves "Leadership Clusters" of campuses working together to create policies and practices that support scholarly approaches to teaching and learning. CASTL's work with scholarly and professional societies—some thirty in all, seventeen of which have received small grants—aims to support the development of vehicles, standards, and communities for the scholarly work of teaching. CASTL provides the primary context for this chapter on the relevance of the scholarship of teaching and learning to new developments in graduate education.

Definitions and Purposes

Before we turn to the context of graduate education, it is useful to consider the origins and character of the scholarship of teaching and learning in a more general way. Many of us in higher education first encountered the phrase in the work of Ernest Boyer, former president of the Carnegie Foundation. In *Scholarship Reconsidered,* Boyer (1990) called for a broader conception of scholarship, one encompassing not only basic research—the scholarship of discovery—but the scholarships of integration, application, and teaching. Since then, other scholars have set about to elaborate and further define Boyer's fourth category. Huber and Morreale (2002) situated the scholarship of teaching and learning in relationship to education research in the disciplines and various educational reform movements. Hutchings and Shulman (1999) distinguished the scholarship of teaching and learning from teaching excellence and scholarly teaching. Hatch and Austin (1999) argued that the scholarship of teaching and learning includes not only the *products* of scholarly inquiry into teaching but "the activities in which individuals and groups engage in order to produce those products" (p. 2). In a similar spirit, Bass (1999, p. 1) defined the scholarship of teaching and learning as an attitude toward "problems":

> In scholarship and research, having a "problem" is at the heart of the investigative process. . . . Asking a colleague about a *problem* in his or her research is an invitation; asking about a problem in one's teaching would probably seem like an accusation. Changing the status of the *problem* in teaching from terminal remediation to ongoing investigation is precisely what the movement for a scholarship of teaching is all about. . . . How might we think of teaching practice, and the evidence of student learning, as problems to be investigated, analyzed, represented, and debated?

The scholarship of teaching and learning can also be defined by its purposes and rationale. Indeed, one of the best ways to understand the scholarship of teaching and learning is as a response to the fact that teaching, as a profession and a practice, has so few established mechanisms for ongoing improvement. Carnegie Foundation President Lee Shulman has written about "pedagogical solitude," the fact that teaching, which would seem to be the most social of academic work, done in community with others, is often much less public than research (1993, p. 6). In fact, teaching is largely private work for most faculty, undertaken without collegial collaboration and review. Habits and conventions that would allow faculty to share what they know and do as teachers, and to build on the work of other teachers, are almost nonexistent. Thus, most faculty members approach their teaching by trial and error.

The contrast with research is striking. When it comes to the kind of scholarship we call research, faculty are expected to have an agenda; their work is expected to progress over time and contribute to the field. Often there are different expectations at different ranks; to become a full professor one must have done research with impact at the national or international level. And there are mechanisms for this kind of career trajectory—fellowships, sabbaticals, mentoring, journals, conferences, rewards of various kinds, and very importantly, a scholarly community in which one's work is shaped, reviewed, valued, and built upon. The purpose of the scholarship of teaching and learning is to bring similar "field-building" mechanisms and habits to the work of teaching, be it in an undergraduate or graduate education context.

Challenges and Strategies

Not surprisingly, the ideas and practices of the scholarship of teaching and learning have both conserving and destabilizing effects for graduate education. On the one hand, a focus on teaching offers graduate students a way to become integrated into professional communities while developing and refining broader skills and abilities. Bringing the scholarship of teaching and learning into graduate education programs is, therefore, an opportunity for enhancing professional socialization and fostering a broader sense of stewardship. On the other hand, the scholarship of teaching and learning can be perceived by some as undermining the scholarship of discovery that lies at the heart of most graduate education programs. To the extent that the emphasis on teaching and learning appears to distract graduate students from their own research careers and their support of faculty research projects, it threatens the cultural expectations and habits cherished by many faculty and administrators. The experience of CASTL offers several lessons informed by both the opportunities and obstacles posed by the scholarship of teaching and learning in graduate education settings.

For starters, CASTL's work suggests that graduate education and the scholarship of teaching and learning can be effective natural partners, with benefits to both. In an essay entitled *Visions of the Possible* describing four models for integrating the scholarship of teaching and learning into the institutional setting, Lee Shulman (1999) proposed that campuses focus "first efforts on an aspect of work that is already central to the research university culture: preparing doctoral students for their work as scholars" (p. 12). Doing so reinforces "the notion that we need to go beyond 'TA training' to address in a much more proactive way the need to prepare graduate students for the full range of scholarships associated with the discipline or professional field—including the scholarship of teaching and learning" (pp. 12–13). Moreover, inviting graduate students into the scholarship of teaching and learning is a way of engaging faculty who might not otherwise be interested. Campuses understand, Shulman noted, "that you can't reshape graduate education without involving faculty as mentors and models. Indeed, engaging faculty through work with graduate students might be seen as part of the 'theory of action'" (p. 13) behind linking the scholarship of teaching and learning with graduate education reform.

A first strategy for making this link is to build on the energy and interests of graduate students themselves as they confront the different values accorded to research and teaching. As Golde and Dore (2001) famously reported, "The training doctoral students receive is not what they want, nor does it prepare them for the jobs they take" (p. 5). In their survey of over four thousand doctoral students in 1999, 83 percent of the respondents cited "enjoyment of teaching" as a factor influencing their decision to pursue a graduate degree, but much smaller percentages reported feeling confident and prepared to take on teaching tasks. Similarly, as a graduate student in a national study by Nyquist and colleagues (1999) put it, "I hear every day that it's an irrational choice to spend time on teaching. I have not felt that teaching is valued within the department. It's belittled, basically—only he who is not a good researcher has to be a good teacher" (p. 24). Treating teaching as scholarly, intellectual work may offer an antidote to this problem, a way of bridging the gap between research and teaching that many graduate students find so jarring. Graduate students can, in fact, be powerful advocates for the scholarship of teaching and learning, especially when they have opportunities to experience and participate in the work themselves.

A second strategy for linking the scholarship of teaching and learning with graduate education reform is to integrate it into the larger graduate education reform movement, treating it not as a self-standing initiative but as one of a number of related initiatives, including Preparing Future Faculty, Re-envisioning the Ph.D., the Responsive PhD, and the Carnegie Initiative on the Doctorate (all described elsewhere in this volume). Like these programs, the scholarship of teaching and learning movement responds to the broader sense of mismatch between graduate education and the demands of the twenty-first century that propels graduate education reform efforts in many settings. Also like these programs, the scholarship of teaching and learning movement seeks to expand the skills and values that students develop during their graduate years and to prepare them for a more extensive range of faculty roles and responsibilities. In this sense, the scholarship of teaching and learning can best contribute to graduate education reform by reinforcing and strengthening the larger set of efforts under way. Indeed, bringing together the groups that share these overlapping goals maximizes the impact of program resources and faculty energy. It also creates a forum in which participants can develop a new vocabulary for graduate education reforms.

The third and most important strategy is to connect the scholarship of teaching and learning to the core business of graduate education. That is, the scholarship of teaching and learning will take hold and make a difference in graduate education settings when faculty members see it not as one more role or task, and not simply as a new focus for the training of their students, but as an integral component of the program's capacity to attract the best students and provide the very best experiences for them. This means using the scholarship of teaching and learning to address questions about the particular challenges of educating students at the graduate level—questions, for instance, about mentoring. What kinds of mentoring activities and roles are most conducive to the growth and professional development of graduate students in different settings and at different points in their work? There are questions, too, about the impact of work as part of a research team on the learning of individual students, and for students serving as teaching assistants, about the impact of teaching undergraduates on their own understanding of their fields and areas of study. In a recent article in *Liberal Education,* Jerry Gaff (2002) observed that there are few empirical studies on best practices associated with student success and failure in doctoral education and little rigorous assessment of alternative educational practices. "Because doctoral education is decentralized," Gaff wrote, "it resembles a 'cottage industry' in which each faculty member establishes his/her own rules, little collective learning occurs, and minimal centralized standards or guidelines are available" (p. 8). In this sense, one might argue that the scholarship of teaching and learning is especially important in graduate education. It is, as noted earlier, the missing mechanism for collective improvement, and as such it should be at the very heart of graduate education reform efforts.

Outcomes

Though the scholarship of teaching and learning has, as yet, only a fragile hold in most settings, signs of progress are increasingly evident on campuses and in other organizations. A literature is growing up around the movement, and new outlets, including a number of electronic journals, are now available. The Carnegie Foundation's Knowledge Media Laboratory offers on-line multimedia exhibits of scholarly work on teaching and learning. An annual event on the scholarship of teaching and learning is held at the American Association for Higher Education's national conference. And some two hundred campuses have participated in the CASTL Campus Program, some of them with an explicit focus on the role of and implications for graduate education. Four

examples from campus work illustrate a range of models and outcomes relevant to graduate education; each employs one or more
of the strategies already noted: building on graduate student interests, integrating the scholarship of teaching and learning into
other graduate education reform movements, and connecting the
scholarship of teaching and learning to the core mission of graduate education.

Campus Developments

Indiana University (IU) has an extensive program to support the
scholarship of teaching and learning; special publications, regular
seminars, and stipends to faculty are among the elements of their
initiative. But one of the most powerful elements in the IU program has been the role of the graduate school, and more specifically, the support of George Walker, past dean of the university's
graduate school and vice president for research. At an inaugural
event for the scholarship of teaching initiative, Walker strongly
endorsed the work and its centrality to the mission of the university, noting that the scholarship of teaching and learning should,
like other forms of scholarly work, receive matching funds from
the school's Office of Research: "I have instructed our office to
make sure that this is a high priority and in no way is given second
place to the matching funds that we provide for research in other
areas" (Walker, 1999, p. 6). The IU program on the scholarship of
teaching and learning has involved educators from across the system, with important leadership coming from faculty and administrators in various roles and offices. For instance, the Office of
Academic Affairs facilitated a process that led to changes in annual
report forms, inviting faculty to include their research on teaching
and learning activities. For the purposes of this volume, however,
IU is an especially relevant example of documenting an effective
connection between the scholarship of teaching and learning and
the enterprise of graduate education. Support from the graduate
school and the Office of Research has strengthened the scholarship of teaching and learning, and the scholarship of teaching and
learning, in turn, has helped to broaden the conception of scholarship at the graduate level. The sociology department on the
Bloomington campus, for instance, requires graduate students in
its Preparing Future Faculty Program to take a three-course

sequence focused on teaching and learning, the third of which requires a project in the scholarship of teaching and learning. One recent project, which the class undertook as a team, allowed students to use the various methods of the discipline (ethnographic study, in-depth interviews, record analysis, and other approaches) to study an experimental pilot program designed to reengineer the IU first-year experience. The results of their evaluation did not support the program's effect on IU's goals, and the pilot program was discontinued. Graduate students thus saw their work having an impact on institutional decision making. In addition, they saw in a vivid and concrete way how the skills and methods of sociology can be brought to bear in new contexts in consequential ways. They are now writing up the work so that various audiences can build on it (Bernice Pescosolido, personal communication with the authors, October 31, 2002).

A similar process can be documented at Howard University, where the graduate school has taken the lead in supporting the scholarship of teaching and learning. Faculty members working with one or more graduate students on projects in the scholarship of teaching and learning in their field may apply through the graduate school for small grants in an annual competition. Participants in the program are then expected to present their findings in a public roundtable; their work may also be grist for a published monograph. In the first round of this program, projects involve nine faculty and nineteen doctoral students in fields ranging from business management to English composition and sociology. Each of the projects entails research on how undergraduate students acquire the language of their disciplines, and each will be assessed, in part, in terms of an expected improvement by undergraduate majors in the capstone experience that Howard requires for graduation. In the context of doctoral education, then, the graduate school sees the scholarship of teaching and learning as an instrument to link undergraduate and graduate education. The program also gives doctoral students an experience that helps them see the pedagogy of their fields as legitimate subjects for scholarly inquiry. According to Graduate Dean Orlando Taylor, Howard expects this program to be an annual competition (Orlando Taylor, personal communication with the authors, October 7, 2002).

The impact of the scholarship of teaching and learning on graduate education can be seen at the University of Michigan in its innovative program established in the chemistry department. Chemical Sciences at the Interface of Education (CSIE) is an interdisciplinary fellowship program for Ph.D. students in chemistry interested in pursuing academic careers. Using the familiar model for training grants, students are supported to do course and project work above and beyond that of their colleagues, with the idea of integrating an emergent area—namely, teaching and learning—into their preparation in chemistry research. In addition to seminars and workshops on aspects of faculty careers such as proposal writing, authorship, mentoring, and the peer review process, the centerpiece of their activities is to design, implement, assess, and document an instructional project. These projects are conducted in collaboration with the chemistry faculty, and generally constitute a reform or innovation that the faculty member was interested in pursuing but did not have the time or energy to complete without assistance. Importantly, the impact of this model is not on graduate students alone. Instructional development teams are generally intergenerational (as in research), involving undergraduate and postdoctoral collaborators. Michigan's undergraduate students enrolled in the new or revised courses directly benefit from these activities as well.

In 2002, the CSIE program entered its fifth year. Early indicators suggest that students who have completed the program will have a strong competitive advantage when seeking faculty positions. According to CSIE Director Brian Coppola (1998), chemistry faculty from outside the University of Michigan who have met these students in a variety of professional settings, such as seminars and conferences, have been impressed by the sophisticated understanding of higher education these students exhibit. "These students will become a new breed of faculty member," Coppola notes. "In every core disciplinary education, there are interdisciplinary areas that are included because a baseline understanding is crucial to one's expertise. To be a faculty member, one's education should bring a person up to speed in the area of teaching and learning in one's discipline as a prerequisite." In addition, CSIE has had an impact on the department's ability to recruit outstanding graduate students. "A number of excellent students have selected our Ph.D. program over departments ranked higher than ours because we openly embrace future faculty development," Coppola reports. A research collaboration recently launched with the Center for the

Study of Post-Secondary Higher Education at the University of Michigan will help CSIE determine whether or not systemic change has resulted from the department's future faculty education in a broadened definition of scholarly development. (For more information, see the CSIE Web site at www.umich.edu/~csie.)

Finally, the University of Colorado documents ways that scholarly work on teaching at the graduate level can contribute to broader change throughout the institution. Recognized by the Woodrow Wilson Foundation as one of the best graduate training programs in the country, the Graduate Teacher Program (GTP) grew from initial concern over the lack of preparation and support for graduate students taking on TA responsibilities to an interest in the longer-term development of graduate students as scholar-teachers. It now offers a certificate to students taking a set number of teaching workshops—an incentive to participate—and provides lead TAs with small stipends to develop graduate student activities inside departments. Serving a graduate student constituency, the GTP provides the "scaffolding" and infrastructure needed to reflect on teaching and learning issues as graduate instructors and future faculty members.

In addition to GTP, another Colorado-Boulder program—the Faculty Teaching Excellence Program (FTEP)—shares many of these features. FTEP recently moved to a next phase of faculty development with its "Department- and Discipline-Specific Program in Learning Goals and Assessment," with the physics department serving as a first pilot site. In conjunction with FTEP and the School of Education, the physics department has instituted a series of presentations on physics pedagogy, a once-a-week department brown bag on teaching improvement, and a possible summer institute for faculty to learn more about learning and assessment. As of fall 2003, several pedagogical models are available on line for other science departments so that they can learn about establishing a similar discipline-specific program. As the pilot program makes clear, FTEP provides different venues in which faculty can "go public" with teaching and learning issues and build on the experiences of others. Incentives for sustained faculty participation in such efforts increased when campus tenure policies were revised in the late 1990s to incorporate multiple measures of teaching excellence and to highlight student learning.

Both the Graduate Teaching Program and the Faculty Teaching Excellence Program benefited from the initial support of "champions" in the administration; both demonstrate the importance of scholarship of teaching and learning "entrepreneurs" and new institutional arrangements. Importantly, both mobilized their constituencies around the notion that teaching practices and student learning are "problems to be investigated, analyzed, represented, and debated" together (Bass, 1999, p. 1). In 2003, the university's Office of Academic Affairs launched a Provost's Seminar on Teaching and Learning to bring the various campus stakeholders to the table to consider how these and other campus teaching and learning initiatives might be better coordinated and contribute to larger change. The presence of four Carnegie Scholars on the Boulder campus has helped catalyze activity across units and programs at both the graduate and undergraduate levels.

Developments in the Scholarly Societies

Campuses are clearly crucial sites for the scholarship of teaching and learning. But the impact, or potential impact, of the scholarship of teaching and learning on graduate education may also be traced beyond campuses. For instance, the movement has made significant inroads through the scholarly and professional societies. Prompted in large part by *Scholarship Reconsidered,* many disciplinary associations have produced statements calling for a broader conception of scholarly work, one that includes work on teaching and learning (see *The Disciplines Speak,* edited by Diamond and Adams, 1995, for a collection of such statements). The American Sociological Association has developed an "audit" to help these organizations assess their progress on these matters (Howery, 1999). Many fields have also responded to recent reports and analyses critical of graduate education, and many have established task forces and standing committees on graduate education that have come forward with recommendations consistent with the central ideas of the scholarship of teaching and learning (though not always using that language). For example, the American Political Science Association recently established the Task Force on Graduate Education; included in its charge is how best to prepare graduate students for the teaching and service responsibilities they will face. In addition, the association launched an annual "Teaching and Learning in Political Science" conference in April 2004 and uses the association journal, *PS,* to focus discussion on the scholarship of teaching and learning—its definition, how it can be used in the discipline, and its relevance to graduate education reforms (Clarke, Meranto, & Kehl, 2002). As reported in Chapter Twelve of this volume, a number of scholarly societies are also working with the Carnegie Initiative on the Doctorate, which invites graduate programs to use the principles of the scholarship of teaching and learning to examine and improve their own practices.

Recommendations

The argument of this chapter is that the scholarship of teaching and learning can bring important "field-building" habits and processes to the work of graduate education, thereby strengthening graduate programs, the preparation of future faculty, and the larger academic culture. Along the way, our discussion of strategies and examples suggests a number of lessons for graduate educators interested in harnessing the powerful ideas and practices of the scholarship of teaching and learning:

- *Link teaching to the field-building mechanisms used in research.* The scholarship of teaching and learning is best seen not as yet another task or area of work—a new specialty for a few faculty, or an added component in a workshop for TAs—but as an integral element of an effective, responsibly functioning educational program. That is, the idea is to bring the values, habits, and skills that are essential to traditional research to bear on the work of teaching and learning and to do so because it is part of our professional responsibility as educators to be continually questioning, gathering evidence, building knowledge, and seeking to advance the enterprise.
- *Reconsider the campus reward system.* Much of the national conversation about the scholarship of teaching and learning focuses on a need to shift the traditional academic reward system. However, this does *not* mean that to advance the scholarship of teaching and learning universities must suddenly "count" teaching the same as research efforts, or that teaching

is research. Advancing the scholarship of teaching and learning *does* mean that discipline-based teaching and learning issues should be seen as appropriate topics for scholarly research and can be advanced in some of the same ways that our understandings of substantive disciplinary problems are advanced. Initiatives at Colorado and Indiana point in promising directions for this rethinking, but more needs to be known about how graduate students and faculty become interested in such work, how it affects their career trajectory and prospects, and where it fits into the larger arc of faculty work (including their work with their own graduate students). Mary Taylor Huber, a senior scholar at the Carnegie Foundation, has completed case studies of four faculty members that will begin to answer these questions.

- *Recognize the disciplinary contexts for the scholarship of teaching and learning.* The discipline or professional field is a crucial context for advancing the scholarly work of teaching and learning. Each field brings its own questions, methods, and rules of evidence to this work, and faculty are much more likely to embrace (or at least to understand) the work if it reflects the culture and character of the field. As a historian working with CASTL put it, "I'm not going to do something [in the scholarship of teaching and learning] with a double blind and proper control groups—all the accoutrements of the scientific approach that an experimental psychologist would want to see. Historians don't do that" (Kelly, 2000, p. 55). Instead, this faculty member used methods from his own field to investigate his students' learning in a Web-based environment. Because it is discipline-based, the scholarship of teaching and learning offers greater incentives for faculty and graduate student participation.

- *Make students participants, not subjects.* A powerful catalyst for action is participation by students, both undergraduate and graduate. Rather than seeing students and their work as the subject of the scholarship of teaching and learning, instructors should seek ways to involve them in the framing and investigation of questions about their learning. For instance, Professor William Cutler, a historian at Temple University and a Carnegie Scholar with CASTL, invited TAs to help investigate his American history course. Their observational journals are part of his course portfolio that is posted on the American Historical Association Web site at http://www.theaha.org/teaching/aahe/aahecover.html (Cutler, 1997).

- *Go public on your campus.* Those committed to the scholarship of teaching and learning should develop campuswide communities where faculty and graduate students can "go public" with their analyses of teaching and learning issues and begin to build on each other's experiences. Such efforts can take many possible forms; campuses often can build on existing but more limited programs and use working groups to scale up these efforts.

- *Tap into work being done beyond the campus.* Participation in national initiatives like those undertaken by the Carnegie Foundation and the American Association for Higher Education can increase the visibility, prestige, and occasionally the resources available to local efforts. There are now notable developments internationally as well, with conferences and publications likely to be of interest to graduate faculty and students.

- *Keep track of progress, which also means defining success.* Higher education needs to develop indicators that will tell us where, when, and how the scholarship of teaching and learning is making a difference in various programs and aspects of the campus culture. Many CASTL participants are concerned, for instance, with tracking how the scholarship of teaching and learning is integrated into promotion and tenure decisions, scholarly discourse, and professional reward structures—publications, grants, and awards. There are questions, too, about its impact on doctoral seminars and extracurricular programs available to faculty and graduate students. Indicators of progress in these areas would give us a better sense of the scaffolding in place for the scholarship of teaching and learning and the areas needing further attention.

Conclusion

We have referred to the scholarship of teaching and learning as a *movement* in this essay. That word is often used casually and prematurely. Certainly the scholarship of teaching and learning is still an emergent phenomenon, fragile in many ways. But in the same way that efforts to "internationalize" or "engender" the curriculum gradually took effect and became part of the landscape of higher education, the scholarship of teaching and learning is now starting to make its mark. Graduate education debates are increasingly inclusive of the many types of scholarship and the language of teaching and learning.

On campuses and in scholarly communities, the language we use to discuss teaching is shifting to a learning-centered vocabulary, and teaching problems are being framed as issues for investigation. Faculty roles are slowly expanding in ways that value the scholarship of teaching as well as the scholarship of discovery, and concomitant changes in reward systems are also emerging. In short, both the language and practice of the scholarship of teaching and learning are increasingly widespread. The next generation of graduate reform faces the task of sustaining this momentum and institutionalizing the scholarship of teaching and learning.

References

Bass, R. (1999). The scholarship of teaching and learning: What's the problem? *Inventio, 1,* 1. [http://www.doiiit.gmu.edu/Archives/feb98/randybass.htm]

Boyer, E. L. (1990). *Scholarship reconsidered: Priorities of the professoriate.* Princeton, NJ: The Carnegie Foundation for the Advancement of Teaching.

Coppola, B. (1998). *Chemical sciences at the interface of education: An infrastructure for developing the scholarship of teaching and learning (SoTL) for future faculty.* Ann Arbor: University of Michigan. [www.umich.edu/~csie]

Clarke, S. E., Meranto, O., & Kehl, J. R. (2002). The CO-CA cluster: Initiatives for preparing future faculty. *PS, 35,* 720–726.

Cutler, William W., III. (1997). *History 67, the United States to 1877: A course portfolio 1996 and 1997.* Washington, DC: American Historical Association. [http://www.theaha.org/teaching/aahe/aahecover.html]

Diamond, R. M., & Adams, B. E. (Eds.). (1995). *The disciplines speak: Rewarding the scholarly, professional, and creative work of faculty.* Washington, DC: American Association for Higher Education.

Gaff, J. G. (2002). The disconnect between graduate education and faculty realities. *Liberal Education, 88*(3), 6–13.

Golde, C. M., & Dore, T. M. (2001). *At cross purposes: What the experiences of doctoral students reveal about doctoral education.* Philadelphia: A Report for The Pew Charitable Trusts. [www.phd-survey.org]

Hatch, T., & Austin, K. (1999). *Toward the scholarship of teaching* (Draft report for the Carnegie Academy for the Scholarship of Teaching and Learning). Menlo Park, CA: The Carnegie Foundation for the Advancement of Teaching.

Howery, C. B. (1999). *An association audit re: scholarship of teaching.* Washington, DC: American Sociological Association.
[http://aahe.ital.utexas.edu/resources/ASA's_association_audit.doc]

Huber, M. T., & Morreale, S. P. (Eds.). (2002). *Disciplinary styles in the scholarship of teaching and learning: Exploring common ground.* Washington, DC: American Association for Higher Education and The Carnegie Foundation for the Advancement of Teaching.

Hutchings, P., & Shulman, L. S. (1999, September-October). The scholarship of teaching and learning: New elaborations, new developments. *Change, 31*(5), 10–15.

Kelly, T. M. (2000). For better or worse? The marriage of Web and classroom. In P. Hutchings (Ed.), *Opening lines: Approaches to the scholarship of teaching and learning* (pp. 53–62). Menlo Park, CA: The Carnegie Foundation for the Advancement of Teaching.

Nyquist, J. D., Manning, L., Wulff, D. H., Austin, A. E., Sprague, J., Fraser, P. K., Calcagno, C., & Woodford, B. (1999, May-June). On the road to becoming a professor: The graduate student experience. *Change, 31*(3), 18–27.

Shulman, L. S. (1993, November-December). Teaching as community property: Putting an end to pedagogical solitude. *Change, 25*(6), 6–7.

Shulman, L. S. (2004). Visions of the possible: Models for campus support of the scholarship of teaching and learning. In W. E. Becker & M. L. Andrews (Eds.), *The scholarship of teaching and learning: Contributions of research universities.* Bloomington: Indiana University Press.

Walker, G. E. (1999, December 4). *The scholarship of teaching.* Address to the meeting of research institutions at Georgetown University, Washington, DC.
[http://aahe.ital.utexas.edu/resources/G_Walker's_speech.doc.doc]

Chapter Nine

Preparing Future Faculty
Changing the Culture of Doctoral Education
Anne S. Pruitt-Logan, Jerry G. Gaff

> *As I look back on the past two years in PFF, I realize that I*
> *have seriously considered my future for the first time—PFF*
> *has forced me to think about my life, my graduate career,*
> *and my future goals in a new light.*
> DOCTORAL STUDENT IN ZOOLOGY

The Preparing Future Faculty Program (PFF) is a national program that offers a new vision and a broader education for doctoral students who seek a career in the professoriate (Gaff, Pruitt-Logan, & Weibl, 2000; Pruitt-Logan, Gaff, & Jentoft, 2002; Gaff, Pruitt-Logan, Sims, & Denecke, 2003). In the twenty-first century, both undergraduate and graduate education are undergoing significant change. In addition to educating doctoral students who aspire to an academic career primarily as researchers, graduate education should prepare them to be competent in the whole range of faculty responsibilities—teaching, research, and service—and PFF strives to do so.

Indeed, a range of studies and reports provides evidence of the need for a program such as PFF. Studies of graduate students (Golde & Dore, 2001; Lovitts, 2001; National Association of Graduate-Professional Students, 2001; Nyquist, Austin, Sprague, & Wulff, 2001) document the need for more information about potential careers, greater attention to teaching, more mentoring, and a closer relationship between doctoral preparation and the realities of faculty work. As discussed in earlier chapters of this volume, investigations that focus on new faculty point to the need for better graduate preparation and clearer expectations about the nature of faculty roles (Rice, Sorcinelli, & Austin, 2000; Sorcinelli, 2001; Trower, Austin, & Sorcinelli, 2001). Research involving Ph.D. alumni, including those employed both in the academy and outside it, also supports the need for more information about careers, more attention to teaching and interdisciplinary work, and greater emphasis on communication, organizational, and teamwork skills (Nerad & Cerney, 2000; Smith & Pedersen-Gallegos, 2001).

Further, several organizations have called for changes of the sort that PFF represents. *Reshaping the Education of Scientists and Engineers* (Committee on Science, Engineering, and Public Policy, 1995), a report issued collectively by the National Academy of Science, the National Academy of Engineering, and the National Institute of Medicine, calls for graduate students and faculty to have better and more up-to-date information about careers and for graduate programs to be more flexible and address the needs of alternative careers. In 1996, the National Association of Graduate-Professional Students (NAGPS) adopted a resolution supporting the PFF philosophy and objectives relating to pedagogical skill building and professional development. In 1998, a report issued by the Association of American Universities (Committee on Graduate Education, p. 21) cited PFF as "one of the most systematic efforts to increase graduate student preparation for teaching." Thus, both empirical evidence and reports from various study groups representing significant constituencies of graduate education coalesce in the call for improved preparation of future faculty.

Since PFF was launched in 1993, approximately four thousand doctoral students have been "core participants" in PFF programs, and many more have occasionally participated in PFF activities and derived secondary benefits. Most of these individuals, like the zoology student cited at this chapter's opening, report that they learned important lessons about their chosen professions and that what they learned was not available elsewhere in their studies. By all accounts, a PFF program, added to any Ph.D. program, constitutes better preparation for the professoriate than the traditional approach that focuses almost entirely on research.

Program Description and Purposes

The key purpose of PFF is to promote expanded professional development for doctoral students. PFF recognizes the compelling need for new faculty members to be effective teachers, active researchers, and good academic citizens who contribute to the betterment of their departments, campuses, and communities. New faculty members at many institutions are expected to conduct research and publish, provide intellectual stimulation to their colleagues, and bring prestige to their institutions. They also are expected to be able to teach and advise a student body diverse not only in race, ethnicity, gender, and other demographic qualities but also in intellectual skill, motivation, and learning style. Further, they are expected to employ powerful modern strategies of teaching and learning, including active, collaborative, experiential, and technological approaches, and to assist with campus initiatives, such as writing across the curriculum, assessment of student learning, and strong general education curricula (Adams, 2002). They must be research mentors to others and experts in various forms of scholarship and be able to engage undergraduate students in research. Many faculty and administrative colleagues report that large numbers of candidates for assistant professor positions are not ready for these demands of the higher education workplace.

Although some doctoral students may become teaching assistants, the reality is that large numbers of graduate students do not have this opportunity. Of those who do, many receive teaching assistant assignments that do not provide opportunities for grappling with the full array of serious intellectual and practical challenges of teaching, learning, and shaping an educational program. The point is not that teaching and professional service should be favored over research experience but that doctoral education for the professoriate should be strengthened by attention to all the elements that characterize an academic career.

PFF embodies some key ideas:

- *The doctoral experience should provide increasingly independent and varied teaching responsibilities as well as opportunities for prospective faculty to grow and develop as researchers.* Apprenticeship teaching, research, and service experiences should be planned so that they are appropriate to the student's stage of professional development and progress toward the degree.

- *The experience should help students begin to understand and appreciate elements of faculty service.* Programs should include opportunities for doctoral students to serve their departments, disciplines, campuses, and communities.

- *Doctoral students should learn about the academic profession through exposure to the range of professional responsibilities in the variety of institutions that may become their professional homes.* This exposure enables them to find a comfortable "fit," providing a context of understanding as they seek to match their own interests and competencies with the needs of departments and institutions. The reality is that those who go on to faculty careers work mostly in institutions that have different missions, student bodies, and expectations of faculty than do the research universities where the doctoral students obtain their degrees.

- *Doctoral programs should formalize a system for mentoring in all aspects of professional development.* Just as students have mentors to guide their research, they also benefit from ongoing relationships with experienced faculty members as they develop their teaching and service expertise. Indeed, students can benefit from multiple mentors. A teaching mentor may be located at a different institution, perhaps one with a mission that is different from that of the research university.

- *Doctoral experiences should equip future faculty for the significant changes taking place in classrooms and curricula.* For example, future faculty should be competent in using technology; knowledgeable about teaching for inclusiveness; familiar with the increasing heterogeneity of students; sophisticated about general education and interdisciplinary curricula; and capable of using active, collaborative, and experiential approaches to teaching and learning.

- *Professional development experiences should be thoughtfully integrated into the academic program and sequence of degree requirements.* Unless leaders of doctoral education are intentional about these matters and structure these new experiences into their programs, PFF activities are likely to be added to an already full program and may increase the amount of time required to earn a degree.

- *Where high-quality teaching assistant orientation and development programs are available, PFF programs should build on them.* PFF is consistent with the best practices of teaching assistant development, while also advancing another, more comprehensive level of preparation.

PFF programs are organized and implemented around the core concept of the "cluster," a new form of institutional collaboration that brings the institutions that hire Ph.D.'s ("consumers") together with the institutions that educate them ("producers"). A cluster is a formal, cooperative arrangement involving doctoral degree granting universities with a range of other institutions or departments—"partners"—in a joint working relationship. Anchored by a doctoral degree granting university, cluster institutions usually include primarily undergraduate institutions such as liberal arts colleges, comprehensive universities, and community colleges. Experience with the different institutions in the cluster helps prospective faculty gain a broad understanding of the higher education workplace.

When PFF began with a grant (Phase 1) from The Pew Charitable Trusts to the Association of American Colleges and Universities (AAC&U) in collaboration with the Council of Graduate Schools (CGS), the purpose was to select institutions to develop model programs with clusters that incorporate the PFF vision and concepts previously described. By means of a national competition under the leadership of Jerry Gaff, principal investigator, 5 universities were awarded grants of $170,000 each, and another 12 universities were given more modest grants. This first phase included 17 lead universities and 68 institutional partners. After three years, it became clear that it was feasible to create clusters, that the new programs operated as intended, and that participants reported very positive outcomes. A second grant (Phase 2) was received to help the institutions institutionalize their programs and spread the ideas and programs to others. In this second phase, 10 of the original participants were selected through a competitive process, as were 5 more that had instituted programs with several PFF elements, giving a total of 15 lead universities and 119 institutional partners. These grants in both phases were awarded to graduate deans, who played leadership roles in creating university-wide PFF programs.

In all these early PFF programs, graduate faculty members also played central leadership roles, but the number of graduate faculty members involved was small. In order to secure greater faculty ownership for PFF, the next step was to enlist disciplinary societies as partners. In the third phase, then, with the leadership of Anne Pruitt-Logan, principal investigator, and with a grant from the National Science Foundation (NSF) to CGS in collaboration with AAC&U, professional societies in the disciplines of chemistry, computer science, life sciences, mathematics, and physics became involved: the American Association of Physics Teachers, the American Chemical Society, the Association for Computer Machinery's Special Interest Group on Computer Science Education, and the American Mathematical Society jointly with the Mathematical Association of America. There were 19 academic departments and 92 departmental partners involved in this third phase. A subsequent grant (Phase 4) from The Atlantic Philanthropies—again with Pruitt-Logan as the principal investigator—added 6 societies in the humanities and social sciences: the American Historical Association, American Political Science Association, American Psychological Association, American Sociological Association, National Communication Association, and National Council of Teachers of English. This phase included 25 academic departments and 130 departmental partners. In each case, the societies held national competitions to award matching grants to departments in their fields to develop model PFF programs and to assemble clusters to implement them. Although the society in the life sciences withdrew, all the others have developed significant PFF innovations, highlighting PFF in their programs and publications and becoming strong advocates for this broader preparation for the professoriate.

PFF has been an unusually successful collaboration between two Washington-based educational associations. As this chapter is being written, all of the grants supporting PFF have been completed, and most campus-based PFF programs continue with institutional support.

Strategies

Campus leaders have been encouraged to develop programs that are in keeping with PFF concepts while also reflecting their own institutions' needs, interests, and circumstances. Important elements that institutions must consider include the nature and location of activities, key institutional players, and management strategies.

Nature and Location of Activities

PFF programs concentrate activities in three different loci: the university, because some learning is general and appropriate for all graduate students; the department, because some learning is particular to the disciplines; and the partner institution, because some learning is dependent on the institutional context.

At the university level, activities often include a course on college teaching and learning, forums on faculty life and careers, discussions of faculty governance issues, and development of professional portfolios documenting students' expertise in teaching, research, and service. Departments usually offer courses on the teaching of their disciplines, provide sequences of supervised teaching experiences, and host discussions in which faculty members from different institutions describe their careers. They also sponsor talks by alumni, who discuss how their graduate programs did and did not prepare them well for their jobs. Specific kinds of program elements found in both university-wide and departmental PFF programs include certificate programs, courses for credit, seminars and workshops, mentoring activities, assessment and evaluation, attention to diversity, informal student activities, and activities and resources through disciplinary societies.

Partner institutions assign a faculty mentor to work with doctoral students, invite students to attend department or faculty meetings, include them in faculty development activities, and offer supervised teaching opportunities. For example, the University of New Hampshire operates both a university-wide PFF program and one located in the psychology department, the latter originally supported by the American Psychological Association. Victor Benassi, associate provost, describing the departmental program, says students are given an orientation to faculty life during the first-year graduate proseminar in psychology and complete a two-year assistantship as apprentices in which they work closely with two or more partner faculty on a variety of faculty-related duties. They also take a two-semester course on teaching before and while they teach their own courses, visit a diverse set of partner institutions, and participate in a university-wide PFF breakfast series during which issues related to faculty careers are discussed with faculty from partner institutions. If they choose, doctoral students may earn a cognate or a master's degree in college teaching. Moreover, they supervise undergraduate students on research projects and get assistance from graduate faculty as they prepare for and undertake the job-search process. Students in the program routinely develop a portfolio documenting their accomplishments in teaching, research, and service as "colleagues-in-training." In addition, the department keeps up-to-date placement information.

Duke University operates a university-wide PFF program—as well as a biology teaching certificate program; the latter is available for postdoctoral fellows and graduate students in the life sciences in the arts and sciences college and the medical school. The content of the certificate program includes a course in teaching and learning in the biological sciences, teaching with supervision, and faculty mentoring. Students develop a teaching portfolio containing materials in each of these areas, a reflective essay, a statement of teaching philosophy, samples of curriculum materials developed, syllabi of courses taught, and teaching evaluations. Partner faculty are involved in both the course and mentoring, and they and their graduate student colleagues can apply for minigrants to support the development of innovative curricula in biology. Students are very positive in their reactions to this program, although formal assessments have not been completed.

Aside from simply assembling a cohort of doctoral students, PFF programs also focus on increasing the diversity of their students so that PFF can help enlarge the pool of faculty of color. These activities include linking with national and university programs designed to increase the number of underrepresented students in various disciplines. For example, Summer Research Opportunity Programs, sponsored by many graduate schools, target undergraduate students to encourage young students of color to enter graduate school. Federal government programs such as NSF's Alliances for Graduate Education and the Professoriate (AGEP) programs and Louis Stokes Alliance for Minority Participation (LSAMP) target underrepresented students in sciences and engineering. The U.S. Department of Education's Ronald E. McNair Postbaccalaureate Achievement Program engages undergraduates in research and scholarly activities to encourage preparation for the professoriate.

Key Institutional Players

PFF programs involve many players, and at their best, incorporate an ethos of collaboration, openness, and inclusiveness. Whether the PFF program is university-wide or departmental, the various players include a program director, graduate dean, other university officials, graduate faculty, partner faculty and administrators, and doctoral students.

PFF program directors are usually faculty members—such as Dick Simpson in political science at the University of Illinois at Chicago—who are committed to the PFF vision and are articulate advocates of PFF. They enlist the support of multiple constituencies and oversee the design and implementation of the program. One of the director's most challenging responsibilities is to assemble a cluster of institutions to participate in PFF and to recruit and support the faculty members who participate.

Graduate deans, such as Orlando Taylor at Howard University, usually are attuned to national needs and trends and have a university-wide perspective that allows them to recognize the value and potential of PFF. Sometimes they initiate the program; in other cases they aid departmentally initiated programs. In either event, they assist the department and key graduate faculty to develop a sense of ownership of the program and give support—financial, political, and strategic—to the program and the director.

Other university officials include provosts, such as Milton Glick at Arizona State University, who contributes budgetary and other assistance for a university-wide program; college deans, such as Gerald Crawley, dean of the College of Science and Mathematics at the University of South Carolina, who lends leadership and financial support for college or departmental programs; and directors of teaching and learning centers, such as Rosalind Streichler, at the Center for Teaching Development at the University of California-San Diego, who helped establish PFF in the physics department. Such officials sanction the program, consult with department chairs and faculty about the value of PFF, and assist in creating policies and programs that enable innovations like PFF to succeed.

Graduate faculty members serve as mentors to PFF students in expanding their skills in teaching, research, and professional service, advise students on other aspects of the academic profession, participate in PFF seminars and workshops, and offer suggestions for improving the program. They also encourage their students to participate, recruit partner faculty, and educate their faculty colleagues who may be skeptical about the benefits of PFF programs.

Faculty and administrators at partner institutions share their distinctive experiences with PFF students. The faculty members mentor PFF students who teach units of courses. They design and implement graduate student internships, serve as guest instructors in PFF courses and workshops, and allow students to shadow them in committee meetings and faculty development activities. Administrators explain their institutions' missions and their faculty search processes, and they help coordinate the relationships among the institutions in the clusters.

Although most partner faculty experience a great deal of satisfaction from fulfilling their roles in PFF programs, explicit recognition is important. A few partner institutions provide salary supplements or workload reductions, and most PFF programs recognize these faculty publicly and give a range of rewards, including acknowledgment in written materials, invitations to scholarly activities, use of libraries and research facilities, and free parking at the university.

Doctoral students themselves are, of course, key players. Doctoral students are usually eager to learn about the academic profession. Those who have already determined that they want academic careers are easy to recruit because they want to learn more about faculty roles at different kinds of institutions. Some PFF students want to explore the possibility of an academic career, and still others believe that the skills they will learn will be useful in almost any career path. In addition to seeking knowledge about the academic profession and developing skills in teaching and working with colleagues, most students want a credential that will give them a competitive advantage in a job search.

The influence of all of these players—program directors, graduate deans, other university officials, graduate faculty, partner faculty and administrators, and doctoral students—is strategic in bringing about robust PFF programs. Clearly, PFF programs involve wide collaboration among interested parties.

Management

How can so many components be orchestrated into a coherent PFF program? The answer is by means of a steering committee representing all participants. This committee plans and oversees the program. Great care must be taken in creating such a complex arrangement because, although partnerships are common in higher education, collaborating is not easy. Overcoming any suspicions and history of tensions between the research university and the primarily undergraduate partner institutions requires skillful negotiating. Specifically, the steering committee determines what leaders and faculty at the institutions believe will be needed in new faculty. It then helps faculty in both the doctoral university and the partner institutions learn about the expectations for faculty participating in PFF and the ways that faculty roles are changing in various institutions.

Leaders of PFF programs, whether departmental or university-wide, assert that establishing and maintaining a program are not costly activities. Yet budgetary support for program management is essential, as are funds for doctoral students' activities and cluster development. Programs usually operate with a combination of funds from a variety of campus units, such as pertinent academic departments, teaching and learning centers, and graduate and undergraduate deans' offices.

These strategies are implemented at different rates, depending on a variety of circumstances: the skill of the director, the ability of administrators to supply resources for the innovation, the willingness of the departmental faculty to encourage student participation, and the agreement of cluster members to collaborate. Moreover, it is essential that the initiator—whether graduate dean, graduate faculty, or other university official—continue to monitor and assist in developmental and implementation responsibilities.

Outcomes

Since its inception, PFF has progressed from a set of ideas to a national movement. The number of university-wide programs has grown from the original 17 to 23, with 44 academic departments involved. It has contributed to the education of about 4,000 doctoral students and involved about 400 graduate faculty and 450 partner faculty as "core participants." Countless more have been peripherally involved. It has partnered with disciplinary societies in 11 fields. In addition, it has spawned similar programs in a number of other universities.

Much assessment has been completed, including visits by a team of evaluators; case studies of PFF programs; surveys of PFF students, faculty members, and administrators (Pruitt-Logan, Gaff, & Weibl, 1998); and a commissioned external evaluation (Thomas, 2002). There have also been annual reports in which cluster leaders indicated progress toward institutionalizing their programs. In addition, clusters have been encouraged to assess their own programs and track their graduates, and most have done so.

From the beginning, students and faculty members have reported an array of benefits for doctoral students:

- Developing expertise as a teacher, articulating a teaching philosophy, and using different approaches to engage diverse students
- Learning about faculty roles and activities
- Understanding the variety of institutions in which graduates may work and the expectations those institutions have for their faculty
- Being mentored by a faculty member at a partner institution
- Developing a network of professional colleagues and other resources
- Clarifying career choices and empowering students for the job market
- Increasing students' self-confidence as academic professionals
- Getting off to a confident start as new faculty members

DeNeef (2002) conducted a survey of PFF alumni who are in faculty positions to determine how the program affected their careers. After surveying individuals in a broad range of disciplines—using a questionnaire and telephone interviews—he concluded that PFF affected the experiences of these individuals in three primary ways. First, the alumni believed that because of their involvement in PFF their graduate student experience was qualitatively different—and better—than it would have been otherwise. Second, they believed that PFF experiences aided them in their job search, with PFF usually credited as a central reason why they received their job offers. Third, they reported that what they learned through PFF helped them get off to a faster and surer start as new faculty members than did their faculty peers.

One of DeNeef's more surprising findings was that PFF alumni were serving as resources to their new faculty colleagues. For example, as noted in DeNeef (2002), Wendy Crone, a new faculty member in engineering at the University of Wisconsin-Madison, reported that the PFF program had provided her with a set of professorial tools from which she could continue to pick and choose as needed. This outcome is common among PFF alumni, according to DeNeef. But in Crone's case, because she had this "basket of tools," her peers were seeking her advice on various professional matters. "I have become a de facto mentor to my colleagues," she observed (p. 16).

A three-year independent evaluation of PFF—supported by the National Science Foundation and The Atlantic Philanthropies—concluded in fall 2003. Although only a small amount of information has been released thus far, the results generally confirm the very positive findings of internal studies.

Drawing from the results of all of the assessments, we conclude that PFF programs indeed function largely as they were conceived and they are notable for several important outcomes:

- Most doctoral students and alumni are enthusiastic about their PFF programs and gain an understanding of faculty roles in different institutions, clarity about choice of career, competence and confidence in their teaching, and credentials that help in the job search.
- Faculty members from partner institutions derive several benefits, including intellectual insights from junior colleagues, fresh ideas about teaching their courses, renewed enthusiasm for their work, and the gratification that comes from helping younger colleagues learn about the profession and their kinds of institutions.

- Graduate faculty members appreciate the professional development opportunities their students gain through PFF programs, and they themselves learn about the roles of faculty at various institutions, the changing job market, and interesting new colleagues.
- Virtually all PFF participants who have been queried—graduate students, faculty members, and administrators—have said they would recommend these programs to others.
- Benefits to academic departments and universities include better recruitment and placement of graduate students and a greater sense of academic community.

Arguably, the benefits listed here outweigh the modest investments of time and money that are required.

Recommendations

Although much has been accomplished through PFF programs, more remains to be done if PFF is to achieve its potential for changing the culture of faculty preparation. The following recommendations pertain especially to the research and doctoral granting institutions, but the last one addresses higher education leaders throughout institutions, associations, and disciplinary societies:

- *Continue to embed elements of professional education into doctoral programs that prepare future faculty.* A fundamental premise of professional education is that one prepares for a profession by experiencing it in the variety of settings in which it is practiced. In a number of the professions, students prepare through internships, residencies, and fieldwork that are not usually part of the preparation for the professoriate. Medical students, for example, serve on hospital floors and in a variety of clinics early in their training, later working as interns and residents with increased responsibilities. Some law students take clinical courses, and others work as interns in law firms or with judges practicing the legal work to which they aspire. Seminarians, while still studying toward their degrees, work in parishes, preach, and minister in homes for the elderly. A new doctor must know a great deal about anatomy and pharmaceuticals but must also have experience treating patients. Similarly, it is not sufficient for faculty members to know only the content of their fields; they also must understand effective teaching and advising and know how to foster learning.

- *Continue to promote inclusiveness to diversify the next generation of faculty.* Despite the many efforts designed to diversify the faculty, college and university faculties still do not reflect the population of the United States. Now that the professoriate is seeing large numbers of both retirements and new hires, a historic opportunity exists to diversify. We should not miss this opportunity.

- *Develop capacities to teach students with different abilities and motivations.* With about 70 percent of the high school cohort attending postsecondary education and large numbers of nontraditional students enrolled, there is a need for new professors to educate a heterogeneous student body.

- *Develop PFF programs in more departments, universities, and disciplinary societies.* Although impressive progress has been made, PFF programs are not accessible to all doctoral students preparing for an academic career. More departments, universities, and disciplinary societies should take steps to provide this education for their students.

- *Sustain PFF programs after the grants end.* Educational programs developed with the support of grants often disappear when the grants end; however, PFF has taken steps to encourage the continuing sustainability of its programs. Institutions were required to match grants and were urged to secure a critical mass of involved students and faculty members, assess their programs to document outcomes, and attain visibility through presentations and publications—all strategies to help them maintain the programs with their own resources. In fact, most PFF programs have continued after the end of grant support.

- *Develop a stronger demand among employing institutions for PFF preparation.* Comprehensive universities, baccalaureate colleges, and community colleges hire the majority of new faculty, and leaders of these institutions are frustrated that faculty candidates lack appreciation for the particular qualities of their institutions and that many would prefer to work elsewhere. If these institutions can form some kind of "consumers' collective" and demand that doctoral degree granting universities provide them with candidates who are better prepared, they could become a powerful market force for promoting better faculty preparation.

Conclusion

After a decade of innovation, we conclude that PFF is an effective complement, even a corrective element, to traditional doctoral education for those students seeking academic careers. Yet the culture and structure of doctoral education cannot be changed overnight; significant change in the culture of doctoral education requires a sustained and concerted effort. PFF is a key strategy in institutional and national efforts to encourage such change. A PFF brochure prepared by the American Association of Physics Teachers (n.d., p. 7) summarizes the enthusiastic attitudes of most who have been involved in PFF: "The changes precipitated by PFF programs constitute a win-win-win strategy: better preparation for doctoral students, better faculty candidates for the colleges and universities that hire them, and stronger, more engaging programs for doctoral degree granting departments."

References

Adams, K. A. (2002). *What colleges and universities want in new faculty* (Preparing Future Faculty Occasional Paper No. 7). Washington, DC: Association of American Colleges and Universities and Council of Graduate Schools.

American Association of Physics Teachers. (n.d.). *Preparing future physics faculty.* College Park, MD: American Association of Physics Teachers.

Committee on Graduate Education. (1998). *Report and recommendations.* Washington, DC: Association of American Universities.

Committee on Science, Engineering, and Public Policy (COSEPUP) of the National Academy of Sciences, the National Academy of Engineering, and the Institute of Medicine. (1995). *Reshaping the education of scientists and engineers.* Washington, DC: National Academy Press.

DeNeef, A. (2002). *The Preparing Future Faculty Program: What difference does it make?* (Preparing Future Faculty Occasional Paper No. 8). Washington, DC: Association of American Colleges and Universities and Council of Graduate Schools.

Gaff, J., Pruitt-Logan, A., Sims, L., & Denecke, D. (2003). *Preparing future faculty in the humanities and social sciences: A guide for change.* Washington, DC: Council of Graduate Schools and Association of American Colleges and Universities.

Gaff, J., Pruitt-Logan, A., & Weibl, R. (2000). *Building the faculty we need: Colleges and universities working together.* Washington, DC: Association of American Colleges and Universities and Council of Graduate Schools.

Golde, C. M., & Dore, T. M. (2001). *At cross purposes: What the experiences of today's doctoral students reveal about doctoral education.* Philadelphia: A Report for The Pew Charitable Trusts.

Lovitts, B. E. (2001). *Leaving the ivory tower: The causes and consequences of departure from doctoral study.* Lanham, MD: Rowman & Littlefield.

National Association of Graduate-Professional Students. (2001, October). *Preliminary executive summary of the National Doctoral Program Survey.* Washington, DC: National Association of Graduate-Professional Students.

Nerad, M., & Cerny, J. (2000, Winter). From rumors to facts: Career outcomes of English Ph.D.'s: Results from the PhDs—Ten Years Later Study. *ADE Bulletin, 124,* 43–55.

Nyquist, J. D., Austin, A. E., Sprague, J., & Wulff, D. H. (2001). *The development of graduate students as teaching scholars: A four-year longitudinal study* (Final Report, Grant no. 199600142). Seattle: University of Washington, Center for Instructional Development and Research.

Pruitt-Logan, A., Gaff, J., & Jentoft, J. (2002). *Preparing future faculty in the sciences and mathematics: A guide for change.* Washington, DC: Council of Graduate Schools and Association of American Colleges and Universities.

Pruitt-Logan, A., Gaff, J., & Weibl, R. (1998). *The impact: Assessing experiences of participants in the Preparing Future Faculty Program, 1994–1996* (Preparing Future Faculty Occasional Paper No. 6). Washington, DC: Association of American Colleges and Universities and Council of Graduate Schools.

Rice, R., Sorcinelli, M., & Austin, A. E. (2000). *Heeding new voices: Academic careers for a new generation* (New Pathways Working Papers Series No. 7). Washington, DC: American Association for Higher Education.

Smith, S., & Pedersen-Gallegos, L. (2001). *The careers and work of Ph.D. scientists: Not simply academic.* Unpublished paper, Bureau of Sociological Research, Department of Sociology, University of Colorado-Boulder.

Sorcinelli, M. (2001). *Principles of good practice supporting early-career faculty.* Washington, DC: American Association for Higher Education.

Thomas, V. (2002). *Evaluation report of shaping the preparation of science and mathematics faculty project.* Washington, DC: Council of Graduate Schools and Association of American Colleges and Universities.

Trower, C. A., Austin, A. E., & Sorcinelli, M. D. (May, 2001). Paradise lost: How the academy converts enthusiastic recruits into early-career doubters. *AAHE Bulletin, 53*(9), 3–6.

Chapter Ten

Re-envisioning the Ph.D.
A Challenge for the Twenty-First Century
Jody D. Nyquist, Bettina J. Woodford, Diane L. Rogers

The idea of re-envisioning doctoral education is not a new one. Re-envisioning the Ph.D. is one more "conversation" in a long history of constructive debates about the doctorate. Various efforts to reconsider doctoral education occurred in the late 1800s and in the midtwentieth century, spawned first by the adoption of the German model of Ph.D. education and later by the post–World War II science research boom. In addition, the GI Bill made college education accessible and created increased demand for Ph.D.-trained faculty as institutions began to expand. In 1965, the National Education Act once again generated interest in graduate training. Although the factors motivating the various conversations were different, in each case participants aspired to help doctoral education reassess its strategies for success in the face of changing social, cultural, and economic realities. This is no less the case for the Re-envisioning the Ph.D. Project, whose purpose is to stimulate a wide-reaching, proactive, and ongoing discussion on the following question: How can we re-envision the Ph.D. to meet the needs of society in the twenty-first century?

Project Description and Purposes

In essence, we are asking if the current paradigm of graduate education at the modern research university is the most appropriate one for the Ph.D. to thrive in the context of increasingly complex demands. Driving the project, and indeed distinguishing it from all previous conversations, is a dual philosophy of inclusiveness and empowerment. By inclusiveness, we mean bringing to the table representatives from all the constituencies crucially affected by the practice of doctoral education. By empowerment, we mean explicitly seeking out strategies for action to enable all constituencies to engage collaboratively in processes of improving doctoral education.

First, let us consider inclusiveness. The Re-envisioning the Ph.D. Project is built on the premise that doctoral education is not *owned* by any one educational level, type of institution, or social or academic constituency. The analytical skills and problem-solving habits developed in Ph.D.'s are of great concern to a range of employers that hire Ph.D.'s both inside and outside of academia. For example, research institutions rely on the preparation of Ph.D.'s who can produce high-quality, cutting-edge research and scholarship. The quality of instructional preparation for Ph.D.'s is of particular interest to institutions whose missions focus on excellence in undergraduate education. Likewise, the relevance of doctoral research is of major significance to commercial successes in business and industry, and to the resolution of our nation's social challenges in government and not-for-profit sectors. The late Thoyd Melton, former graduate dean of North Carolina Agricultural and Technical State University, captured the inclusive premise of the Re-envisioning philosophy particularly eloquently during an interview conducted for the project (Nyquist & Woodford, 2000, pg. 4) when he declared that a new vision of the Ph.D. is

> a community problem. It is going to require input from federal agencies, input from industry, input from academia and from others who hire Ph.D.'s. What we have not done is sit at the same table and declare what the ground rules are going to be, because no one party can change effectively what we are trying to do.

To engage all parties in articulating a new vision, the project conducted what we described as an environmental scan of the landscape of doctoral education. Its purpose was to assess widely held concerns about the current model as well as to map out the array of innovative practices that we knew were emerging on campuses and in other organizations to address those concerns. After more than four hundred interviews with leaders inside and outside academe, supplemented by focus groups and e-mail surveys, the project identified Ph.D. stakeholders: doctoral students, research-extensive and -intensive universities, teaching-intensive colleges and universities, K–12 education, business and industry, government and government funding agencies, foundations and other nonprofits, disciplinary societies, educational associations, governance boards, and accrediting agencies. Collectively, the groups represent dynamic and interconnected spheres of influence on Ph.D.'s.: those who *prepare* them, those who *fund* them, those who *hire* them, and those who *influence* the doctoral enterprise in important ways, including the students themselves.

At the same time the project has identified and included all stakeholder perspectives, it has proceeded to foster an ethos of action and empowerment. Thus, it has created several resources to help change agents—be they students, faculty, administrators, funders, or employers—formulate a collective action agenda in response to the results of the research:

- A national-international Web site, currently receiving over 320,000 hits per month, that serves doctoral stakeholders as a clearinghouse for transformative ideas and strategies
- An extensive bibliography of over seven hundred entries addressing doctoral education
- A compilation of more than three hundred "Promising Practices," representing innovations in doctoral education from 153 different institutions
- A national working conference, a landmark event that drew together leaders from all the groups with a role to play in imagining the future of the Ph.D.
- A collection of resources for obtaining a Ph.D. and subsequently obtaining employment
- A collection of over forty recent studies in doctoral education
- Approximately five hundred external partners that have links from their sites to the Re-envisioning Web site
- An ongoing virtual discussion that currently involves over four thousand stakeholders from all sectors

The project's overarching assertion is that evolution in our social, economic, and cultural realities creates new circumstances for, and therefore, new challenges to, our educational processes. The doctorate is not exempt from these forces, despite the belief of some that the key to advancing higher orders of knowledge is the doctorate's ability—indeed, its charge—to exist in isolation from the clutter and noise of mundane human affairs. We prefer to think of the Ph.D. as an eternally valuable idea with universal applications that deserves to be continually renewed. As addressed in a longitudinal study (Nyquist et al., 1999; Nyquist, Austin, Sprague, & Wulff, 2001) and discussed in Chapter Three, doctoral students report that their experience does not adequately prepare them to meet the demands of a changing academy and society. Nerad and Cerny (2000) reported in their study of over six thousand Ph.D.'s that many faculty hold negative attitudes toward jobs outside of major research universities, and few encourage students to seek nonacademic jobs in business, government, or nonprofit sectors (see Chapter Seven). This incongruence, or what Golde and Dore (2001; see Chapter Two) have called a "mismatch" between the training students receive and the opportunities they actually seek, need not remain an enduring problem. Simply stated, any creative endeavor, whether commercial, artistic, or educational, must, from time to time, reassess its goals and its tools in relation to the wider context in order to remain successful. To do this, doctoral education should encourage "multiple models of excellence" (Atwell, 1996). To safeguard its vitality, including its very raison d'être, the Ph.D. must get to know change, and must embrace it.

Within this larger discussion of reform, as Austin and Wulff argued earlier in this volume, are the particular issues pertaining to the preparation of faculty to enter a higher education system undergoing major transformations. Being a faculty member in this brave new world is daunting in and of itself. New approaches to how we learn, teach, and govern are occurring globally as well as in the United States. The Glion Declaration (Hirsch & Weber, 1999), for instance, authored by an international group of educational leaders, argues that higher education faces unique responsibilities and opportunities at this time. These challenges involve "providing new structures, flexible career paths, and selective support for new patterns of creative inquiry, effective learning, and responsible public service" (p. 180). Achieving higher education's future goals will require faculty members to be prepared differently than they have been in the past. Our research and that of others has confirmed this need. For the purposes of this book, this chapter focuses on themes in the research and recommendations from our project that relate *only* to the preparation of aspiring faculty in higher education. Broader issues involving all of the stakeholders and the preparation for Ph.D.'s for a variety of careers are discussed in *The Ph.D.: A Tapestry of Change for the 21st Century* (Nyquist, 2002), in *Re-envisioning the Ph.D.: What Concerns Do We Have?* (Nyquist & Woodford, 2000), and on our Web site at http://www.grad.washington.edu/envision.

Themes and Strategies

Interviewees from a variety of institutions in higher education highlighted concerns about whether doctoral education prepares its graduates to achieve success in the many colleges and universities that make up the higher education landscape (Nyquist & Woodford, 2000). Participants in our study expressed a healthy skepticism as they raised such questions as these:

- Do aspiring faculty make *informed* choices about careers in the many kinds of higher education institutions: research universities, teaching-intensive universities, liberal arts and community colleges, electronic universities, specialized colleges, for-profit educational institutions? Do they understand the differing missions, structures, and expectations of each kind of institution, including the realities of part-time and temporary appointments?
- Are aspiring faculty prepared well enough for the multitude of responsibilities involved in the roles of faculty members, which include teacher, researcher-scholar, mentor, advisor, and liaison to the greater society where their expertise is needed?
- Are aspiring faculty ready to work productively with student populations who are diverse not only in race but also in age, preparedness, and family and work responsibilities?

- Are aspiring faculty well versed in applying learning theory responsibly, in experimenting pedagogically, testing the results, and experimenting again, informed by the analysis?
- Are those aspiring to research institutions prepared to manage research labs, procure external funding, and meet the publication criteria?
- Are aspiring faculty who are not heading into research universities willing to be generalists, to teach across disciplines, to work in departmental structures different from their doctoral programs, and to develop more nuanced understandings of how learning occurs in varied institutional contexts?
- Can aspiring faculty employ new technologies in their research and teaching, and can they provide distance and on-line learning?
- Do aspiring faculty recognize the global dimensions and potential for international partnerships in the educational enterprise?

Our respondents maintained that obstacles to dealing effectively with these concerns persist. Further, they referred to unexamined assumptions—or to what we discuss in this chapter as myths—under which much of doctoral education continues to operate. *By myths we do not mean untruths or wrongs. Rather, we mean that when traditional ways of doing things go unexamined in the face of new circumstances, they can engender misconceptions about our educational reality, and thus perpetuate beliefs and practices that inhibit the full potential of the Ph.D.* Re-envisioning the Ph.D. is about unlocking that full potential of the doctorate.

In what follows, we examine three pervasive myths about doctoral education, delineate what hundreds of project participants articulated to be the reality for preparing aspiring faculty, and present strategies we developed to begin to dispel and replace the myths with realistic understandings. The chapter concludes by highlighting key recommendations for various stakeholders about how to embrace that reality successfully and how to adopt practices more aligned with it.

MYTH ONE: Research institutions are solely responsible for determining the preparation of future faculty, who should emerge
as Ph.D.'s in the tradition of their mentors.

As noted earlier, the American higher education landscape com-
prises a full range of institutions with differing charters, missions,
and need. As Boyer (1990) asserted, "Today's higher education
leaders speak with pride about the distinctive missions of their
campuses" (p. 53). If an institution's mission is clearly defined and
implemented, it will make prominent a particular culture and standards of excellence for scholarship. Faculty in all types of institutions must be scholars; however, the distinctive mission of each
institution will shape what specific aspects should be prioritized.
For research institutions, discovery and invention are the first priority. For teaching-intensive institutions, scholarly teaching, interdisciplinary and integrative approaches, and outreach to the
community usually are priorities. In professional, religious, or tribal
institutions, service can be an especially important focus, with an
emphasis on meeting community or societal needs. Faculty members in any institution are responsible for performing well in all
the varieties of scholarly activity, but priorities and focus will differ
from setting to setting.

These institutional priorities translate into concrete expectations for faculty performance. Research institutions require substantial research and publication, including the procurement of
external funding, the mentoring of graduate students, and in the
sciences, the management of labs and teams. Faculty roles at master's level institutions commonly involve managing multiple classes,
supervising teaching assistants, and meeting research expectations
that may involve small laboratories and steady, but fewer, publications. Faculty in liberal arts colleges must be adept at teaching general education courses and working across disciplines and in
departments with structures quite different from those of their doctoral programs. In some cases, faculty members may be the sole
representatives of their disciplines. Community colleges, which are
hiring Ph.D.'s in greater numbers, need faculty whose teaching
competency is unquestionable, particularly with first-generation
and part-time students whose academic preparation may be incomplete. Best suited to teaching-intensive institutions are faculty who

are versatile in their intellectual expertise, responsive to the instructional needs of widely diverse student populations, able to develop a range of effective pedagogies, and creative in their scholarship and research, which usually is not supported by large grants.

The variation in missions, priorities, and resulting performance expectations is particularly relevant in terms of academic roles for new doctoral graduates. According to the *Doctoral Recipients from United States Universities: Summary Report 2001, Survey of Earned Doctorates,* over 48 percent of all newly minted Ph.D.'s take their first jobs in academia, but only a small percentage of these jobs are located in research institutions (National Science Foundation et al., 2002). Instead, the employers span the entire range of Carnegie's Classification of Institutions of Higher Education (Carnegie Foundation, 2001) and include research universities (extensive and intensive), master's comprehensive institutions, four-year baccalaureate colleges, two-year colleges, a variety of specialized institutions (medical, law, art, music, professional, theological, and others), and tribal colleges. As previously noted, although all of these institutions value excellent scholarship, many of them do not place their primary emphasis on discovery research. As a result, when bringing in new faculty, these institutions face particular difficulties in socializing graduates who have been exposed solely to the research institution paradigm and experience.

Increasingly, then, graduate faculty at research institutions are called upon to develop students with professional competencies appropriate to the variety of hiring institutions. Recognizing the power of scholars within a discipline in a research institution is essential. Their priorities are the most influential on the lives of doctoral students. As Adams emphasized in her statement on what colleges and universities want and expect in new faculty, "The attitudes and goals of graduate faculty members are particularly important, since they are the mentors and advocates for the pool of future faculty" (2001, p. 12). Furthermore, she offered concrete recommendations for what graduate faculty should do to prepare students for positions in teaching-intensive colleges and universities:

- Introduce students to new pedagogies; become involved with, and knowledgeable about, such areas as active learning, field-based learning, diversity, and technology.

- Provide students with more than just the experience of teaching classes; provide constructive feedback on performance and participation in group discussions about creative teaching approaches, problem solving, and advising.
- Assist students in preparing for successful job searches at diverse institutions, including helping students gain professional experiences not usually found in research institutions.
- Provide opportunities for graduate students to visit more than one type of institution so that they can see differences and similarities across campuses.

Jerry Gaff (2002), in describing the Preparing Future Faculty Program (discussed in Chapter Nine), extended the list of needed competencies, asserting that because "professors, like other professionals, share responsibility for governing their organizations, we believe that graduate students should learn about the academic profession, colleges and universities as organizations, and relationships between professors and their institutions—in short, about academic citizenship" (p. 6). Thus, circumstances and patterns of employment in the academic marketplace mean that graduate faculty have a significant opportunity, and an ethical responsibility, to expose their students to the variety of expressions of scholarship in research, teaching, and service as well as to prepare them for the various concepts of shared governance that provide the foundation of educational institutions.

Preparing students with the range of competencies, however, is a tall order and certainly not one that doctoral institutions can fulfill in isolation. Instead, the need for such competencies requires a new kind of collaboration among not only the institutions that prepare doctoral graduates but also those that hire them. As Frank Rhodes (1999) argued in writing about the characteristics of the "new university," rapidly changing circumstances and dwindling resources require that institutions learn to be constructively partnered to succeed in these times. Research universities need to depend more heavily on teaching-intensive institutions in seeking to enrich the experience of the aspiring faculty they train. Partnerships between the institutions that prepare and those that hire the majority of Ph.D.'s can lead to mutually beneficial outcomes and more seamless relationships for both entities, especially if doctoral students are at the center of innovative experiences such as pedagogical internships and multiple mentor programs. Preparing institutions benefit by exposing their doctoral students to the varying competencies needed to function effectively as faculty members in settings where they are likely to find employment, settings with missions often quite different from those of doctoral institutions. Teaching-intensive institutions benefit by becoming more proactive about shaping the future faculty they need and exposing their undergraduates to the excitement of advanced learning that doctoral students bring.

In addition, all involved in the partnerships that Rhodes (1999) described need the kinds of information that can help them in the process of preparing doctoral students adequately. Accordingly, the 2000 Re-envisioning the Ph.D. National Conference, held in Seattle, Washington, invited representatives from each stakeholder group to articulate what contributions they could make to doctoral education as well as the contributions they desired from others. Detailed summaries can be found in the "Sector Meetings" section on the project's Web site: http://www.grad.washington.edu/envision/project_resources/metathemes.html.

The Web-based information exchange began efforts to clarify expectations for Ph.D.'s who will obtain employment in various kinds of institutions. Corroborating accounts of what hiring institutions need in new faculty are collected under "Ph.D. Resources, What Employers Want in New Faculty." This collection includes statements from institutional leaders such as Jolene Koester, president of California State University at Northridge; Kathrynn Adams, interim dean at Guilford College; Leo Lambert, president of Elon University; and others. The statements are unique because they are public descriptions of competencies needed by new faculty who aspire to academic careers in various kinds of institutions. The statements represent clear evidence that exclusively preparing doctoral students to follow in the footsteps of their mentors is an insufficient model for the academy as a whole, and for individual doctoral students aspiring to become faculty in the rich array of institutions of higher education.

Re-envisioning the Ph.D. offers faculty, administrators, and students from the entire spectrum of higher education a forum and a set of resources for engaging in a more constructive dialogue on doctoral education and on the future of the professoriate. Graduate faculty are the first to admit they cannot effect these changes alone. They need the advice and engagement of hiring institutions unlike their own to generate new forms of mutual understanding and to create more robust educational experiences to help their students succeed.

MYTH TWO: The only intellectual endeavor truly worthy of a Ph.D.'s time is traditional disciplinary research.

Just as faculty lives are transforming to meet the changing needs of higher education, so are the possibilities for creative work across the multiple facets of faculty roles. It is no longer the case that traditional disciplinary research questions provide the only path to worthy scholarship. In *Scholarship Reconsidered,* Boyer (1990, p. 27) challenged the scholarship of discovery as the single dominant model in higher education:

> The richness of faculty talent should be celebrated, not restricted. Only as the distinctiveness of each professor is affirmed will the potential of scholarship be fully realized. Surely, American higher education is imaginative and creative enough to support and reward not only those scholars uniquely gifted in research but also those who excel in the integration and application of knowledge, as well as those especially adept in the scholarship of teaching. Such a mosaic of talent, if acknowledged, would bring renewed vitality to higher learning and the nation.

Boyer's challenge to the academic community was to establish a more generous definition of scholarship, one that includes the scholarship of discovery, the scholarship of integration, the scholarship of teaching, and the scholarship of application (or, as it is currently called, the scholarship of engagement). Each of these areas of erudition provides opportunities for the rich, stimulating, analytical thinking, testing, and reporting for which faculty members are trained.

Now, intellectually compelling questions are emerging from new efforts to understand how students learn a discipline, how disciplines relate to one another, and how communities outside the academy can benefit from the scholarly expertise of members of the academy.

These theoretical and practical puzzles expand the possibilities for our research and problem solving and contribute to creative inquiry, experimentation, assessment, publication, and critical advances in applying the knowledge we create. For example, The Carnegie Academy for the Scholarship of Teaching and Learning (CASTL) (discussed in Chapter Eight) is an exemplary model for enabling faculty to examine their teaching and their students' learning, reflect on and analyze what they find, and make accessible to others the lessons learned. Deeply embedded into the disciplines, this approach allows faculty as scholars to investigate their own practices in their own classrooms. As reflected in *Opening Lines* (Hutchings, 2000), participants in CASTL speak of their experiences with the same enthusiasm they reveal when talking about traditional research discoveries. For example, one of those participants exclaimed, "In the last six months, I've learned a lot more than in the previous twelve years about how my students learn and about how to create the kind of classroom climate it takes to facilitate that learning" (p. 50). In each case where the Re-envisioning the Ph.D. Project included interviews with CASTL scholars, our data echoed faculty members' enthusiasm for new questions on disciplinary *learning* and revitalized commitments to what they were discovering. For example, one of our interviewees said, "I feel renewed. This is difficult, frustrating, exhilarating work. I am as excited about what I am doing as I was when I did my dissertation work many years ago and really discovered something important." Another reported, "I love this work! It is probably the most intellectually compelling set of questions I have ever pursued: How do novice learners understand the discipline about which I am so passionate?"

The National Research Council's work on the science of learning also contributes to this body of intellectual work. The science of learning seeks to understand how we can obtain a cumulative knowledge base on thinking and learning, and how we can make it accessible to practitioners. As Branscomb, Holton, and Sonnert (2002) suggested, "We need new avenues for capturing the wisdom of practice, and we need a new kind of professional who can bridge the worlds of research and practice" (p. 409).

Although not as well developed as the scholarship of teaching and learning, the scholarship of engagement reflects increasing efforts to create partnerships between the community and academia. Scholarly engagement has been the focus of several recent national conferences. This work seeks to address problem-based, complex questions that require building new relationships for both creating and sharing knowledge with the community. As James Applegate (2002) asserted, "We must help future colleagues develop their own vision for how to assume the stage as engaged public intellectuals with their research and teaching" (p. 4). Such a professional seeks diverse ways to use expertise, pursue and investigate important questions, and share findings with various communities. This bridging may require the four forms of scholarship: discovery, integration, teaching, and engagement. Aspiring faculty, especially those establishing careers in teaching-intensive colleges and universities, need preparation not only as teaching scholars but also as scholarly citizens. Such a need further dispels the myth that scholarly curiosity is only satisfied through traditional, highly specialized disciplinary research and is only meaningfully expressed in refereed disciplinary journals. A conception of "faculty work" that ignores the potential of the scholarship of teaching and learning and the scholarship of engagement is too narrow a definition of intellectual work for the variety of higher education institutions that employ Ph.D.'s.

The Re-envisioning the Ph.D. Project has produced several resources for supporting creative approaches to scholarship in teaching and engagement. The Selected Bibliography contains over seventy recent articles, books, reports, and conference proceedings on teaching and more than twenty on the subject of service and scholarly citizenship. In addition, a section entitled Ph.D. Resources provides articles and inventories whose topics include incorporating technology, teaching and course portfolios, evaluation, assessment, syllabus development, teaching styles, instructional models, and more. We offer these resources to aid institutions of all types in promoting more generous notions of the scholarly endeavor.

MYTH THREE: Graduate faculty members know what is best for their doctoral students' career choices in academia.

To begin to appreciate the importance of dispelling this myth, we have to recognize that dramatic changes in student characteristics are reshaping the goals of aspiring Ph.D.'s. The contemporary doctoral student population is significantly different from that of fifty, thirty, or even fifteen years ago. According to the *Doctoral Recipients from United States Universities: Summary Report 2001, Survey of Earned Doctorates,* 44 percent of doctoral students today are women (National Science Foundation et al., 2002). The *National Postsecondary Student Aid Study: 1999–2000* reports that 41 percent are pursuing the degree on a part-time basis (Riccobono et al., 2002). These numbers, of course, vary significantly across the spectrum of arts and sciences and professional schools. On average, today's doctoral student is thirty-three years old, is likely to bear weighty family responsibilities, and may bring other professional experiences to doctoral study. In addition, although the doctoral population is becoming more ethnically diverse, retention and completion rates remain a significant challenge. For example, minority students struggle to see their own values reflected in their institutions' values. In a study of African American doctoral students, Antony and Taylor (2001) found, "These students are unable to reconcile the incompatibilities between their own values and those required for success as a member of an education faculty" (p. 204). All these factors influence the choices that aspiring faculty make throughout their graduate experience, especially in the directions they choose for their careers.

In fact, students today proceed through their doctoral programs with far more varied career goals than many of their predecessors. Furthermore, they want their mentors to value and respect these goals. The National Association of Graduate-Professional Students (NAGPS), in the Executive Summary to their 2001 survey (see Chapter Four), stressed that student satisfaction is strongly linked to choice. In that survey of thirty-two thousand, students reported that they want to be prepared to make informed choices about their future careers based on accurate information and that they want those choices to be respected. Even among those seeking to join the professoriate, multiple aspirations need to be acknowledged. One of our project's interviewees, previously the chair of a large language department, described the challenge this way: "Research faculty need to realize that maybe one in ten of students in their seminars will land a position like their own." Many of the other nine will seek promising faculty careers in the diverse array of institutions described earlier, in which expectations of hiring committees vary greatly from those of graduate advisors.

The reality is, however, that appropriate support from faculty is not always present. In speaking for his colleagues, a science professor confessed, "There is resistance to understanding that not everyone who gets a Ph.D. is going to be emulating the career of the mentor." Damrosch (2000, p. B24) also commented on this situation:

> The problem today is that less and less often do we find a one-to-one correspondence between a student's needs and a sponsor's interests and abilities. . . . Even for a student who finds a classic mentor and thrives as a disciple, it can come as a rude shock to find that hiring committees may no longer be so interested in snapping up a younger model of an older approach.

In addition, given the priorities of the academic reward structure, research-oriented graduate faculty may not always be well informed about students' changing goals or about the realities of faculty work in other settings. As noted earlier, employers in other settings place great value on the teaching, service, or outreach roles of their faculty, and on clear indications of mastery of these competencies in their new hires, competencies with which research faculty traditionally have less experience and knowledge. Although this lack of information is understandable, it nonetheless weakens doctoral graduates' chances for academic success. In a recent study, over 60 percent of doctoral student respondents reported experiencing unsystematic guidance on their teaching, and nearly 40 percent said they received little guidance on the nature of academic careers (Davis & Fiske, 2001). In such cases, Ph.D. students are left to their own devices to remedy these deficiencies, if they are fortunate enough to become aware of them in time.

The good news is that there is now a wider acknowledgment of these challenges. More expansive conceptions of possible Ph.D. careers have begun to proliferate. One of our interviewees asserted, "What we as faculty need to do is be creative about allowing our students to see a broader range of life and career opportunities." In the last few years, initiatives have emerged in response to the concern and the need to provide support for faculty in research institutions to develop broader conceptions of their students' future in academia. A highly successful exemplar is the national Preparing Future Faculty Program (PFF) (discussed in Chapter Nine). Based on the concept that mentors who have successfully navigated professional career paths are the best sources for students who desire to emulate them, PFF facilitates partnerships between preparing and hiring institutions to expose aspiring faculty to the array of faculty roles in settings other than traditional doctoral programs. Seminars, institutes, and workshops help students navigate academic career options more strategically, and the partnership model stimulates opportunities to revise doctoral program practices.

To help spread these and other innovations nationally, the Re-envisioning the Ph.D. Project collects hundreds of Promising Practices and, as already noted, organizes them into a publicly accessible compilation available at www.grad.washington.edu/envision/practices/introduction.html. For example, a special endowment, the Huckabay Fellows Program at the University of Washington, enables students to collaborate with faculty, often from another campus or another discipline, to design and carry out innovative curricular projects on teaching and learning. The Professional Development and Community Engagement Program at the University of Texas at Austin partners with faculty from across the disciplines to offer doctoral students courses that develop talents and competencies for academic as well as other careers. Through synergy groups and core curriculum, students learn to identify and pursue their passions both inside and outside the academy, and to solve problems in diverse social realms. Duke University has posted statistics on its graduate programs on the Web, including summary data on gender, nationality, ethnicity, admission and matriculation figures, median GRE scores, number of Ph.D.'s awarded annually by department-program, time-to-degree statistics, attrition, graduation rate, and placement data. This helpful resource for doctoral students also allows the institution to look across units on quantitative measures of Ph.D. attainment. Arizona State University's Preparing Future Professionals Program is geared to developing and implementing practical career-professional development services for doctoral students. Workshops and educational forums include subjects in career exploration, goal setting, résumé development, interviewing, business writing, presentations, and starting a business.

As these and other innovations become more widespread in doctoral granting institutions, they create increased avenues for academic career exploration for students. Although most graduate faculty do not have direct knowledge of the professional realities of other types of institutions, these developments are key in helping them become more aware of the training mismatch, of the strategies needed to address it, and of the ways they can provide better guidance to assist Ph.D. students to obtain their goals.

Outcomes

The project's mission has been to advance the national and international conversation in doctoral education and become a catalyst for collaboration in various initiatives, programs, and efforts. This mission has meant bringing together stakeholders from all sectors: the students themselves; those who prepare students; and those who hire, fund, and influence doctoral education. Highlighting models and disseminating information to these stakeholders have been the strategies the project has used to empower those involved in transformation projects and transformation efforts. As we previously indicated, one of the outcomes of our work has been the creation of an internationally recognized Web site. Currently it serves as the largest Web-based clearinghouse of information and resources in doctoral education transformation.

Another outcome contributing to the national conversation is the dissemination of written materials to support strategic deliberations among faculty, students, administrators, and leaders from other sectors. A brief description of the study on which the project was based, *Re-envisioning the Ph.D.: What Concerns Do We Have?* (Nyquist & Woodford, 2000), now in its fifth printing, has been distributed to over seven thousand constituents and disseminated at dozens of national conferences and meetings. In 2002, the PDF version was downloaded from the project's Web site more than thirty-seven thousand times. The Re-envisioning agenda has appeared in many national publications, including the *Chronicle of Higher Education*, Council of Graduate School's *Communicator*, American Association for Higher Education's *Change* and *Bulletin*,

American Psychological Association's *Monitor*, National Science Board's *2001 Science and Engineering Indicators*, *Hispanic Outlook in Higher Education*, the *Chicago Tribune*, and newsletters of a wide variety of professional societies. Nationally, the project has had the opportunity to present research findings and initiate discussions with many doctoral stakeholders. Presentations have been given at nine national association meetings, three national councils, eleven research-extensive universities, six foundation meetings, and four government agencies. This wide dissemination has broadened the project's scope and influence by making public the news and inviting others directly into the conversation.

Also at the national level, at least two new initiatives have taken shape as a result of Re-envisioning the Ph.D. research and activities: the Carnegie Foundation's Initiative on the Doctorate and the Woodrow Wilson Foundation's Responsive PhD Initiative. Described in the chapters that follow, both of these efforts are attempts to put the Re-envisioning themes into action by continuing to study how students become teaching scholars and by encouraging the adoption of innovative practices at a wide range of Ph.D.-producing institutions.

At a local level, the project has worked with more than forty-seven academic departments at the University of Washington to develop their programs further to improve the graduate experience. The Re-envisioning staff work across the campus by providing workshops, speaking at faculty meetings, consulting with faculty committees, serving on task forces and committees, presenting at university group meetings, organizing campus conferences, researching information, conducting local surveys, and responding to hundreds of individual inquiries about developments in doctoral education. Re-envisioning staff have consulted department by department, faculty member by faculty member, to assist in reflection, deliberation, and change as graduate faculty struggle to find time for rethinking one more aspect of the university and their lives. The project has also yielded many campus-specific print and electronic resources to enhance mentoring. These resources are then shared nationally as examples that can be adapted, adopted, or recast for particular applications.

Recommendations

The Re-envisioning the Ph.D. Project looks at the assumptions about doctoral education that have dominated the enterprise for the last several decades and helps doctoral stakeholders imaginatively envision the future of the degree by actively collecting and coordinating a broad range of perspectives and resources. When reflecting on the project as a whole—the concerns expressed by our interviewees, the calls for action made by many national leaders, the statements of need on the part of hiring institutions—and on the implications of the various projects represented in this book, we are struck by a remarkable convergence of proposals (Nyquist, 2002). Altogether, they help constitute a new vision of the Ph.D. enterprise, a new paradigm of reflective thought and concerted action. This new paradigm, applied to preparing tomorrow's faculty, presents to all of us the following challenge: the doctorate should function as an induction into a rich and complex learning profession, not only into a discipline. That is, doctoral education should continue with the goal of delivering robust training in the disciplines (and increasingly across the disciplines), while also making greater strides in guiding students' understanding of the various facets of the professoriate *as practiced in the wide range of institutional contexts.*

From the collection of resources and perspectives informing this project, we have distilled ten recommendations to assist doctoral education in meeting this tremendous challenge:

- Doctoral granting institutions should prepare students with a more realistic, versatile notion of the academic profession in which teaching, research, and service roles find equally challenging but different expressions, depending on institutional context.
- Faculty in doctoral programs should use wider parameters to examine the academic career pathways available to their students by assessing the placement data for *all* their doctoral graduates (not only those who attain positions in research institutions), and they should integrate this fuller, more transparent picture into doctoral student mentoring.

- Institutional leaders should affirm with graduate faculty and administrators the importance of faculty mentoring for students with diverse backgrounds and goals and encourage multiple mentoring approaches through appropriate policies and incentives.
- Students should be assigned teaching experiences within a model of progressive development, increasing their exposure to greater pedagogical responsibility, subject matter diversity, learning theory, and technology.
- Doctoral programs should provide opportunities for students to engage in professional self-assessment; this process could involve feedback from a committee of mentors (including faculty from other institutions) who share responsibility for integrating needed experiences into students' doctoral training.
- Teaching-intensive institutions must ensure that their hiring practices truly reflect the value systems underlying their missions; they must not allow their hiring practices to become obfuscated by the prestige culture of higher education.
- Teaching-intensive institutions need to communicate more explicitly the qualities they seek in new faculty; they should require professional portfolios that emphasize teaching and service as well as research and provide feedback to preparing institutions on how well the graduates hired do in their institutional settings.
- Hiring institutions should seek opportunities to help graduate faculty understand the scholarship that is accomplished in their settings and to offer doctoral students real experiences in their institutions—for example, through innovative faculty mentoring initiatives, academic shadowing, pedagogical internships, and faculty exchanges.
- Doctoral students should be more proactive about seeking needed information and appropriate mentors for their career goals and researching best practices through investigating initiatives and resources and circulating information to other students.
- Those who prepare, fund, hire, and influence doctoral graduates should seek more ways to partner on initiatives to improve the Ph.D. because such partnerships increase the resources available for experimentation and expand accountability for change.

Conclusion

In this chapter we have focused on our project's effort to envision a new paradigm for preparing aspiring faculty. Preparation for the academic profession is an important component of what is also a broader goal of the Re-envisioning the Ph.D. Project: to develop a paradigm that extends the assets of doctoral education within and beyond the world of academe. Rhodes (1999, p.170) underscored the complexity of this larger goal:

> No university, however large, can be truly comprehensive in its programs. Nor should it seek to be. If the university is to meet the increasing range of societal needs, it will require new alliances within the academic community and new partnerships outside it, with communities; local, state, and national agencies; corporations; foundations; hospitals; professional associations; scholarly societies; and other institutions—from other universities, schools and colleges to federal research laboratories—to enrich and extend its scholarly work and support its services.

Although Rhodes's and Re-envisioning's proposals are certainly ambitious, we are heartened by the already tremendous accomplishments of innovators from the full spectrum of stakeholders, accomplishments that the project has brought to national attention through its research, Web resources, and collaborative agenda. As few as five years ago, many doubted that such diverse groups would have anything constructive to say to one another over the contentious issue of modifying doctoral education, let alone experiment with new ways of working together for a common goal. The two new national initiatives and changing practices at many research institutions are excellent examples of collaborative action resulting from Re-envisioning dialogues; they represent the outcomes of both inclusiveness and empowerment. Countless more action-oriented conversations are occurring in the hallways of universities, corporations, government agencies, and schools, marking a significant turning point in what is quietly, yet persistently, becoming a national movement to re-envision doctoral education for the twenty-first century.

Acknowledgments

This project was supported by a grant from The Pew Charitable Trusts and by the Graduate School of the University of Washington. The opinions expressed in this chapter are those of the authors and do not necessarily reflect those of the funding organizations.

References

Adams, K. A. (2001). *What colleges and universities want in new faculty* (Preparing Future Faculty Occasional Paper No. 7). Washington, DC: Association of American Colleges and Universities and Council of Graduate Schools.

Antony, J. S., & Taylor, E. (2001). Graduate student socialization and its implications for the recruitment of African American education faculty. In W. G. Tierney (Ed.), *Faculty work in schools of education: Rethinking roles and rewards for the twenty-first century* (pp. 189–209). Albany: State University of New York Press.

Applegate, J. L. (2002). *Engaged graduate education: Seeing with new eyes.* Washington, DC: Association of American Colleges and Universities.

Atwell, R. H. (1996, November 29). Doctoral education must match needs and realities. *Chronicle of Higher Education, 43*(14). [http://chronicle.com/che-dat/articles.dir/art-43.dir/issue-14.dir/14b00401.htm]

Boyer, E. L. (1990). *Scholarship reconsidered: Priorities of the professoriate.* Princeton, NJ: The Carnegie Foundation for the Advancement of Teaching.

Branscomb, L. M., Holton, G., & Sonnert, G. (2002). Science for society. In A. Teich, S. Nelson, & S. Lita (Eds.), *American Association for the Advancement in Science: Science and technology policy yearbook* (pp. 398–433). Washington, DC: American Association for the Advancement of Science.

Carnegie Foundation for the Advancement of Teaching. (2001). *Carnegie classification of institutions of higher education* (rev. ed.). Menlo Park, CA: The Carnegie Foundation for the Advancement of Teaching.

Damrosch, D. N. (2000, November 17). Mentors and tormentors in doctoral education. *Chronicle of Higher Education, 47*(12), B24.

Davis, G., & Fiske, P. S. (2001). The 1999 PhDs.org graduate school survey report of results. *Making Strides, AAAS Directorate for Education & Human Resources Programs, 3*(1), 6–8.

Gaff, J. G. (2002, Summer). The disconnect between graduate education and the realities of faculty work: A review of recent research. *Liberal Education, 88*(3). [http://www.aacu-edu.org/liberaleducation/le-su02feature.cfm]

Golde, C. M., & Dore, T. M. (2001). *At cross purposes: What the experiences of today's doctoral students reveal about doctoral education.* Philadelphia: A Report for The Pew Charitable Trusts.

Hirsch, W. Z., & Weber, L. E. (1999). *Challenges facing higher education at the millennium.* American Council on Education, Series on Higher Education. Phoenix: Oryx Press.

Hutchings, P. (Ed.). (2000). *Opening Lines: Approaches to the Scholarship of Teaching and Learning*. Menlo Park, CA: The Carnegie Foundation for the Advancement of Teaching.

National Association of Graduate-Professional Students. (2001, October). *2001 National Doctoral Program Survey*. Washington, DC: National Association of Graduate-Professional Students. [http://survey.nagps.org/]

National Science Foundation, National Institutes of Health, U.S. Department of Education, National Endowment for the Humanities, U.S. Department of Agriculture, & National Aeronautics and Space Administration. (2002). *Doctoral Recipients from United States Universities: Summary Report 2001, Survey of Earned Doctorates*. Chicago National Opinion Research Center. [http://www.norc.org/issues/sed-2001.pdf]

Nerad, M., & Cerny, J. (2000). Improving doctoral education: Recommendations from the PhDs—Ten Years Later Study. *Council of Graduate Schools Communicator, 33*(2), 6.

Nyquist, J. D. (2002). The Ph.D.: A tapestry of change for the 21st century. *Change, 34*(6), 12–20.

Nyquist, J. D., Austin, A. E., Sprague, J., & Wulff, D. H. (2001). *The development of graduate students as teaching scholars: A four-year longitudinal study*. Seattle: University of Washington, Center for Instructional Development and Research.

Nyquist, J. D., Manning, L., Wulff, D. H., Austin, A. E., Sprague, J., Fraser, P. K., Calcagno, C., & Woodford, B. (1999). On the road to becoming a professor: The graduate student experience. *Change, 31*(3), 18–27.

Nyquist, J. D., & Woodford, B. J. (2000). *Re-envisioning the Ph.D.: What concerns do we have?* Report for the Re-envisioning the Ph.D. Conference. Seattle: University of Washington, Center for Instructional Development and Research. [http://www.grad.washington.edu/envision/project_resources/concerns.html]

Rhodes, F. H. (1999). The new university. In W. Hirsch & L. Weber (Eds.), *Challenges facing higher education at the millennium* (p. 170). American Council on Education, Series on Higher Education. Phoenix: Oryx Press.

Riccobono, J. A., Cominole, M. B., Siegel, P. H., Gabel, T. J., Link, M. W., & Berkner, L. K. (2002). *National Postsecondary Student Aid Study, 1999–2000 (NPSAS, 2000)*. (Methodology Report NCES 2002–152). Washington, DC: National Center for Education Statistics, Office of Educational Research and Improvement, U.S. Department of Education. [http://nces.ed.gov/pubs2002/quarterly/summer/5–1.asp]

Chapter Eleven

Toward a Responsive Ph.D.

New Partnerships, Paradigms, Practices, and People

Robert Weisbuch

"A value," Emily Dickinson wrote, "must struggle to exist." Doctoral education is a value that struggles to exist. The experience of, say, an aspiring doctoral student in medieval history and another in biophysics will vary so vastly—in coursework and the notion of a course, in what one field calls scholarship and the other, research, in disciplinary conventions and approved professional outcomes— that their same-named degrees will seem to be awarded on different planets.

The American doctorate is a radically underdetermined degree. It connotes nothing more than what each authorized area of academic endeavor defines as "expertise." This is one reason why the Ph.D. compels interest, for it is—or rather, its many forms are— so clearly an invention. It is also highly effective, or at the least very popular, and this is fascinating as well, because doctoral education constitutes by far the most locally controlled, decentralized level of education in our system.

No wonder, then, that the administrative structure for the Ph.D.—the graduate school and its underfunded dean—struggles to exist as well, and sometimes fails. At some universities, graduate deaning is a subfunction of the office of research; at a few, the job simply does not exist, dissolved into the various college or school deanships. Even where there presides an autonomous dean, that autonomy is largely fictional, because the dean must seek alliances with the discipline-based chairs and college-based deans to accomplish much of moment. Follow the money and it leads away from the graduate school to the faculty salary budgets of the other deans.

In all, it is fair to ask whether doctoral education is a meaningful concept. Our answer, aside from the struggle to exist, is that it *ought* to exist, that academic life and its benefits to the world improve mightily when graduate education exists robustly. The initiative that the Woodrow Wilson Foundation calls the Responsive Ph.D. is our attempt, in partnership with fourteen universities, both to strengthen the presence of a varied but holistic doctoral education within the academy and to encourage a far more dynamic interchange between social and academic realms. But this response to the shaky existence of a unified doctoral education, that it should exist strongly within a university and grow beyond it, requires a defense, and that defense has determined the shape of the Responsive PhD. I want here to support the notion of a holistic treatment—and enactment—of doctoral education and then to describe our project in relation to that.

Start with the structural issue of the graduate school. It is because the graduate deanship is an "invent-a-job" that it too compels interest. Some graduate deans indeed serve tea more than they serve purposes. But most pilot a usefully wayward bus across the gridlines of the disciplines. En route, they collect intellectual capital and create community for what are not, after all, random planets but a single campus, a United Nations of discovery, an ultimately common endeavor.

And doctoral education itself does exist, actually, as well as technically. Although each discipline determines the nature of its expertise as defined by the doctorate, these decisions are not made in a cultural bell jar. (As just one example of a huge agreement across disciplines, scholarship or research has trumped teaching, for better and for worse.) In fact, several recent studies reveal common dissatisfactions—and even areas of satisfaction, always harder to acknowledge—among doctoral students in all disciplines.[1]

Program Description and Purposes

Woodrow Wilson took from The Pew Charitable Trusts the task of deriving four basic themes from these studies, translating findings into answering practices, and sharpening recommendations for action. Institutional change is at the heart of the initiative, which aims to identify good models of innovation and promulgate them nationally. For this daunting effort we chose graduate schools as partners, attempting to achieve a diversity of institutions with respect to geography, public or private status, and resources and history.[2] The project will become more and more inclusive as it develops, but for a first stage we looked for graduate schools with an activist record that also offer a variety of doctoral degrees across the arts and sciences.

Among these graduate schools, we sought to identify a range of demonstration projects or experiments, elicit comments on what does and does not work and what stimulates evolution in the thinking of deans, enabling them to build on reforms they had already begun. To advance this process, Woodrow Wilson sponsored Responsive PhD roundtables on each of the fourteen partner campuses. Teams of faculty, students, administrators, and business and community leaders assembled, under the auspices of the graduate schools, to consider local changes made in the doctorate, discover new priorities, and propose new strategies. Roundtable participants emerged, often after several follow-up sessions, with action plans. They then shared their proposals with department chairs, graduate student groups, other faculty, and provosts. And to encourage a cross-fertilization of ideas, the foundation brought the fourteen graduate deans together twice.

As we draw on both the existing research in the area and the experience of these fourteen partners—their sense of what works and what matters—we hope to synthesize the various conversations and findings about doctoral education into a shared national agenda.

Themes and Strategies

Together, the foundation and its partners developed four themes to ground the Responsive PhD Initiative: *new partnerships, new paradigms, new practices,* and *new people.* The first, a set of structural principles, might be less truly a theme than an underlying foundation for the other three. Get that one wrong, and work on the other three will go for nothing.

New Partnerships

The new partnerships portion of the Responsive PhD promotes more active partnerships with constituencies inside and outside the university. Fundamentally, we are concerned with how the doctorate gets built. We start by acknowledging the decentralized nature of the Ph.D., our most balkanized and least regularly evaluated level of education. The passionate commitment of the faculty to this level of education indeed depends on such local control. But so much and so local, so without the voices of constituencies from outside the departmental lounge?

Many doctoral programs manage themselves wonderfully well. But in general, when governance is lacking—and particularly when constituents' interests are not represented—habit rules and self-interest lurks. When a group, like an individual, speaks only to itself, it is a sign of dementia. But to assume the bad will of the faculty, or its recalcitrance, as some of the studies appear to do, is unfair—for when has the faculty been invited to consider even these findings, much less to engage in a thorough and rigorous but guiltless self-examination?

On the one hand, the faculty makes the decisions. Any improvement in doctoral education depends utterly on the will and energy of the faculty. No imposition from outside can do more than play at the edges. On the other hand, those faculty decisions have effects far beyond the faculty and its degree granting institution, for many of the human products of those programs end up working not only in very different kinds of educational places but also in business and government. Thus the nature and quality of doctoral education is hardly the concern of the graduate faculty alone. Jody Nyquist's Re-envisioning the Ph.D. Project represented, for the first time, the views of all those who are crucially affected by the practice of doctoral education (see Chapter Ten). A first dialogue was initiated between the producers and the consumers, so to speak, of doctoral graduates. We seek above all to make that national dialogue local and constant, to promulgate, discipline by discipline, a kind of conversation that has never taken place, so that decisions about doctoral practice can be based on an authentic range of perspectives.

To achieve that kind of informed policymaking requires far more than the occasional good-spirited meeting. It requires an active partnership among interested parties, everyone from the entire professoriate, including those at small colleges, four-year comprehensives, and community colleges, to leaders in business, government, cultural institutions, and the schools. We have tried that approach at Woodrow Wilson in another of our initiatives, the Humanities at Work, where we seek to extend the reach of these supposedly insular disciplines beyond the academy into social realms. There, the results for all concerned have been life-changing. Postures literally straighten when I say to graduate students in the humanities, "Three months from now you on average will have an offer to teach part-time at a college in a part of the country where you don't really want to be. Or you can have that offer and three others from A.T. Kearney, Microsoft, and the National Park Service." I often add that I myself might well have chosen the lousy academic job, but it would have been by choice and that would have made all the difference. Faculty in these disciplines actually and increasingly welcome this perspective, for it suggests that these disciplines can serve not merely to critique reality but to constitute it.

The kinds of largely untried partnerships we imagine in the Responsive PhD would be full of dangers and replete with missteps. To the extent our partner institutions have experimented with it, however, the results are powerful. Moreover, the faculty has participated without much defensiveness and shown an impressive capacity for change. "Order me and I will fight you to the death," one faculty member wrote. "Invite my expertise and there is nothing I won't do for you."

The very process of this initiative seeks to practice what it preaches. Deans meet with a range of faculty and students at each of their campuses and then with one another. They also meet with the far larger number of representatives from the sectors beyond the research university. Just now we are comparing action proposals from each of the participating universities and finding surprising degrees of overlap. And now also the deans are creating local councils with students, faculty, and their own alumni representatives from business, government, and a real range of educational institutions.

What gets said in these expanded conversations? There is a deep theme reflected in the name of the project. Here are some piquant samples from a prototype of the new continuing conversation we propose, taken from interviews conducted by one of the projects that inspired and influenced our own, the University of Washington's Re-envisioning the Ph.D., as reported in Nyquist and Woodford's (2000) summary of concerns:

Research university faculty member:	There is resistance to understanding that everyone who gets a doctorate isn't going to be emulating the mentor's career. We as faculty need to be creative about letting our students see a broader range of life and career opportunities.
Urban college dean:	Our new faculty members do not understand students for whom school comes after family and job. Sometimes I don't think they even like this type of student, but they represent our livelihood.
Graduate student:	The academic environment is still very insular. And our society is not insular, and people who are well prepared should have a multitude of experiences and interactions with people in different sectors. And that's still not happening, it's still not there. And it's desperately needed.
Business leader:	You develop vision by climbing hills . . . so you actually recognize there's much more to see than you've been looking at.
Business leader:	Graduate education . . . needs to skate to where the puck is. [pp. 9–27]

Even if, like me, you believe that graduate education also sometimes requires skating to where the puck *is not,* there is a consensus here worth minding. It was made into a parable by a young faculty member at a Woodrow Wilson forum: "It's as if they spent years training me to know everything about the roller-coaster. But now I'm in charge of the whole amusement park. I need to know about safety and publicity and all the other rides. No one had taught me about them. . . . No one had even told me they existed."

The Responsive PhD does not mean letting the tail wag the dog, does not mean that doctoral education needs to respond to every immediate social challenge. But it does mean to let the dog out of the cage—it means, that is, to extend the reach (and to make it two-way, the responsiveness) of academic learning. To accomplish such an enlargement, the disciplines need not sacrifice their occasional distance from the immediate social noise—a distance sometimes required for far-flung thought—but they do need to become more responsive to the world in those ways that make them humanly worthy in the first place.

That is where we see this dialogue between the producers and consumers of doctoral education leading. Others will interpret the conversation differently, and it will take unexpected turns as it develops over the decades. But whatever the conclusions and whatever actions may be pursuant to them, by creating this dialogue the graduate school comes to exist more fully. Faculty members hear colleagues in distant disciplines for the first time, as well as non-faculty citizens of their own discipline. Those alums previously loyal solely to the specific program they attended now become university citizens in a far larger community. From solo to chorus, from cacophony to some harmony—if the Responsive PhD could achieve any single thing, making this expanded conversation a national norm would be the easy choice, for it would make the faculty truly cosmopolitan in its decision making.

New Paradigms

I hope, however, that we do not *have* to choose among the key emphases of the Responsive PhD, because each—partnerships, paradigms, practices, and people—implicates the rest. The new paradigms theme, for instance, concerns promoting truly adventurous scholarship and connections across disciplines while preserving rigor. Yet this theme is the close companion of the partnerships we just discussed, for the nature of scholarship depends crucially on the opportunities for outreach and ingress. (Just so, its enactment includes the issues of teaching and the applications of knowledge that new practices treat. And its subjects and methods depend in real part on the nature of its practitioners, or new people.) Yet I want to pause for a moment to discuss the choice of scholarship as its own area of concern.

Many doctoral initiatives appear to view scholarly research as the Evil Empire, overwhelming other concerns. In fact, there is no reason to apologize for the fact that scholarship is the soul of the Ph.D. In doctoral education, a person on fire with an interest gets the go-ahead to take that interest to its limit, to engage with mystery, and to seek to make our world more habitable and rich. Scholarship is also the content of teaching and its formal identity, given that teaching is finally about strategies for discovery. By scholarship, we push back the night. Research is that without which the doctorate is a ringer. Anything that might dilute a student's passionate immersion in a discipline should be refused—anything, as in anything.

But one can be fierce against dilution and yet intrigued by dilation, by a more generous opening out of learning, by new paradigms of scholarship. Can we, in Bruce Alberts's nice phrase, learn to "cross the T, to add breadth to depth?" As another business leader quoted in the Re-envisioning summary said, "The sin is that people get the impression that going narrow and deep is the essence of the doctorate, but the essence is really trying to be critical and original and to do things on your own. We need people who are intellectually adventurous" (Nyquist & Woodford, 2000, p. 27).

By making scholarship the enemy, some critics of doctoral education overlook a questioning of scholarly practice. It is not the case that everything is fine in regards to scholarship and research training. Instead, the Responsive PhD asks: In each discipline and among them, what encourages adventurous scholarship? What retards and discourages it?

To get at answers, each discipline must do something very difficult, must come to comprehend that its practices are a matter of choice rather than nature. Each discipline has its own anthropology, and it can become self-comprehending only by seeing itself in relation to other tribes. For example, when we look at two extremes of mentorship—the practice in the humanities and some of the social sciences for a dissertation advisor to meet with a student perhaps once a month, and the very different life of the science and engineering laboratories, where professor and student interact daily—we give each a chance to see a different possibility and to learn newly about itself, about how dangerously laissez-faire the dissertation process can become in the humanities, about how prematurely narrowing and overdetermining the life of the laboratory may be.

Beyond the need for looking at one another is the question of working together. Interdisciplinarity is universally praised for sponsoring adventurous learning and just as universally underfunded. Its many forms are also woefully underassessed.[3] Cherry-pie virtue turns to cherry-bomb warfare as the departments and interdepartmental programs battle over rights and faculty. How a university administers the interdisciplinary in relation to the disciplines remains one of the most fraught problems, economic and academic at once.

Furthermore, bland praise of the interdisciplinary sacrifices intellectual opportunities of key import. The interdisciplinary often arises because the world beyond academia needs something that crosses the academic boundaries or because a scholar in one discipline is led by her research to questions that land her beyond the line. Such an occasion is a freshening moment; it is the very history of knowledge in the making. But some such moments may be unique (some may even be unfortunate!), whereas others are endemic. The deeply contentious nature of the interdisciplinary—it seeks, after all, a reorganization of knowledge—should lead to very exciting debate, allowing the traditional disciplines a new understanding of themselves in the process. And the variety of this genre—ranging from a single individual's perspective to the very different circumstance of a multidisciplinary group to which each individual brings a disciplinary perspective—barely gets acknowledged.

The interdisciplinary, then, is a special concern of new paradigms. Most graduate students (six out of ten) desire collaboration across disciplinary lines, but only 27 percent believe their programs prepare them for the possibility (Golde & Dore, 2001). And among six thousand graduates interviewed ten years after earning the doctorate, the top ranked recommendation was to maintain an interdisciplinary focus and to go for breadth (Nerad, 2000). The universities of the Responsive PhD already had responded most actively to this concern. Michigan's May Seminars bring together students and faculty on a common theme from across the disciplines. At Washington University, dissertating students meet through the summer on a multidisciplinary basis. At the University of Texas at Austin, the Professional Development and Community Engagement Program gathers students from across the disciplines to consider means of applying knowledge beyond the academy and to form teams to take up social challenges. Arizona State University offers special fellowships to encourage interdisciplinary dissertations, and Duke University allows students to take courses toward a cognate master's degree at no additional charge. A large number of universities now are inhabited by the National Science Foundation's highly innovative Integrative Graduate Education, Research and Teaching Program, which is furiously multidisciplinary to real effect.

But no graduate dean would claim yet to have capitalized fully on the opportunities. And it is here that the graduate school has a huge opportunity—for where else will the questioning, the assessing, and the mixing and matching occur?

New Practices

To put it plainly, *new practices* concerns teaching and service, by which we really mean the application of expertise in the broader society. Service, one might laugh, that lame notion, the joke category in tenure decisions? But in fact both terms require rejuvenation, for reducing the preparation of graduate students as educators to the status of teaching is to impoverish the issue.

But begin with just plain teaching. In most programs, graduate students teach what the faculty does not wish to teach—introductory composition, language instruction, calculus, whatever else gets dubbed (going again to our other abused term) a service course. In many of the science and engineering disciplines, teaching is what a student does to stay alive if no research fellowship comes through. These practices imply to the next generation of teacher-scholars a disastrous notion of the worth of pedagogy. And a disheartening 63 percent of respondents report "their program or institution does not carefully supervise teaching assistants to help them improve their teaching skills" (Davis & Fiske, 1999, p. 4).

To be ashamed of this lack of regard for teaching is not a bad first step. But it is no solution for the economic issues that have contributed to the practice, whereby the least experienced faculty teach the least experienced undergraduates. How might departments redeploy their current resources to provide a progressive set of pedagogical experiences for doctoral students? We are going looking for success stories and we mean to retell them compellingly. One particularly promising tactic at Duke University requires of each program a plan for such a developmental set of teaching experiences as a requisite for departmental funding.

But beyond teaching—and beyond the myriad activities like creating a curriculum or mentoring individual students or inventing courses that are included in the expansive term "pedagogy"— I note that I received my doctorate without spending so much as a half hour learning about the educational landscape. Most doctoral students have spent their young lives at privileged institutions and most will work elsewhere even if they stay in academia. (It is wildly controversial to suggest that there are important roles for doctoral graduates in K–12 education and that very controversy only signals the terrible gap—more absolute in the United States than in any other country—between higher and public education.) The fact that we award the highest degree to students so often educationally illiterate is simply weird. It is an anomaly that both the Preparing Future Faculty Program and the National Science Foundation's K–12 initiatives have tackled with some success. But we are far from that norm where doctoral students would routinely experience a spectrum of teaching experiences. As Chris Golde and Tim Dore report, "There is a three-way mismatch . . . between the purpose of doctoral education, aspirations of the students, and the realities of their careers—within and outside academia. The result: students are not well prepared to assume the faculty positions that are available, nor do they have a clear concept of their suitability for work outside of research" (Golde & Dore, 2001, p. 5).

Teaching beyond all classrooms anywhere is a definition that might provide some life to the tired notion of service. Service has come often to mean nothing more than participation on university committees, where it might more rightly connote the rigorous application of knowledge to the social sphere. The next generation wants the opportunity. Over half of doctoral students want to provide community service, whereas less than one in five report being prepared to do so (Golde & Dore, 2001). At the University of Texas at Austin, the Professional Development and Community Engagement Program is the most thorough attempt to do just that, and it enlists dozens of faculty and hundreds of students in courses designed to stimulate the intellectual equivalent of tech transfer. The University of California-Irvine runs a set of programs called the Humanities Out There (HOT), which reach out, in practical and inspiring ways, to the schools and to cultural institutions at large. Several of our Responsive PhD universities—Yale University, Washington University in St. Louis, The University of Pennsylvania—have created graduate career offices that for the first time provide expert advice to graduate students so that they can be more creative in considering their options. Arizona State University's Preparing Future Professionals and the University of Colorado-Boulder's Windows on the World both bring together alumni and current students with faculty to encourage a new, extra-academic reach for the disciplines.

Our own experience at Woodrow Wilson has convinced us that students benefit immensely when faculty no longer conceive of themselves as guiding the next generation of teacher-scholars but as guiding the next generation of intellectual leaders, some of whom may become teacher-scholars. In our Humanities at Work effort, we found forty corporations and cultural institutions willing to hire doctoral graduates in positions that would employ their training meaningfully. Think what each university might do in this regard by working with alumni and regional businesses and non-profits! But more tellingly, we also gave small stipends in our practicum grant program to current doctoral students who wished to apply their learning to extra-academic venues for a summer. A student in American studies writing on the Latino arts movement of the 1960s found a graphic arts cooperative in East Los Angeles that had valuable documents it did not know it possessed. He created archives and gave a citywide exhibit at the end of the summer. An anthropology student at the University of Texas worked in a home for delinquent girls who had been abused as children. She applied everything apt from her discipline—dance, autobiographical writing, folklore—to help these young women improve their images of themselves. A comparative literature student worked with lawyers in Washington, D.C., on a war against hate literature; a philosophy student worked in his university's medical school on the ethics of transplants and also counseled transplant patients.

We have over one hundred such examples, surprising but convincing in their application of academic knowledge, and the reports of the students are strikingly in agreement. To a person, they note a new appreciation of the power of their discipline, a sense of how much they might accomplish in various venues, and an improvement in the writing of the dissertation because of the experience. It is not that all of them will now opt for nonacademic employment, but they have learned something about the power of their expertise in the world at large. And that is what the Responsive PhD most centrally concerns.

New People

Thus far, we've been thinking about the *what* of doctoral education and neglecting the *who*. *New people* is concerned with effectively drawing in and preserving diversity in the doctorate. Defenders of doctoral education often cite as evidence of success the large number of students who leave their homelands to earn a doctorate in the United States. This is a worthy point, but it contains an embarrassing counterpoint, one exposed anew in the aftermath of the September 11 attacks. As the federal government narrows immigration opportunities, universities worry that their research labs will go understaffed. Such a worry need not occur, of course, if we were as effective in educating our own population as we are in attracting international students. The number of African American, Hispanic, and Native American Ph.D.'s remains terribly low despite a tremendous number of worthy efforts by nonprofits and government agencies. Women have made more progress, but numbers are distressing in some disciplines there as well. At present, diversity in doctoral education lags far behind the achievements of business, government, and professional schools.

In our eighteen months of convenings, the Responsive PhD has focused on four approaches for democratizing doctoral education. The first is to coordinate the various funding and fellowship efforts. A dual grant from the Atlantic Philanthropies and the Andrew W. Mellon Foundation is providing funding for a report from which we hope to initiate a legislature of funders—that is, a new degree of coordinated effort among the foundations, agencies, and universities to ensure greater diversity in the graduate student cohort across the disciplines.

A second approach involves presenting doctoral education more aggressively in the earlier stages of education. If up to 70 percent of Latino students who attend college begin in community college (and often do not go on to four-year universities), then that is where the graduate school must make a connection. And well before then, in middle school, students make course decisions that determine their college eligibility. The graduate school, in other words, will not succeed by focusing alone on undergraduates but must participate in earlier stages of education to enlarge the eligible cohort. This kind of outreach in no way precludes the current efforts, such as those associated with McNair and with National Science Foundation programs such as the Alliances for Minority Participation (AMP) and Alliances for Graduate Education and the Professoriate (AGEP), efforts to make the most of that undergraduate cohort by providing bachelor's students with early research opportunities and graduate students with the support that will encourage their success. But it does mean going to places where we have not been.

Those students of color who do get to graduate school, according to an American Council on Education report, "do not feel mentored and . . . do not feel supported in the way that White students are. . . . This sense of isolation and lack of support was nearly universal among the minority graduate students with whom we met" (Fine Knowles & Harleston, 1997, p. 6). Yet even White students voice a similar complaint: "An overwhelming number of students reported that . . . mentoring needs to begin earlier, be more systematic, be based on a multiple-mentor model, and formally include teaching and curriculum concerns and career planning" (Nyquist & Woodford, 2000, p. 20). A new project led by the Mellon Foundation with assistance from Woodrow Wilson will focus on the mentoring shortfall, for minority students and for students at large.

Yet finally, it may be that all of the other concerns of the Responsive PhD can make themselves good in terms of this vital challenge to diversify the American intellect. Is it possible that so few students of color undertake the doctorate because, however undeliberately, the doctorate has imaged itself as abstract, irrelevant, White? There has been no deep questioning of how the background of practitioners affects the content and method of academic disciplines. In fact, according to a report prepared for the Compact for Faculty Diversity, students of color "are more interested than their White counterparts in collaborating in interdisciplinary research" (Golde, 2001, p. 10), and a greater percentage of doctoral students of color look to nonacademic careers (Golde & Dore, 2001). One of the healthier aspects of the national life, fully evident in academia, is the desire of people from oppressed groups to give back, to stay connected to their communities, and to make their individual success helpful for others in that population. A responsive Ph.D. affords the doctorate a reasoned urgency, and it encourages those kinds of connectivity for all students.

Outcomes

The roundtables have yielded some compelling, concrete, early results, and several institutions already have begun to implement their ideas.

- Out of Yale University's roundtable process came a pilot program for an alumni networking database that will put students, faculty, and alumni into direct contact. The intent: to help scholars refine research ideas, give students new career connections, and engage alumni more directly in department life, encouraging them to illustrate how they apply their own doctoral expertise to their work beyond academe. The pilot, a collaboration among the graduate school, the alumni association, and the graduate career center, began in fall 2002.
- At the University of Texas at Austin, action teams explored new forms of the dissertation and the application of new knowledge to pedagogical and community issues. A new graduate course has emerged, From Dissertation to the Profession: Teaching by Design, in the graduate school's Professional Development and Community Engagement Program. The intent is to help students see their work in new and exciting ways, and motivate timely completion of the dissertation. This program, which houses an extensive curriculum, blends internships and seminars to create connections between academia and the public and private sectors.
- In conjunction with a project supported by the Carnegie Foundation's Scholarship of Teaching and Learning (SoTL) Program, Howard University focused its roundtables on strengthening pedagogical scholarship, especially in relation to teaching diverse populations. In fall 2002, Howard's graduate school created its first Research on Scholarship of Teaching and Learning Awards.

The program encourages dynamic collaborations between student-faculty teams who research novel pedagogical approaches and then test them in undergraduate courses. An annual public forum will showcase the recipients' work.

- Transparency of information emerged as a top concern in doctoral education at Duke University, Indiana University, and the University of Washington. The graduate schools are proposing new guidelines for departments to make information on a range of matters—academic and nonacademic placements, disciplinary or cultural expectations, time to degree, and the like—more publicly available to new and prospective Ph.D. students. In some cases, information requirements are tied to annual budget approvals.

- Through its roundtables, Washington University in St. Louis developed a dynamic plan to engage doctoral students in the national debate on emerging trends in doctoral education. In October 2003, as part of its sesquicentennial celebration, the university hosted the Future of Graduate Education conference. Students engaged with many of the Responsive PhD themes.

As significant as these outcomes on individual campuses are, equally important are the institutions' desires to learn from one another's work. Several institutions have expressed interest in adapting the University of Texas at Austin's Professional Development and Community Engagement Program. Others are proposing mentoring guidelines similar to the University of Michigan's well-known faculty and student mentoring handbooks. And Yale University's new alumni networking project is an obvious test case for other institutions looking to engage their Ph.D. alumni more effectively.

Through careful study of these and other demonstration projects at the fourteen Responsive PhD partner institutions, a new vision of doctoral education is emerging, in more than just words—in concrete practices illustrating the dynamic holism of a more robust doctorate.

Recommendations

A thorough assessment of many of the efforts that grew out of these initial Responsive PhD roundtables will require a test of time. Even in medias res, however, exemplars at our participating universities and others point toward several basic recommendations:

- The central notion of a graduate school requires strengthening so that it can become a vital force in breaking down barriers between programs and sponsoring a more cosmopolitan intellectual experience for doctoral students.
- Changes in doctoral policy, as well as in the ultimate standards for the doctorate in each field, should emerge from a continuous dialogue among the faculty who teach doctoral students, the students themselves, and the representatives of diverse sectors that employ doctoral graduates.
- Departments and graduate schools need to involve Ph.D. alumni more substantively in doctoral training.
- Doctoral students need both departmental and extradepartmental structures to give their concerns a strong and effective voice.
- Information about doctoral education, program expectations, and career prospects must be more transparent to students from the moment they begin to consider a Ph.D.
- Doctoral programs urgently need to expand their approaches to mentoring, such as through team mentoring, particularly in order to attract and retain a diverse cohort of students.

Conclusion

This is the first major published work on the Responsive PhD in its short existence. A more comprehensive synthesis of the early project experience is still in the making. Three publications will appear in early 2004: a review of the best work the initiative has found for carrying out these recommendations, a report on assessing innovation at the doctoral level, and the previously mentioned study (funded by the dual grant from the Atlantic Philanthropies and the Mellon Foundation) on the funding of minority students. Later in 2004, the University of Michigan will publish a book of essays on public scholarship that grew out of a Responsive PhD conference in Ann Arbor on that topic.

But although all of this writing might please a researcher, and pleases us, it also worries me. We already have hundreds of pages of recommendations on doctoral education and not a lot of lived change. To help address this issue, we are performing with our partner institutions an inquiry on how best to gauge the effectiveness of the new practices they implement.

The Responsive PhD hopes to challenge itself with a certain degree of impatience. In the last few years, a number of national foundations have decided to delete higher education as a category for funding. Although funders claim any number of reasons for these decisions, it is hard not to worry that perceived inaction is among them. "We spend millions on universities and we just don't see the change," a foundation officer told me. "When we spend the same amount on any other issue—world hunger, population control, disease—we see a great deal more results."

Of course, this is not entirely fair. Universities do indeed change very slowly, but they also change profoundly. (Schools come up with a new panacea every few weeks and really do not change very much at all.) Even so, a critical habit of mind can create the unintended result of extreme stodginess. I think, for instance, of all those raging departmental debates over the canon in my own field. The net result introduced many new female authors and writers of color, and that was great. But the number of African Americans who earn doctorates in English has not improved over this period very much at all, for we as faculty failed to connect to community organizations or the schools. Hermetic revolutions do not cut it.

The Responsive PhD, in other words, ought to be assessed less by the wisdom of its words—though publication is indeed one form of action—than by what it achieves in real places for real students and faculty and by what it thereby achieves by encouraging them to become more responsive to a world that is urgently real. The Responsive PhD begins, then, when the language ends.

Acknowledgments

Dr. Bettina Woodford not only reviewed the research studies for this chapter but played a leading role in defining the four themes of the Responsive PhD Initiative. She has also served superbly as its initial program officer at the Woodrow Wilson National Fellowship Foundation. The Responsive PhD was made possible in part through the generosity of The Pew Charitable Trusts.

Notes

1. For a listing of the full range of inquiries conducted over the last decade, from individual studies to research commissioned by government and educational agencies, see the Responsive Ph.D. initiative's resource Web page: http://www.woodrow.org/responsivephd/responsive_phd.html.

2.   The institutions include, in the Northeast, The University of Pennsylvania, Princeton, and Yale; in the South, Duke, Howard, and the University of Texas; in the Midwest, Indiana, the University of Michigan, Washington University, and the University of Wisconsin; in the West, Arizona State University, the University of California at Irvine, the University of Colorado at Boulder, and the University of Washington. Earl Lewis, graduate dean at Michigan, is the national chair of the initiative. Robert Thach, graduate dean at Washington University, leads the Deans' Group. Jody Nyquist, Associate Dean for Professional Development at the University of Washington, leads the Sectors Group. They are joined by Debra Stewart, president of the Council of Graduate Schools, Catherine Stimpson, graduate dean at New York University and a trustee of the Woodrow Wilson Foundation, and George Walker, leader of the Carnegie Fund initiative in doctoral education, on a central advisory board.

3.   The careful discussions and assessments conducted by the Henry R. Luce Foundation, sponsor of a number of interdisciplinary professorships at various universities, are an important exception to this rule.

References

Davis, G., & Fiske, P. (1999). *The 1999 PhDs.Org graduate school survey report of results.* [http://www.phds.org/reading/nsbhandout.html]

Fine Knowles, M., & Harleston, B. (1997). *Achieving diversity in the professoriate: Challenges and opportunities.* Washington, DC: American Council on Education.

Golde, C. M. (2001, January). *Findings of the survey of doctoral education and career preparation: A report to the Compact for Faculty Diversity.* Unpublished manuscript, University of Wisconsin-Madison.

Golde, C. M., & Dore, T. M. (2001). *At cross purposes: What the experiences of doctoral students reveal about doctoral education.* Philadelphia: A Report for The Pew Charitable Trusts. [www.phd-survey.org]

Johnson, T. H. (Ed.). (1960). *The complete poems of Emily Dickinson.* New York: Little, Brown.

Nerad, M. (2000, April 14). The PhDs—Ten Years Later Study. Presentation at the Re-envisioning the Ph.D. conference.[http://www.grad.washington.edu/envision/project_resources/2000_conf_pages/2000_panel_surveys.html]

Nyquist, J. D., & Woodford, B. J. (2000). *Re-envisioning the Ph.D.: What concerns do we have?* Seattle: University of Washington, Center for Instructional Development and Research. [http://www.grad.washington.edu/envision/project_resources/concerns.html]

Chapter Twelve

The Carnegie Initiative on the Doctorate

Creating Stewards of the Discipline

George E. Walker

A review of national studies recommending improvements in graduate programs leads to the observation that there are a few important issues that have continued to draw attention for several decades. Among these issues are diversity, interdisciplinary or multidisciplinary opportunities, financing Ph.D. education, time spent in Ph.D. programs, quality and structure of mentoring, admissions standards, heterogeneity of the undergraduate background, relevancy of high-stakes assessment such as the Ph.D. qualifying exam and the final thesis oral, the form and content of the thesis, the Ph.D.-postdoctoral transition, the job market, and the breadth of career options considered appropriate by faculty and graduate students. It is sobering to realize that already in the 1950s many of these were subjects of concern and deliberation. Most have been discussed in some detail in national reports that are sitting on our shelves, and many of our faculty would naturally list half of these topics if asked about Ph.D. educational issues at a cocktail party. The meaning of some of the words may have changed over the years, but the issues have been surprisingly constant. I have heard it said that many of these issues simply reflect unchangeable boundary conditions like "the market," conflicting priorities of the faculty, economic resources, and empowerment, and although they can be discussed, there really is not much to be done. We shall see. These issues may be among those that leaders of the disciplines see as most important or solvable. If they do, the Carnegie Initiative on the Doctorate (CID), which is the focus of this chapter, should be helpful in implementing proposed solutions.

As an introduction to the CID, some comments on doctoral education as currently practiced in the United States may be helpful. First, current Ph.D. degree training reflects attributes of our society. It is *ruggedly individualistic;* there is no strict government oversight or set of national tests. There are many different types of Ph.D. granting departments in a discipline. The departments distinguish themselves through the accomplishments of their faculty and students, not by government licensing. Second, departmental faculty and graduate students are drawn from the entire world, not just the United States. In fact, *openness to talented scholars from around the world* continues to be a great source of intellectual and economic strength both in the academy and in the public sector. Third, Ph.D. departments often pride themselves on a *competitive* (almost capitalistic) *intellectual environment* that rewards most those who excel in activities that have been deemed high priority (mainly research productivity) in major Ph.D.-producing departments. This directly affects the Ph.D., which is a "research degree."

Although there may be some important negative consequences associated with our cultural Ph.D. mindset, overall the system works quite well. Certainly, the U.S. Ph.D. degree is highly respected. Many of the best and brightest from the world come to our institutions (some staying to become leaders in U.S. industry or universities and to contribute to U.S. government initiatives), and the accomplishments of our graduates in all areas of the arts and sciences and professions are outstanding.

And yet, there is always the possibility that we are settling for good in some areas while excellence remains outside our crowded vision. Most would argue that periodic program review is highly desirable to allow Ph.D. programs to evolve to meet changing expectations, challenges, and opportunities. But these reviews, if they take place, can be largely perfunctory because of busy schedules and the tyranny of near-term high priorities. The basic philosophical underpinnings and consistency between goals and practices in doctoral programs are often not reviewed by departments in depth because of time considerations. The CID proposes to help address this problem.

In this chapter we briefly describe the CID and its purpose, discuss some of the guiding themes and strategies for the program, and conjecture about possible outcomes. We conclude by briefly identifying some of our recommendations based on our work in the initial stages of the CID.

Definitions and Purposes

We at Carnegie believe that a more holistic conception of the Ph.D. holder would be helpful in discussing some of the goals of doctoral education. As a basis for discussion, we believe it is important to address the question, "What is the purpose of doctoral education?" In thinking about this question, we have identified three desired characteristics of a mature disciplinary scholar or leader that the Ph.D. should produce. Ideally, a Ph.D. holder should have the following abilities:

- *Generate* new knowledge by conducting research and scholarship that make unique contributions and meet disciplinary standards of credibility and verifiability.
- Critically *conserve* history and foundational ideas of a discipline while constantly evaluating new knowledge claims and determining how the discipline fits into the broader intellectual landscape.
- Effectively *transform* existing knowledge and its benefits to others through application, teaching, and writing. Whether working in a classroom, nonprofit or governmental organization, industrial setting, or policy arena, a steward must be able to convey information about the discipline through speaking or writing to technical and lay audiences and across traditional disciplinary boundaries.

Each of us may have a favorite word or phrase to describe someone with these scholarly characteristics. In our discussions at Carnegie, we have found it useful to designate a scholar who has the potential for generation, conservation, and transformation as a *steward of the discipline*. Words have differing connotations for different people, and thus the following discussion should be taken as an explanation of what we mean by disciplinary steward.

Disciplinary stewards are those responsible for preserving the essence of their fields while simultaneously directing a critical eye to the future, those to whom we entrust the vigor, quality, and integrity of the individual disciplines. The CID materials and project make frequent reference to creating a steward of the discipline as shorthand for the desired outcome of a doctoral program experience. To answer the question with which we began, we believe that the purpose of Ph.D. training should be to create stewards of the disciplines, scholars who are caretakers of the disciplines. We also believe that the framework of stewardship offers a broader conceptualization of doctoral education than the present graduate experience usually does.

With the creation of stewards as the desired outcome, then, the Carnegie initiative has been conceived as a multiyear research and action program designed to enrich and invigorate doctoral education by supporting departments in their efforts to structure their programs to that end. Planning for the initiative began in 2001, and the current phase of the project will extend through 2006. Thus, our effort is very much a work in progress. As it proceeds, the initiative will continue to work closely with the disciplinary communities and selected departments in six fields of study. The Carnegie Foundation will continue to facilitate the work of the partnering institutions as discussed later in this chapter. More detailed and current information on the initiative can be viewed on our Web site at http://www.carnegiefoundation.org/CID. The next section of this chapter provides a more detailed discussion of the CID, including the overriding themes around which we have designed the program and a summary of strategies that will be part of Carnegie's role in supporting the departments that participate.

Themes and Strategies

As a preliminary step in developing the plan for the CID, we interviewed dozens of disciplinary leaders, or stewards of the disciplines. The encouraging news was that they were eager to discuss the issues of importance in their disciplines at some length and felt the Carnegie initiative is timely. In fact, their input and suggestions were crucial in: confirming that the disciplines we have selected for initial involvement are ripe for a program like the CID, agreeing that serious collective faculty deliberation at the department-program level is important, and suggesting particular areas as grist for the deliberative mill in given disciplines.

Using the ideas gleaned from these interviews, the foundation is partnering with approximately six to eight departments, or programs, in each discipline, in an effort characterized by departmental action in the following areas: in-depth study of the current doctoral program with consideration of the alignment of desired outcomes and present procedures, proposed new departmental initiatives, implementation of proposed initiatives, and assessment and wide distribution of the results of the new departmental experimental efforts. In essence, then, the CID has been designed around conceptual analysis, experimentation, and evaluation and dissemination. These interacting themes provide the bases for Carnegie's work with the selected departments.

Conceptual Analysis

One theme that permeates the CID is that bringing about meaningful change is a process of ongoing reflection and discussion. Such conceptual analysis has been especially prevalent in initial departmental discussions in the program and will continue to establish the directions as the departments proceed. During conceptual analysis, disciplinary teams from selected departments have worked to refine what stewardship means in that discipline and to identify implications for the way graduate education is structured in those departments. Through the CID, we at the Carnegie Foundation are providing special opportunities for departments and programs to *reflect on the goals* or *expected outcomes* for their doctoral programs and to determine whether existing curricula, practices, and assessments of graduate student progress are robustly contributing to those outcomes. Ultimately, we seek to help departments understand the core processes of doctoral education in each discipline.

At the heart of the conceptual analyses are the disciplines. We believe not only that the formulation of the stewardship lies in the disciplines but also that the process for creating stewards may differ by discipline. Consequently, we have designed the program in the context of individual disciplines, realizing that there will be disciplinary insights as well as cross-disciplinary insights to be gleaned. The disciplines included are chemistry, English, history, mathematics, neuroscience, and education, including both educational psychology and curriculum and instruction. Among the reasons for the selection of these fields are the following: together they span a broad intellectual spectrum that includes the humanities, social sciences, sciences, and professions; they produce a relatively large number of doctorates; and together they provide a mix of the proportion of graduates who enter various career paths. Several of the fields involve the teaching of large numbers of undergraduates, and one of the fields, neuroscience, is intrinsically interdisciplinary.

For purely logistical reasons, we divided the six disciplines into two groups. In late summer 2002, the invitation for participation was mailed to over 150 universities in the first group, consisting of chemistry, English, mathematics, and education. The deadline for interested departments to respond was October 15, 2002. We were delighted by the magnitude of positive responses, with approximately eighty-five proposals from departments. In every field, there were high-quality proposals from nationally respected departments prepared to examine their Ph.D. programs seriously in hopes of implementing new initiatives. The diversity of institutions submitting proposals also was extremely gratifying. We have recently extended a similar invitation to doctoral granting departments in the second group, history and neuroscience.

As we have reviewed proposals from the first four disciplines and made selections for final participation, we have proceeded with specific criteria in mind. We have selected departments that can demonstrate ability and willingness to advance the goals of the CID. We expect the selected departments to have a critical mass of students and faculty who are willing to think deeply about the foundations of their graduate programs. Through their proposals, departments must have indicated willingness to experiment by trying new initiatives and then assessing these initiatives and disseminating more broadly the lessons learned. We wanted to include departments that have respected doctoral programs with a track record of placing some Ph.D. graduates in tenure-track positions in doctoral granting departments. Furthermore, we sought fertile institutional settings that are supportive of the departments' involvement in the CID—perhaps by providing appropriate supplementary resources. Finally, we thought it would be useful to have participation in a range of types of institutions—public and private—to ensure that lessons learned are translatable to a wide variety of institutional settings.

Also central to the selection of participating departments and the resulting conceptual analyses are willing faculty leaders who are themselves stewards of the disciplines. The faculties in the local departments, rightly so, are in charge of their Ph.D. programs. These scholars are necessarily strongly influenced by their own experiences in graduate school and strengthened in their beliefs by their own successes in their fields, especially the tenured, highly respected leaders in the disciplines. It is just these faculty who are absolutely essential in both discovering areas where programs can be enriched and implementing suggested changes. Because of the nature of prestige and funding, the disciplinary societies and funding agencies are crucial partners in the reflective improvement process. But it is the scholars in the discipline who have a special role in discovering the need for and then implementing change. This group of leaders—the respected scholars in the departments or programs under consideration—must be convinced that some changes are needed and that the CID provides a useful process for addressing the needs. The process will only proceed if it begins with their reaching these conclusions through departmental deliberative processes. This basic assumption has been a key starting point for the theme of conceptual analysis in the CID. Because disciplinary leaders in the department have not been front and center in other studies, this feature distinguishes the CID from other national movements.

For the first group of disciplines, the conceptual, reflective stage occurred during the 2002–03 academic year. Departmental discussions took place on the purposes of doctoral education and the expected skills, experiences, and outcomes for graduates of these Ph.D. programs. Important baseline data, if not already available, was collected and examined during this period. The time frame for discussion was designed to allow for serious deliberation about the relevancy of various components of each program in leading to the desired outcomes. During the summer of 2003, disciplinary meetings were convened at Carnegie for the first four disciplines to share the results of their deliberations and to discuss their planned initiatives.

It is during the initial deliberations of conceptual analysis that we expect continuing differences of opinion or priorities among the faculty in a given department over various aspects of the doctorate program. However, we have also observed that a practical consensus develops among a critical mass of the faculty that certain new approaches are important to initiate or that existing initiatives need to be broadened, strengthened, or assessed. As committed departments have found either mismatches or the need for additional practices during this process, we have encouraged them to *experiment* with new initiatives that can be evaluated to determine if they indeed contribute to strengthening the program.

Experimentation

The second theme that runs through the activities of the CID is experimentation. After conceptual analysis, participating departments experiment with various approaches, trying to implement suggested ideas to create stewards in the disciplines. Currently, departments in the first cohort already are discussing possible new aspects of their programs with the full knowledge and cooperation of the departmental faculty and graduate students. In essence, these departments have committed to experimenting with adaptations in their programs and implementing changes that foster development of disciplinary stewards. The CID will be facilitating the work of these departments in carrying out their experimental efforts. We expect the experiments to be ongoing for several years and pursued in partnerships, not only between the departments and the Carnegie Foundation, but also among the universities of the departments involved, funding agencies, and scholarly societies. Naturally, departments will want to implement the changes in ways that facilitate the important next stages—assessment of the value of the new initiatives, and dissemination of lessons learned—which begins in 2004.

Evaluation and Dissemination

The ongoing evaluation phase will require some *research* to determine the usefulness of the conceptual analysis, the experiments, and their implementation. The process of assessment will begin with the initial deliberations of the departments on their existing doctoral program and will continue as they gather appropriate evidence on the outcomes of their new initiatives. For this part of the process the baseline data obtained early in the conceptual phase will be very valuable for comparative purposes. In addition, the initiatives that the departments conceive, and their subsequent implementation, should be evaluated with the same purposeful attention that is brought to bear in their disciplinary research and in such areas as the scholarship of teaching.

It is important to make public the thinking of the departments in addressing their Ph.D. programs in the same way that peer-reviewed disciplinary research is made available to the practitioners of the discipline. Therefore, throughout the initiative, we will be distilling the results of discussions and research and sharing them with the doctoral education and disciplinary communities in order to disseminate more broadly the lessons being learned.

Carnegie's Ongoing Role

The Carnegie Foundation will continue to provide expertise and modest resources to facilitate each partnering department's pilgrimage through all stages of the CID process. One strategy we will use is to facilitate several different types of meetings: campus-based for each program, cross-site for each discipline, and programwide for assessment and integration. A variety of products will result from the initiative: models of experimental doctoral programs, research and analysis of the experiments and seminars, and institutional and policy-level recommendations. During these meetings, the partnering departments will have the opportunity to share their ideas with others and have access to leaders with extensive experience in areas of relevance to the partnering departments' disciplines.

Although not intended to be complete, the following list of ideas highlights some of the specific ways in which Carnegie will continue to be involved with departments. During the past year, we have been visiting participating departments to help facilitate discussions if needed, provide Carnegie-commissioned essays by respected leaders on issues of relevance for the project, and provide reference and background materials that provide context for the departmental deliberations. We will continue to convene sessions at Carnegie similar to those conducted during the first summer after departments begin their deliberations—to facilitate departmental implementation plans, and to share ideas and lessons learned. Such sessions are expected to continue on a regular basis for several years. As the project progresses, Carnegie is committed to providing expertise, and in other crucial ways, to facilitating the assessment and dissemination of the results of the departmental initiatives. We will cooperate with departments to obtain additional resources for their exploratory endeavors.

Outcomes

The lasting positive impact of the CID depends importantly on the centrality of the disciplines chosen, the positive reputation and commitment of the participating departments and their leaders, the institutionalization, and thus the sustainability, of the new practices, and the wide dissemination of the assessed results. The credibility of the entire exercise depends on the leadership of respected scholars in the fields chosen—at both the departmental and national levels. For this reason the involvement and strong support of disciplinary leaders, national professional societies, and private and governmental funding agencies are key. The cooperation and support of other national Ph.D.-strengthening efforts will be helpful to the CID as well as to the other programs themselves. The several national projects are quite complementary—the CID being an in-depth action program led by leaders in a few disciplines and involving a few well-respected programs in those disciplines.

Let us now *imagine* that it is about a decade into the future. There is a good departmental response to the CID and every stage of the project has gone well, although almost certainly not as planned. What outcomes have occurred and what impact has the Carnegie initiative had?

First, it is important to note that the outcomes obtained would not have been possible without the serendipity of excellent timing, the cooperation of many disciplinary leaders and professional societies, the work and leadership of other successful national initiatives, the funding agencies, and most of all, the faculty and graduate students of the participating departments. The rapid dissemination of the lessons learned from the new exploratory practices and the careful evaluation of the many successful efforts allowed the impact of the initiative to spread and be quickly institutionalized in research universities throughout the country. The initiative was aided significantly by the informed changes in the evaluation criteria for a wide variety of grant proposals by public and private foundations.

One striking outcome has been the emergence of a cadre of scholarly leaders or stewards of the discipline who are able to function even more effectively in diverse environments. Leaders in the private and public sectors have repeatedly commented on this and complimented the nation's research universities for building stronger and enriched graduate programs. Graduate students and faculty have commented that their level of personal satisfaction has significantly improved as their teaching and research productivity and quality have made assessable gains. The large number of outstanding international students seeking admission to our Ph.D. programs has continued to rise, but what is most striking is the increased number of highly motivated and gifted domestic undergraduates who are choosing to enter doctoral programs in a wide spectrum of disciplines. Of course, an important outcome is the significant increase in the job market because of the general agreement in the United States that the Ph.D. educational experience is invaluable for leadership roles in most areas of endeavor in the increasingly information-based economy. One positive outcome has been that faculty in a wide variety of undergraduate institutions are not only more effective in educating undergraduates but also speak more highly of the value of their own graduate experience.

To the delight of the academic research establishment, funds for research and the support of graduate education have shown unusual growth in the last couple of years. Some believe this has occurred because scholars have become more adept at explaining to the general public the importance of research and graduate education. Others attribute it to the astounding successes recently obtained by scholars who work creatively to solve problems in settings where several disciplinary cultures must work together.

Fundamental gains in public appreciation of research as well as the new research breakthroughs have come from the increased diversity in and access to doctoral programs that were facilitated by initiatives spawned by the CID and kindred programs. The fact that new paradigms and approaches have been so numerous and successful at the frontiers of knowledge is attributed by some to the greater presence of different cultural perspectives in the Ph.D. population. To be sure, departmental efforts in recruiting and creating a fertile learning environment for people with diverse needs and perspectives has been fundamental to many of these successes.

Other direct and indirect outcomes are attributable in part to the CID initiative begun over a decade ago. There is now a strong national network of support and habit of mind for a continuing systematic examination of doctoral programs so that they will remain vigorous. In fact, there is a strong legitimacy for acts of discussing, making explicit and public the principles and assumptions that guide departments in the implementation of their graduate programs. Many books, articles, and publicly accessible Web sites have arisen from the CID project, and these tangible deliverables play an important ongoing role in strengthening programs so that they can do an even better job of educating doctoral students to be stewards of the disciplines. Space does not permit more complete elaboration, but all in all, doctoral education, and therefore, all sectors of society, have been enriched by the results of this and related efforts to advance learning in the broadest sense at our schools and universities.

Let us work cooperatively to make this imagined future a reality.

Recommendations

Although it is premature to list a series of recommendations associated with a project that has been in place for such a short time, some basic assumptions and initial lessons learned may be helpful:

- *Serious deliberation by respected scholars at the department-program level is a prerequisite for improvement of doctoral programs.* As argued earlier, such change in the quality of graduate preparation requires the participation and commitment of departmental scholars. Also important, though, is the realization that this process should be part of the ongoing lives of the departments and not just a onetime event. One way to perpetuate such ongoing reflection, adaptation, and assessment is to make sure that graduates leaving their Ph.D. granting institutions are prepared to assume roles as disciplinary stewards once they move into their careers.

• *Cooperation is essential with other credible movers in the discipline, such as professional societies, funding agencies, and leading educators.* Like others in this volume who have argued the importance of the collective in moving forward to improve doctoral education (see Nyquist, Woodford, & Rogers, Chapter Ten, this volume), we are convinced that commitments from respected leaders representing all the relevant constituencies are essential to the success of a program such as the CID. Thus, the Carnegie Foundation will continue to seek opportunities to facilitate such collaboration across groups as part of the program.

• *Assessment and public dissemination of the departmental initiatives are crucial for informing the discipline on the evolution of outstanding doctoral programs.* The synergy resulting from groups working together and sharing information and lessons provides the best chance for moving us forward on the important issues in doctoral education. Although the disciplinary perspective is key, it does not preclude the possibility of collaboration within disciplines and across disciplines and with other constituents interested in graduate education.

Conclusion

This brief summary of the CID is being written in the early iterations of the program. We are still in the beginning stages of working with departments. We have had numerous discussions with disciplinary leaders and have given numerous talks at professional disciplinary meetings and general higher education conferences, to groups of department chairs, and at various funding agencies. We have had two meetings with our advisory committee and are planning annual meetings in the future. We have commissioned essayists on topics of importance for the project; we hosted a meeting of these Carnegie essayists, and we now have final drafts from ten of them. Each essay is terrific and will provide an excellent basis for departmental deliberations. The responses at all stages of the CID process have been outstanding, both in quality and magnitude.

At this point, however, we do not know exactly what experimentation, evaluation, and dissemination will take place because that will not depend on Carnegie alone but also on the efforts and priorities of our partners. All of our efforts to date have been well received with regard to timeliness, importance, and general appropriateness of the CID. But we do not know for sure where the deliberations and initiatives will lead. We have reserved the dance hall and the band, and are ready for the festivities to begin. We know that many have responded positively to our invitation to dance, and are now even out on the dance floor. Although we do not know yet exactly what forms or steps each department will take, we have every reason to be optimistic that the dance will be a success.

Acknowledgments

An initiative of this scope requires the active leadership of many outstanding educators—a national advisory committee, disciplinary essayists, and several senior scholars from the Carnegie Foundation are a few of the key extradepartmental participants. Additional information is listed on our Web site. I want especially to thank Dr. Donald Kennedy (President Emeritus and Bing Professor of Environmental Sciences, Emeritus, Stanford University; and Editor-in-Chief of *Science*) for his leadership as chair of the committee, and acknowledge the crucial contribution of two of my colleagues at Carnegie: President Lee Shulman and Senior Scholar Chris Golde, the research director for the Carnegie Initiative on the Doctorate.

Chapter Thirteen

Michigan State University's Conflict Resolution Program

Setting Expectations and Resolving Conflicts

Karen L. Klomparens, John P. Beck

Graduate education is a key activity of higher education, contributing to the creation of new knowledge and advancing our society (Tinto, 1993). Yet nationwide, only 50 percent of all doctoral students complete their programs (Bowen & Rudenstine, 1992). The graduate education process involves myriad opportunities for miscommunication, misunderstanding, and conflict to occur, which contribute to this low success rate. As a student progresses through his or her program, the guidance committee or the major professor or faculty advisor become the locus of the educational community (Tinto, 1993). Not surprisingly, doctoral students regard their relationships with faculty members as the most important element in the quality of their graduate experience, but many also have reported it as "the single most disappointing aspect of their graduate experience" (Hartnett & Katz, 1977, p. 647).

Research has also shown that students who are given useful and explicit early information about program expectations develop better working relationships, are more committed to their programs, and are more productive as measured by numbers of future publications (Bauer & Green, 1994; Green, 1991). Hartnett and Katz (1977) postulated that clarity about expectations results in increased accountability on the part of both graduate students and faculty members. Studying students who did not complete doctoral degrees, Lovitts (2001) reported that doctoral degree completers identify academic integration (interactions with faculty and other graduate students, and a connection with life in the discipline) and an understanding of informal expectations as the most important factors contributing to successful graduate education. The lack of mutually understood expectations and the conflicts that may subsequently arise between faculty members and graduate students damage these fundamentally important relationships and contribute to the low completion rate.

There is increasing national recognition of the serious nature of interpersonal conflicts between graduate students and faculty. Holton's 1995 book, *Conflict Management in Higher Education,* did not mention conflicts between graduate students and faculty. In her second volume in 1998, however, this issue received attention, and most recently Warters (2000) highlighted the importance of conflict resolution in graduate education.

Conflict inflicts heavy costs on graduate students, faculty members, and administrators, as well as on the department and university. Whether the lost time and opportunity for the graduate student who does not complete his or her degree; the lost institutional investment when students depart; the damage to departmental culture and reputation; or the time and energy that conflict diverts from the university's core missions of teaching, research, and outreach, all are real costs that can be avoided, or at least, minimized.

However, many of the strategies for conflict resolution in higher education, such as peer mediation and formal grievance processes, are based on the needs and experiences of undergraduates. The results of the application of many of these strategies to graduate education are inconsistent because of the huge differences between what these strategies offer and the context in which they are applied. They are not designed to maintain the faculty-graduate student relationship, but rather are set in the process of fact finding, mounting an evidentiary rationale one against the other, assessing blame, and staking a claim for redress. The close working relationship between a graduate student and an individual faculty member or a small group of faculty that characterizes graduate education does not readily lend itself to the easy use of strategies such as going through formal grievance procedures or simply leaving the relationship or program. Exit may mean the end of a student's career at the specific institution. Furthermore, personal rancor, resulting from either exiting or formally bringing forward a grievance (even a successful grievance), may lead to problems that follow the person to other institutions, either as a student or as a professional. These processes are inadequate because they often run counter to the ongoing important relationship and communication requirements that link advisor and advisee. In fact, graduate students often avoid these processes for that reason.

On our own campus at Michigan State University (MSU), graduate student and faculty focus groups, surveys of current graduate students, and a survey of Ph.D. alumni, as well as input from the ombudsman, the university's Intellectual Integrity Officer, and officers of the Council of Graduate Students, indicated that the lack of mutually understood expectations creates great potential for interpersonal conflict in the graduate education process. Our survey results also underscored that students' greatest dissatisfaction was with departmental, mentor, and advisor-related communication issues. They reported specific concerns about orientation, guidance committee interactions, appropriate student progress, faculty feedback, quality of advising, and faculty receptiveness to student input. We suspect that this pattern of concerns is similar at other "research-extensive universities" (Carnegie, 2000), a conclusion that has largely been supported by Golde and Dore's (2001) national survey data (see Chapter Two) and Nerad and Cerny's (2000) study, PhDs—Ten Years Later (see Chapter Seven).

Both students and faculty in focus groups at Michigan State University cited interpersonal conflicts as formidable barriers to success in graduate education and recognized these conflicts as posing a different and more difficult set of challenges than students face as undergraduates. The graduate students in the focus groups expressed the belief that because they are quite vulnerable, conflicts they face with faculty supervisors are either irresolvable or resolvable only by their paying a high price for voicing their concerns, especially in a formal grievance procedure. The students were very conscious of the power differential between them and faculty members; they believed that even winning a "victory" could result in irreparable professional harm with respect to financial support, letters of recommendation, and entry into the disciplinary field. Faculty, department chairs, and others cited concerns about the time required to resolve conflicts and the resulting reduction in both faculty and student productivity.

Recognizing the human and institutional costs of conflicts involving graduate students and the limitations of available avenues for successful resolution of conflicts, the graduate school at MSU initiated a program in 1996 designed to recast conflict resolution from the confrontational, positional approach—based in blaming and right-wrong dualities—to an interest-based approach that lays the basis for more creative and amicable problem solving. This chapter describes our experience with this program at MSU, our change in focus to avoiding conflicts through better setting of explicit and mutually understood expectations, and our conviction that the program presents a transferable model that may be used to affect retention positively on other campuses as well.

Program Description and Purposes

Michigan State University's interest-based approach, although not new in the practice of general negotiation and conflict resolution, had not been applied to graduate education. We believed that it held great promise as an alternative to high-stakes grievance-driven and position-based methods. As we developed the program, however, we realized that the technique of conflict resolution was not the sole determinant of our program's possible success. The interest-based approach needed to be part of a shift in emphasis away from the resolution of conflict between faculty and graduate students to its avoidance through proactive setting and communication of mutual expectations. We termed this process "making the implicit explicit."

We initiated the program—entitled Setting Expectations and Resolving Conflicts—to see if we could transfer to the enterprise of graduate education the systematic use of interest-based approaches employed in environmental disputes, labor-management negotiations, and international relations. Program development was supported by the Fund for the Improvement of Post-Secondary Education (FIPSE) (from 1997 to 2000) and by the William and Flora Hewlett Foundation (from 1997 to 1999) and was a team effort that included the two authors, graduate students Julie Brockman and Jennifer Eyelans Oxtoby, and R. Sam Larson, Ph.D., an independent consultant specializing in organizational change. Janet Lillie, Ph.D., of the MSU Department of Communications, designed and now presents our companion workshop in communication skills.

We developed a set of workshops that used short video vignettes as conversation triggers to teach faculty and graduate students interest-based approaches to setting expectations and resolving conflicts. We also developed a workshop for graduate students alone (without faculty members present), in which they could try out the approach in a safe and supportive environment. In designing the workshops, we ensured that the necessary content was included, but we were also sensitive to time constraints for both faculty members and graduate students.

Strategies

Interest-based approaches involve several steps: the individuals agree on the issue needing resolution; they identify the underlying *interests* they believe are linked to the issue and the outcome they desire (the "position" they hold); they identify all other individuals who have a "stake" in the resolution of the conflict and their interests; and finally, they craft options that meet the individual and mutual interests of everyone involved and form the basis for successfully addressing the issue in a way that each person will find acceptable. These strategies counter traditional "positional" approaches used in bargaining, in which the focus is the position of each individual rather than the underlying interests and concerns of all persons, positions that each may strongly defend from attack and to which they become increasingly committed (Fisher & Ury, 1991). With traditional approaches, agreement may reflect a mechanical "spelling out" of the differences between final positions, rather than a solution to the issue in dispute that is carefully crafted to meet the legitimate interests of the individuals. Not infrequently, positional negotiation strains and sometimes shatters the relationships between the individuals—relationships that are of fundamental importance for doctoral education.

Often, the best option for resolving a conflict may not be a simple compromise between stated positions. When two individuals share their underlying interests, it moves them from a linear argument—in which usually inflexible positions are stated, often fixing all possible solutions between the stated desired outcomes—to a comprehensive discussion approach that can result in a wider and more creative set of solutions.

Interest-based approaches rely on five main strategies: the discussion is focused on the problem and not on the people involved; the focus is on the needs, desires, interests, and fears underlying the stated positions; a variety of options are generated that advance shared interests and creatively reconcile differing interests before a final decision is made; the participants engage in a fair testing of the options to determine their goodness as complete or partial solutions to the issue and how well they meet the stakeholder interests (truly the test of the goodness of any solution); successful decision making and ongoing evaluation lead to a negotiation process whereby the individuals are willing to be flexible and to reenter the process again later as the context changes.

In our two- to three-hour Setting Expectations and Resolving Conflicts workshops—which are attended by both faculty members and graduate students in departmental settings or by graduate students alone in groups that span disciplines—we use thirty- to ninety-second video vignettes to spark discussion and teach the basic principles of interest-based approaches. We designed more than fifty vignettes depicting a wide range of issues that can lead to conflicts or describing implicit expectations not made explicit. Issues highlighted include changing guidance committee members, "even more" revisions to a dissertation, authorship issues, data access, working with faculty, teaching assistant issues, and balancing family and graduate studies. Video vignettes are more lively than reading a case study. Furthermore, the venues portrayed by the vignettes, as well as the physical attributes and mannerisms of the characters, also provide "teachable moments." Following is an example vignette script and related questions that are used in the workshops.[1]

Professor: Gloria, why did you cancel your discussion section of my course yesterday?

Graduate student: My daughter, she woke up with a temperature and she was sick. I didn't have anyone to take care of her at the last minute, so I had to stay home. I'm a single parent. There was nobody to call at the last minute.

Professor: Do you realize that this is the third time that this has happened this semester and that undergraduate students are beginning to complain? If you don't take care of this situation soon, it may affect your ability to be assigned a section next semester.

General Questions Related to This Vignette

1. What is happening in this interchange?

2. How realistic is the interchange?

3. What does each of the characters want from the other person, or from the situation?

4. Are there others, not in the vignette, who are affected by the situation? What do they need in the situation described?

5. What questions do we need to have answered to analyze this situation?

6. What policy or expectations might have helped avoid this situation?

7. What are the emotions portrayed in this vignette? Where do they have their origin?

8. What can we reasonably expect to be the next step in this situation?

Specific Questions Related to This Vignette

1. What are the various responsibilities being explored in this vignette?

2. The title of this vignette, "Double Bind," implies that there are dueling priorities or responsibilities at play. Discuss who is in a double bind and what the dueling priorities are.

3. What constitutes a professor's responsibility to the students in his or her course? Is the graduate teaching assistant's responsibility any different? If so, what are the differences and where do these get articulated?

4. What are the possible consequences facing all players in this situation if it is not resolved?

5. The professor makes a statement about Gloria not being able to "be assigned a section next semester." Is this a threat? How does this statement affect the situation?

6. How does the location of the interchange affect how we view it? What are some other "locations" where this issue could be discussed? How might the change of location affect the situation and the interchange?

Selecting vignettes that are closely aligned with the interests of the specific participants—for example, lab-based vignettes on ownership of scientific data are relevant to those in the sciences—allows the facilitator to focus on those important, and perhaps even contentious, issues most likely to provoke discussion. Participants can then safely explore the issues presented in the vignette, as well as learn interest-based approaches to resolve them. In our experience, participants often generate creative solutions to the conflicts depicted in the vignettes and begin to discuss expectations that might be made explicit in order to prevent the conflict in the future.

The Setting Expectations and Resolving Conflicts Program has several facets. Participants learn interest-based approaches and skills for negotiation and conflict resolution. They participate in the facilitated discussions that use the video vignettes as triggers to conversations about specific areas of possible conflict and differing expectations in disciplines, or more generally, in graduate education. In situations where faculty and student groups work together, participants have used interest-based approaches and skills to establish collective departmental understandings of expectations and responsibilities. Written materials provided in the workshops describe the philosophy and skills of interest-based negotiation strategy. Participants practice these skills by developing frameworks for setting expectations and applying these frameworks to scenes depicted in the vignettes.

The workshops highlight a number of key concepts. We emphasize that early attention to setting expectations can help avoid conflicts. We show that early attention to resolving conflicts is a key to success, because, as time passes, things are said and done by students and faculty members that often significantly limit options for satisfactory resolution. We also spend considerable time discussing how expectations are set and who sets them. We believe that explicit, shared expectations are the fundamental keys to improving retention.

We are also careful to define our own assumptions early in the workshop, such as these: Not all issues are negotiable. Conflict itself is neither good nor bad (and is, in fact, how we advance knowledge in the academy), but rather it is how conflict is handled that may be defined as good or bad. The power differential between faculty members and graduate students will never be equalized, because faculty have expert power as well as other forms of power. Finally, we should not expect 100 percent graduate student retention and completion.

As noted earlier, we also have added a workshop on communication skills for graduate students alone, at their request and by recommendation of our national advisory committee. This workshop, which uses the same video vignettes as the Setting Expectations and Resolving Conflicts workshops, provides additional practice, skills, and information to help the students talk effectively with faculty members. It reinforces the practice and use of the interest-based approaches to setting expectations and resolving conflicts.

Outcomes

Program participants gain skills in communication, conflict resolution, and teamwork that improve the quality of graduate education and serve students and faculty members throughout their careers. The program also increases graduate student participants' academic integration and socialization into the disciplines. To date, outcomes can be determined both from evaluation data and from observations of institutional impact.

Evaluation Data

The MSU program attracts approximately one hundred students to the workshops offered by the graduate school each semester. In addition, the approach and vignettes have been used by MSU's Intellectual Integrity Officer, Women's Resource Center, Office of the Provost Teaching Seminar series, and faculty members in orientations and doctoral proseminars. Going beyond MSU, we have presented workshops to deans and assistant and associate deans during the Council of Graduate Schools preconference programs. We have also conducted workshops and train-the-trainer sessions at Kansas State University, Pennsylvania State University, University of Minnesota, University of Michigan, and other institutions.

At the beginning of each of fifty-seven workshops we sponsored at MSU and elsewhere during a three-year period of FIPSE evaluation, we asked participants to complete a registration form. We calculated that 561 faculty, 737 graduate students, and 30 postdocs—for a total of 1,328 individuals—attended the interest-based

Setting Expectations and Resolving Conflict workshops. To evaluate the immediate impact of the workshops on cognitive and affective learning goals, we administered a survey to participants immediately following the workshops. In addition, we measured long-term understanding and use of the approaches through a survey administered to workshop participants several months after they attended a workshop.

The surveys administered at the conclusion of each workshop provided useful findings: 65 percent of the participants could correctly state an expectation as a well-defined interest; 62 percent could articulate an expectation that would meet the needs of both parties; 89 percent were ready to use the interest-based negotiation skills presented in the workshop; and 83 percent said they would use these skills if they had an opportunity to practice them more. In addition, 94 percent found the workshop to be somewhat or very helpful in recognizing their own expectations of graduate education; 88 percent found the workshop to be somewhat or very helpful in their understanding of what others (depending on the respondent, either their major professors or their graduate students) might expect of them; and 92 percent said the workshop was very or somewhat helpful in their thinking about the long-term impacts of relationships with major professors or graduate students. In the survey administered several months after students attended the workshop, many reported sharing their expectations with their major professors, identifying parties associated with expectations, and considering the interests of parties associated with expectations.

The observations of a few student participants, taken from the project evaluation for FIPSE, also illustrate some of the outcomes of the project:

> I was exposed to this workshop during my first semester on campus and I think it's one of the best things I did in terms of shaping my expectations for my doctoral plan of study. It helped me to realize that conflict is inevitable and that even though I'm a student I can negotiate with faculty. I learned to look for the [reasons] underlying . . . positions. . . . I've used these skills in setting expectations for my assistantships, and thus far, conflicts have been handled before they escalate.

I was very hesitant to confront my advisor about my needs in terms of comps and/or thesis. As it turned out we negotiated a compromise that was much more helpful to me in both my professional and academic goals, and the end result means I have negotiated several new opportunities. I think these workshops were very helpful.

Institutional Impact

The focus on how explicit expectations are set also has influenced graduate program review at MSU. While acknowledging that many expectations about graduate education are implicit (a core tenet of our program), the workshops highlight how clear communication of formal expectations reduces the guesswork for students and prevents conflict. Graduate program review, therefore, includes an examination of graduate handbooks for explicit language about formal, and even informal, expectations. Further, training sessions conducted every fall semester for new and returning graduate program secretaries and coordinators pay considerable attention to the key role that clarifying expectations, while considering the interests of all stakeholders, plays in student retention and success.

Overall, from 1996 to 2002, the doctoral retention-completion rate at Michigan State University has improved from 53 percent to almost 59 percent, although the retention-completion rate for doctoral students nationally has not changed in thirty years. We believe that the frequent opportunities provided for students and faculty to participate in this program, the consistent use of the interest-based language and process by the graduate school personnel, and the focus on the improvement of doctoral student retention throughout all of our activities (for example, a graduate handbook template and use of completion rates in our formula for allocating fellowship funds) have all contributed to the improvement of this measure at MSU.

Recommendations

The experiences at MSU, as well as at other institutions that have adapted the strategies discussed here, indicate that a program specifically designed for graduate students and faculty members that focuses on setting expectations and helping participants develop skills in conflict resolution makes a significant impact. We urge other institutions to initiate such programs, and we offer here some final recommendations:

- *Use graduate school–sponsored workshops on setting expectations and conflict resolution to provide safe contexts for students to discuss issues of concern.* The workshop setting provides a context in which students can strengthen social connections with one another. Graduate school–sponsored workshops also increase the visibility of university personnel, who can provide a safe environment for students to discuss issues of concern and seek advice outside the context and power structure of any particular department. This safe environment is particularly attractive to international students, nontraditional students, and students from underrepresented groups.

- *In addition to graduate school–sponsored workshops open to all graduate students, situate interest-based conflict resolution training in departments as well.* Departments are the place where implicit understandings and organizational folklore often affect the lives of graduate students and faculty members. Interest-based approaches can be useful to departments in several different ways. First, faculty members working as a departmental group without graduate students can use interest-based approaches to discuss their understandings of key departmental policies and goals. When departmental faculty have agreed about a framework—a safety net of common expectations—they can build on this framework to talk with student advisees about setting individual expectations and goals. A second approach, which we believe holds great promise, is a joint training and expectation-setting experience involving *both* graduate students and faculty in a single department, unit, or subspecialty. Graduate students and faculty can gain a common understanding of the problematic areas in graduate education (authorship, financial support, and so on), explore areas that may not be sufficiently explicit, and build a web of departmental understandings and expectations inside which faculty and students are expected to operate. Absent departmental meetings of faculty, or of faculty members and students together, individual faculty members who are knowledgeable about the cultures in their departments can still use interest-based expectation setting to interact with their own advisees.

- *Articulate compelling incentives for students and faculty members to participate in an interest-based workshop on setting expectations and learning conflict resolution skills.* The incentives for involvement in this program are to improve the climate for graduate education in the department and to avoid miscommunication and conflicts that can take faculty and student time and attention, as well as other resources, away from more productive endeavors. In addition, we have found that individual faculty members are more likely to participate in this program if there is discussion of the research that links early and explicit communication to productivity for faculty and for their students (Green, 1991). Good working relationships between faculty and graduate students contribute positively to perceptions about the quality of departments and institutions.

Conclusion

The setting expectations and resolving conflicts program initiated at MSU and adopted at a number of institutions helps graduate students and faculty members set mutual expectations and place interests, not positions, at the center of joint discussions. When implicit interests and desires are made explicit, the creation of multiple options and solutions becomes more likely when conflicts arise. Although an interest-based negotiation strategy or approach is not "rocket science," it is more complex to teach than one might expect. The approach represents a fundamental change of culture as well as a habit of mind that requires multiple experiences with the process in order to break away from the positional mindset. The results are worthy of the effort, however. Students and faculty who participate report increasingly positive departmental climates and improved retention and completion rates. This modest program, not requiring extensive resources, has the potential for significant impact in improving graduate education.

Note
1. Published materials further describing this program, including all program vignettes on videodisk, are scheduled to be available in the near future. Currently, more information, including sample vignettes, is available at the following Web site: http://grad.msu.edu/conflict.htm.

References

Bauer, T. N., & Green, S. G. (1994). Effect of newcomer involvement in work-related activities: A longitudinal study of socialization. *Journal of Applied Psychology, 79*(2), 211–223.

Bowen, W. G., & Rudenstine, N. L. (1992). *In pursuit of the Ph.D.* Princeton, NJ: Princeton University Press.

Carnegie Foundation for the Advancement of Teaching Classification. (2000, August). A new way of classifying colleges elates some and perturbs others. *Chronicle of Higher Education,* A31–A41.

Fisher, R., & Ury, W. (1991). *Getting to yes: Negotiating agreement without giving in.* New York: Penguin Books.

Golde, C. M., & Dore, T. M. (2001). *At cross purposes: What the experiences of today's doctoral students reveal about doctoral education.* Philadelphia: A Report for The Pew Charitable Trusts. [www.phd-survey.org]

Green, S. G. (1991). Professional entry and the advisor relationship: Socialization, commitment, and productivity. *Group and Organization Studies, 16*(4), 387–407.

Hartnett, R. T., & Katz, J. (1977). The education of graduate students. *Journal of Higher Education, 48*(6), 646–664.

Holton, S. A. (Ed.). (1995, Winter). *Conflict management in higher education.* New Directions for Higher Education, No. 92. San Francisco: Jossey-Bass.

Holton, S. A. (Ed.). (1998). *Mending the cracks in the ivory tower: Conflict management strategies for higher education.* Boston: Anker.

Lovitts, B. E. (2001). *Leaving the ivory tower: The causes and consequences of departure from doctoral study.* Lanham, MD: Rowman & Littlefield.

Nerad, M., & Cerny, J. (2000, Winter). From rumors to facts: Career outcomes of English Ph.D.'s: Results from the PhDs—Ten Years Later Study. *ADE Bulletin, 124,* 43–55.

Tinto, V. (1993). *Leaving college: Rethinking the causes and cures of student attrition.* Chicago: University of Chicago Press.

Warters, W. C. (Ed.). (2000). *Mediation in the campus community: Designing and managing effective programs.* San Francisco: Jossey-Bass.

Part Four

Synthesis, Lessons, and Future Directions

This part of the book consists of the final chapter, in which we consider the threads running through the research and action projects highlighted throughout the book. The chapter represents synthesis, analysis, and reflection. Initial synthesis appears in summaries of the research studies and action projects. Analysis and additional synthesis lie in our efforts to present our conclusions based on the research studies and action projects. The chapter is reflective inasmuch as we offer implications for strategic action that follow from each conclusion, as well as our vision for future directions of importance to researchers, institutional leaders, and others involved in preparing the next generation of faculty. We hope this chapter will help readers make use of what already has been learned and developed concerning graduate education as they continue their own efforts to support and prepare those pursuing paths to the professoriate.

Chapter Fourteen

Future Directions
Strategies to Enhance Paths to the Professoriate
Donald H. Wulff, Ann E. Austin

In the preceding chapters, we have brought together the voices of researchers, institutional leaders, and program directors who are working to improve doctoral education. Gathering this major research in one place enables us to look across studies to reflect on recurring findings and identify implications for action. Furthermore, reviewing the experiences described by those who are developing innovative programs offers insightful lessons for other leaders seeking effective strategies to improve graduate education. Juxtaposing the research studies with descriptions of significant programs demonstrates that efforts are already under way to respond to concerns about the preparation of future faculty and indicates areas in which to focus ongoing efforts.

We have organized this final chapter into four broad sections. In the first two sections we briefly highlight the research presented in Part Two of this volume and then the programs—the action projects—described in Part Three. In the third section we identify five key conclusions about helping doctoral students succeed and offer specific strategies related to each one. In the final section of the chapter we identify six major challenges that we believe will be ongoing issues that will need to be addressed to enhance the preparation of the next generation of faculty.

Highlights of the Research Studies

The six studies highlighted in this book all focus on the graduate school experience, but they each emphasize particular questions about that experience and use a range of approaches and research methodologies. The chapters in Part Two describe these individual studies and their results in detail; here we simply review their distinctive features.

Four of the studies sought to capture students' views of the graduate experience while the students were in the midst of it. Using a survey of doctoral students in eleven arts and sciences disciplines at twenty-seven universities, the Golde and Dore study (Chapter Two) collected data from more than four thousand doctoral students concerning their perceptions of various aspects of their graduate experience. In their chapter in this volume, Golde and Dore focused on comparisons between participants in two of the disciplines, English and chemistry. The National Doctoral Program Survey (Chapter Four), described by Fagen and Suedkamp Wells and sponsored by the National Association of Graduate-Professional Students, is especially distinguished by being designed and conducted by graduate students themselves. Using what they term a "viral publicity mechanism" to spread the word about the Web-based survey, the researchers were able to gather more than thirty-two thousand student responses from almost five thousand doctoral programs in almost five hundred universities in the United States and Canada. The results and recommendations from this set of studies will serve not only to improve graduate student experiences but also to assist graduate students in preparing for faculty careers.

Two of the other studies used qualitative rather than quantitative approaches to gather information about the graduate student experience. Although they studied fewer students, the researchers were able to probe deeply into students' views. In their longitudinal study of graduate students as teaching scholars (Chapter Three), Wulff, Austin, Nyquist, and Sprague used intensive interviews repeated with sixty-six participants in a range of departments at three institutions over a four-year period to focus on graduate students' own voices in describing their professional development. Antony and Taylor (Chapter Five) also used a qualitative strategy, conducting intensive interviews with twelve graduate students in six colleges of education to provide opportunities for the students to offer narratives about their socialization experiences in graduate school.

The last two studies focused on scholars who were no longer in graduate education but were looking back on the experience. Lovitts (Chapter Six) sought to learn more about why students depart from graduate school prior to completion. Methodologically, she used a combination of surveys, telephone and in-person interviews, and site visits to explore departmental contexts. Finally, Nerad, Aanerud, and Cerny (Chapter Seven) drew from a large-scale survey of almost six thousand individuals in six disciplines who had completed doctoral degrees at sixty-one institutions from 1982 to 1985, ten to fourteen years prior to the time of the study. This study also involved in-depth interviews with a small group of the participants and some information collected years earlier when the dissertations had been filed.

Highlights of the Action Projects for Reform

Along with the research studies and the efforts on individual campuses, the action projects described in Part Three of this volume represent what Nyquist, Woodford, and Rogers (Chapter Ten) say "is quietly, yet persistently, becoming a national movement to re-envision doctoral education for the twenty-first century." As part of the national movement, the programs have made distinctive contributions in propelling institutions forward and in providing examples, suggestions, and possibilities for adaptation.

The Scholarship of Teaching and Learning Movement

The scholarship of teaching and learning movement, described by Hutchings and Clarke (Chapter Eight), encourages academics—both graduate students and faculty members—to use in the work of their teaching the same skills and habits of systematic inquiry that they employ in their research. As the movement urges academics to engage in teaching as an intellectual, scholarly activity, it also is helping future faculty members take teaching seriously. A number of major research universities and scholarly organizations are integrating principles from the scholarship of teaching and learning movement into specific professional development programs to prepare the future professoriate.

Preparing Future Faculty

The Preparing Future Faculty (PFF) Program, described by Pruitt-Logan and Gaff (Chapter Nine), is one of the most established action projects. With a decade of history, PFF has had a major impact on the national conversation about the kind of preparation that is appropriate for aspiring faculty members, including preparation for teaching in institutions different from the research universities where they train. Through PFF, universities and colleges have worked together to explore the abilities that prospective faculty will need and provide opportunities for graduate students to visit, interact with faculty, and intern at the kinds of higher education institutions in which they may seek employment.

Re-envisioning the Ph.D.

Another major national initiative, the Re-envisioning the Ph.D. Project, described by Nyquist, Woodford, and Rogers (Chapter Ten), has been a catalyst for far-reaching conversation and cooperation among the many stakeholders interested in graduate education. A key question at the heart of the Re-envisioning project is this: "How can we re-envision the Ph.D. to meet the needs of society in the twenty-first century?" One of the project's most important contributions was to convene critical stakeholders—those who prepare and hire new Ph.D.'s, as well as those who fund and influence graduate education—to discuss the purposes and practices of graduate education, and strategies for improvement. Outcomes of this influential project include a summary of the perspectives of primary stakeholders, a major conference of the stakeholders, and a highly used Web site that provides recent studies, bibliographies, and a bank of strategies designed to improve graduate education and the preparation of future faculty.

The Responsive PhD Initiative

The Responsive PhD (Chapter Eleven), an initiative of the Woodrow Wilson Foundation, is bringing together fourteen universities to partner for purposes of developing models of innovation in graduate education that can be disseminated nationally.

With the broader goal of supporting innovation in graduate education, the project emphasizes four themes, all of which are relevant to preparation of the future professoriate. The first is new partnerships that bring into dialogue a range of constituencies, including voices from various types of educational institutions, the academy, business, and government. The second is new paradigms that emphasize the scholarship at the heart of the Ph.D., the possibilities offered by connections across the disciplines, and the potential, in Robert Weisbuch's words, of "adventurous scholarship." The third theme emphasizes practices that prepare a new "generation of intellectual leaders" with abilities as teachers, appreciation of service and engagement, and understanding of "the power of their expertise in the world at large." The fourth area of emphasis for the project is new people, who bring greater diversity and democratization to graduate education. Although still in its early years, this project has produced some promising institutional outcomes: greater transparency about information and processes in participating doctoral programs; more effective mentoring, especially for underrepresented students; new kinds of dissertations involving the application of knowledge to pedagogical and community issues; and new alumni networks and databases to link graduate students with those working in their fields outside academe.

The Carnegie Initiative on the Doctorate

The Carnegie Initiative on the Doctorate (Chapter Twelve) is another action initiative designed both to have an impact on the national conversation about improving doctoral education and to develop and offer models for effecting such improvement. The project focuses on preparing doctoral students as "stewards of the disciplines" who are committed, in the prose of George Walker, to "preserving the essence of their field while simultaneously directing a critical eye to the future." Practically speaking, the Carnegie initiative is bringing together six to eight departments in each of six fields—chemistry, history, English, mathematics, neuroscience, and education—to work together to improve preparation of doctoral students as disciplinary leaders for the future. Participating departments reflect on their programs' intended goals or outcomes, experiment with new initiatives for improving students' learning, assess the impact of those initiatives, and disseminate lessons learned.

Setting Expectations and Resolving Conflicts

Developed at Michigan State University, the Setting Expectations and Resolving Conflicts Program, described by Klomparens and Beck (Chapter Thirteen), trains faculty members and graduate students to engage in discussing, clarifying, and setting mutual expectations, a process the authors call "making the implicit explicit." Such a process directly addresses the concerns evident in the research on graduate education that students often experience uncertainty about the expectations embedded in their graduate programs. Of equal import, the program recognizes that students may bring unrealistic expectations to the graduate experience. Both these situations can be handled through processes that help students and faculty members learn how to set mutually agreed upon expectations. While better setting of explicit and mutually understood expectations helps students and faculty avoid conflicts, the program also trains participants in an approach to conflict resolution that seeks to meet the interests of all parties involved. The program exemplifies strategies for getting new graduate students off to a good start, strengthening advising and mentoring relationships, and preparing graduate students with skills in using an interest-based approach to conflict resolution. All are relevant to their future professional work.

Conclusions and Strategies to Enhance the Doctoral Experience

The studies and action projects described in this volume differ in focus and design or implementation. As a group, however, there are similarities and consistencies in their results, recommendations, and strategies. In reviewing them, five major conclusions emerged for us about ways to enhance the graduate experience for individual students. Others involved in graduate education reform can gain assurance from the similarities in the approaches and recommendations across studies and projects that led us to these conclusions.

In presenting our conclusions about supporting individual doctoral students, we first explain the importance of each conclusion and then discuss the implications for strategic action. We address the implications particularly to graduate deans, department chairs, and faculty members who work with graduate students and seek to improve their experience. Although we have focused the book on strategies for improving graduate preparation of the future professoriate, some of the suggestions will enhance the doctoral experiences of not only the next generation of faculty members (and help ensure that they remain in school and complete the doctorate) but of all graduate students regardless of career aspirations.

Conclusion 1: Students Need Help Getting Started in Graduate School in Ways That Promote Success

In discussing her research in Chapter Six, Lovitts pointed out that, in order to succeed, students need to develop what she calls "cognitive maps" of their departments' formal requirements as well as informal expectations. Weisbuch in Chapter Eleven on the Responsive Ph.D. mentioned the importance of transparency, making elements of graduate programs clear for students. In their recommendations based on the study of graduate students, Fagen and Suedkamp Wells in Chapter Four suggested a similar strategy.

Often, however, when students enter programs, faculty members do not provide explicit information about requirements, expectations, and major stages of the process. When faculty do provide formal handbooks with important information, the informal norms and expectations may remain unspoken. Left on their own, students often derive their understandings from their own observations and from peer interactions. Both of these sources can be useful; nevertheless, mixed and contradictory messages from the environment can increase confusion about what students observe. In addition, peers may not always have complete information and accurate perceptions. Incomplete or incorrect information about requirements, norms for interaction between faculty and students, and informal expectations can undermine the progress of students before they get adequate opportunity to understand what is involved in graduate study.

At the same time that faculty are working to present accurate information, they should remember that the students are striving to develop increasing competence in many areas of their lives. There is a lot of information for students to assimilate, so providing the appropriate amounts and kind of detail about requirements and expectations is particularly important. For many students, this period is one of intense development, which, as Wulff, Austin, Nyquist, and Sprague emphasized in Chapter Three, includes tremendous change for the students. As they are evolving in their understanding of what it means to be teaching scholars, students often are also undergoing great adaptation in their personal lives and needs. Finding ways to provide the most useful information to help students balance their individual developmental needs with the requirements and expectations of the department is thus imperative.

Entrance and Orientation: Implications for Strategic Action

- *Plan a thorough orientation.* A carefully planned orientation that helps new graduate students gain clear understandings about graduate study is a critically important first step. Such an orientation should offer a transparent view of what is to come. There should be information about the program—for example, how it is organized; the specific formal requirements, benchmarks, and time lines that students will be expected to meet; the informal expectations about how students progress; the kinds of research and teaching in which students will be involved; and norms related to graduate education in the discipline or field and in the specific institution and department. There also should be some guidance about what students can expect from advisors and suggestions for productive ways to interact with them, other faculty members, and fellow students. In instances in which students are obtaining degrees through distance learning programs, such orientations are even more important. All told, a carefully designed orientation can help students and faculty set an appropriate foundation while also dispelling misunderstandings about what graduate study involves.
- *Use initial goal-setting meetings.* Such meetings can begin to address the fact that students enter graduate study with strong expectations, passions, and goals of their own. Some of those

aspirations may provide an important driving impetus; others may be unrealistic enough that they present special challenges for students or faculty. Although those individual needs and expectations are certainly important, they should be balanced against requirements and expectations of the departments and the institutions. Having students discuss with their faculty advisors their aspirations and goals provides opportunities for important reflection as both explore and clarify mutual expectations. Furthermore, such interactions provide opportunities for faculty to be reminded and to acknowledge that students are in the midst of complex development involving not only their scholarly work but also their personal lives.

Conclusion 2: Key to the Success of Doctoral Students Is the Extent to Which They Connect with the People and Cultures of Their Departments

From the start of their doctoral programs, students need to be developing a sense of belonging and integration. For this reason, many of the innovative programmatic efforts have solid grounding in disciplinary or departmental contexts, and indeed many of the findings of the research studies reinforce the importance of such connections. In her chapter on factors that contribute to students' decisions to leave doctoral study, Lovitts (Chapter Six) made a compelling argument for the importance of social integration as a major component affecting such choices. The assistantships, the opportunities to participate in the life of the department, and as both Wulff, Austin, Nyquist, and Sprague (Chapter Three) and Lovitts suggested, even the availability of office space that brings students into interaction with other students and with faculty members contribute to the extent to which students are haves or have-nots in the departmental environment. Focusing specifically on Black graduate students, Antony and Taylor (Chapter Five) also emphasized how important it is for students to feel welcome in their programs. They reported that underrepresented students sometimes felt that others approached them with stereotypes that undermined their confidence and sense of belonging. If students are ultimately to become faculty members, they must complete their doctoral work. Thus, the issues of integration and connection within doctoral cohorts, both for on-campus and distance learning programs, are important considerations for faculty members interested in strengthening the preparation of future faculty.

Opportunities for Connection: Implications for Strategic Action

- *Cultivate a sense of intellectual belonging.* Besides ensuring that students get an appropriate initial orientation, an important issue already discussed, faculty members can promote additional approaches to help students feel that they belong in the department. Helping students secure adequate funding is a first step. Fellowships, assistantships, and other awards are especially helpful. If assistantships involve office space near other students, social integration is fostered every day. Travel awards for students to present at conferences convey recognition for their achievements and also provide opportunities for them to interact and feel connected with other aspiring scholars as well as with faculty members. Opportunities to serve on departmental or college committees also bring students into proximity and interaction with faculty members and other students and indicate confidence in the quality of the students' contributions.

- *Encourage informal interactions.* Faculty members who welcome the opportunity to interact informally with graduate students contribute to a departmental culture that is supportive of and encouraging for students. In some of the qualitative studies, graduate students commented on the difficulties they sometimes have in finding occasions to interact informally with faculty members about academic life and career goals. The more faculty members are open to such occasions, and in fact, explicitly provide opportunities for such casual interactions as lunches or coffee with students, the more students feel connected to the life of the department and field.

Conclusion 3: Doctoral Students Need Preparation for a Broader Conception of the Faculty Role

As the research studies and action projects attested, students need greater systematic preparation for careers as faculty members. In terms of teaching, graduate students often do not have opportunities to learn about the full range of teaching options, including technology-based strategies, and the usefulness of various approaches in different disciplines, with diverse students, and for different purposes. Furthermore, although doctoral students may gain experience as teaching assistants, they do not always move through progressively more demanding teaching assignments, that enable them to develop systematically as teachers. Learning how to advise and developing a philosophy as a teacher are other aspects of learning to teach that often are not included as part of the graduate experience.

Even though doctoral students are usually better prepared as researchers than as teachers, research preparation is not always comprehensive. For example, experience with grants, mastery of the complete array of steps in the writing and publishing process, and ways to approach interdisciplinary collaborations are skills not necessarily included in each student's research preparation.

In addition, despite the increasing importance given to outreach at most universities and colleges, the research studies in this volume showed that most graduate students have very little understanding about professional service, outreach, and public engagement and about how such activities might be part of their work as professors. Furthermore, few students are aware of faculty responsibilities as institutional citizens, in terms of academic governance, committee work, and institutional and departmental leadership. Handling ethical issues that confront faculty members is another area in which graduate students are usually only minimally prepared. Examples of ethical issues needing greater attention include approaches to handling student dishonesty, engaging in appropriate relationships with colleagues and students, deciding authorship on collaborative projects, using research funds appropriately, and determining ownership of data and patents. Overall, students need to be supported as they develop along the many professional and personal dimensions required for faculty work.

Preparation for the Faculty Role: Implications for Strategic Action

- *Provide systematic preparation for teaching.* Doctoral programs should provide students with an array of teaching opportunities that become progressively more demanding and require more responsibility. Students who aspire to the professoriate may begin helping with a section or lab but ideally will have opportunities later in the program to teach alone with more responsibility. In addition, students need opportunities to learn about and try various teaching strategies appropriate to their fields. Students also should have opportunities to learn about the different kinds of teaching situations in which they may find themselves, including classes of various sizes, and the different teaching environments across institutional types (community colleges, liberal arts colleges, comprehensive institutions, and research universities). Faculty supervisors or advisors should provide systematic and insightful feedback about the graduate student's development as a teacher. On many campuses, centers specializing in issues of teaching and learning also are available to assist in such preparation.

- *Provide thorough preparation for research.* Many graduate students participate in supervised research duties or on research teams. However, they do not always experience all aspects of the research process, from the development of an initial idea to the writing of the final paper or report. More thorough and explicit research preparation would ensure that students learn about each part of the research process, including grant writing, teamwork and collaboration, and data collection, as well as analysis, report preparation, and presentation of findings to interested audiences. Research preparation also should help students develop skills in sharing research findings with nonacademic groups, such as community members, schools, and civic groups.

- *Prepare aspiring faculty for service and other aspects of academic life.* Students need to understand that faculty members have responsibilities beyond research and teaching. Thus, effective graduate preparation for the professoriate should provide opportunities for students to learn about and develop abilities across the full array of duties. Approaches should include learning about the scholarship of engagement, including making important links across one's teaching, research, and service. Students also should learn to use their scholarly expertise to engage in service useful to an array of constituents and to participate successfully in institutional citizenship responsibilities (including skills useful for committee work, leadership, and collaboration on departmental and institutional projects). Institutions and departments also should ensure that students are aware of and prepared to handle the complex and challenging ethical dimensions of all aspects of faculty work.

Conclusion 4: Doctoral Students Need Ample Career-Planning Information and Opportunities

Both the research studies discussed in this volume and programs such as Preparing Future Faculty described by Pruitt-Logan and Gaff (Chapter Nine) suggest that, in terms of academic careers, graduate students too often do not gain a full understanding of the academic labor market. Often students need more information on the array of institutional types in the higher education sector and the different forms that academic work takes in different kinds of institutions (work as a community college faculty member is different in some ways, for example, from work as a liberal arts or research university professor). Although students lack knowledge of many aspects of academic life, what they do observe as they watch their own faculty members often leads them to question their interest in faculty work. Some students wonder, for example, whether it is possible to lead lives that balance personal commitments with professional duties and whether the academic world actually will enable them to pursue their intellectual passions in the ways they wish. Central to these concerns are the pressures and time demands that aspiring faculty members say they observe in their professors. Often students do not find avenues in their graduate experiences to make sense of these observations and discuss concerns with interested faculty members.

As much as graduate students are unfamiliar with all aspects of academic employment, they usually know even less about employment options outside of academe. Students have little exposure to ways in which their academic abilities can translate into nonacademic employment, and in fact, participants in several of the studies were quick to note that they did not feel comfortable even admitting to their advisors that they were interested in exploring such work.

Graduate students are also still much too uncertain about the job-search process. Some of the studies indicated that students sometimes felt that their departments and advisors provided inadequate guidance, effectively leaving them on their own to figure out next steps after completion of the degree. As the results reported in Nerad, Aanerud, and Cerny (Chapter Seven) suggested, students need more practical advice on the mechanics of the job search. This situation often is exacerbated by the failure of some departments to provide data on completion rates and career placement outcomes of recent graduates.

Career Preparation: Implications for Strategic Action

- *Prepare prospective faculty for a changing context.* A great challenge confronting today's faculty members is to prepare doctoral students for a workplace and society that are changing very rapidly. The educational changes accompanying technological innovations, the new students entering the academy, and the different kinds of faculty appointments (the increase in term appointments compared with traditional tenure-stream appointments, for example) are only some of the many rapidly changing aspects of faculty work. Current faculty members in graduate departments must acknowledge that, if they wish to prepare aspiring faculty members for future challenges in the academy, they cannot simply "clone" themselves as they prepare their students.

- *Help students prepare for an array of academic options.* As many of the programmatic efforts we have seen in this volume emphasized, aspiring faculty members should have opportunities to learn about the range of academic institutions and the differences in faculty work depending on where they are employed. They should also have opportunities to examine the implications of different kinds of appointments—term or contract, part-time versus full-time, tenure-stream versus non-tenure-stream. The process of learning about these options should include consideration of their own goals, hopes, and expectations for their professional and personal lives. To provide such exploration opportunities, faculty advisors may have to help students connect with faculty members at other institutions and ones who have chosen different kinds of career paths than the advisors have. Students also should learn how expectations, needs, and norms in their particular disciplines will influence their options. Graduate students in physics, for example, who wish to engage in highly technical or specialized research may not find the equipment they need if they take a position in a liberal arts college. New graduates in English, however, may find that that same liberal arts college provides them with a good environment for writing a first novel while they also focus on teaching.

- *Create awareness and knowledge of nonacademic options.* Although this volume focuses on preparing graduate students for careers as faculty members, these same graduate students should have opportunities to explore nonacademic careers as well. Academic work should be an affirmative choice, made in the context of thorough knowledge of all of one's options. Faculty members can invite graduates or others who have forged careers outside of academia to visit the campus to discuss their work with graduate students. Because many graduate students are reluctant to admit that they might wish to explore nonacademic work options, it would be helpful if faculty members conveyed their openness to discussing the range of career choices that students may be considering.
- *Arrange discussions about choices in faculty work.* Faculty advisors can begin discussions with graduate students by talking about the choices they have made in their own careers and how and why they made those choices. The studies indicate that students welcome opportunities to talk with faculty members about such issues as forging a professional-personal balance in their lives, handling dual-career situations, pursuing intellectual passions and establishing their appropriate place in a faculty career, making decisions about which institutional leadership responsibilities to assume, relating research and professional service, and determining when and why to select one position over another.
- *Provide completion rates and placement information.* Graduate programs should provide prospective, entering, and continuing students with accurate data on completion rates of recent classes as well as summaries of work placements of graduates.
- *Offer job-search guidance.* Graduate schools or departments should offer students information about job searches. Students need to know how to write a vita, prepare letters of inquiry and application, and present themselves in interviews. Examples and workshops to address these issues can be very useful.

Conclusion 5: Carefully Constructed Advising and Mentoring Relationships Are Important to the Success of Graduate Students

As programs attempt to orient students, connect them to departmental and institutional cultures, and incorporate other suggestions from the previous conclusions, it is essential to incorporate good advising and feedback throughout the process. Unfortunately, the guidance provided is too often inadequate. As the research in this volume suggested, feedback to students about their work and progress was often insufficient, irregular, and unfocused. Students often referred to the unexpected barriers they felt they confronted in their graduate education, challenges that might have been minimized through more careful and regular advising. In the absence of extensive advising, students often turn to peers for guidance, and this strategy, although useful in many ways, is not a substitute for thoughtful advising and guidance from a faculty member. All of the programmatic descriptions either implicitly or explicitly suggested the importance of opportunities to work closely with mentors or advisors. As Klomparens and Beck pointed out in describing Michigan State's Setting Expectations and Resolving Conflicts Program in Chapter Thirteen, both graduate students and faculty members benefit from opportunities to negotiate mutually productive and rewarding relationships.

Advising and Feedback: Implications for Strategic Action

- *Establish standards for advising.* Universities and departments should establish standards for advising, which might include guidelines for the frequency of meetings and the kinds of issues that advisors should discuss with advisees. Departments should establish expectations and guidelines about how often formal progress reports should be prepared and discussed between advisors and students. Guidelines also should establish how students make changes or seek recourse if there are problems in an advising relationship.
- *Clarify advisor responsibilities.* Faculty members need to understand their responsibilities as advisors and the importance of solid advising relationships. Faculty members should share with students the responsibility of initiating meetings and developing good relationships. When advisors discuss their own career paths and show how they have created meaningful work and personal lives, students have important role models for their own development as future faculty members. Advisors and mentors can play a particularly significant role in helping students explore how their passions and interests relate to priorities in their disciplines and departments. Advisors also have

a responsibility to help students make sense of the often conflicting messages that faculty members receive each day about life in academia, expectations in their field, and various demands on their time.

- *Encourage graduate students to interact with a number of faculty members.* Students often benefit from significant relationships with more than one faculty member. Of course, disciplinary cultures may influence whether a student works with several faculty members or primarily interacts with one. Certainly, the opportunity to interact with at least one faculty member who is available to provide regular feedback and guidance is very important, but additional relationships can offer alternative models of how faculty work is done and how faculty lives are constructed.

Looking to the Future: Ongoing Challenges

Our focus in this volume has been the strategies for reform suggested by both research and action projects. In this final section, we offer an agenda—based on our observations, analysis, and reflections—that we believe will be important for the future of the movement to improve the preparation of the professoriate. We present the agenda as our vision of the responsibilities and challenges confronting all involved in doctoral education. The vision includes involving multiple stakeholders; promoting diversity; honoring disciplinarity while developing interdisciplinarity; engaging in experimentation; planning for evaluation and research; and handling constraints of time, economic pressures, and the reward structure.

Involving Multiple Stakeholders

Several chapter authors have discussed the importance of including a variety of stakeholders in decision making about graduate education. In the evolution of graduate education, there was a time when institutions could decide, pretty much in isolation, what the purpose of doctoral education would be and how it could best be carried out in major universities. When graduate education began in the 1800s, for instance, students were much more homogeneous, in both their needs and their expectations for graduate education. Times have clearly changed, however, and strong influences exist today that go beyond the confines of the traditional campus communities.

As various authors in this volume have noted, it is not enough to have campus faculty and administrators involved in conversations about graduate education. Rather, many different individuals—current doctoral students, graduates now in the workplace, and various stakeholders who hire and provide funding—have important stakes in the qualities, abilities, and skills of the doctoral student who emerges as a graduate. Even individuals in the general public, driven by concerns about rising costs and the quality of undergraduate education, have begun to offer their perspectives on what graduate education should accomplish. Many of the action projects discussed have benefited from the perspectives of diverse constituent groups. The Re-envisioning the Ph.D. Project (Chapter Ten), in particular, provides an excellent example of the usefulness of conversations among representatives of constituent groups. For us, as for many of the authors in this volume, continuing to include this broad range of perspectives is an imperative for the future.

Promoting Diversity

As the academic community looks to the future and the preparation of individuals who will fill the faculty ranks, those who design graduate programs should listen particularly carefully to graduate students themselves, a group with diverse perspectives and backgrounds whose perspectives may sometimes be overlooked. Any changes in graduate education will require greater understanding and appreciation for the diversity represented among students and future professors. Special attention should be directed to what the current system does to encourage or discourage diversity in its ranks.

The significance of this challenge has captured the attention of disciplinary associations and funding agencies, many of which have made issues related to diverse graduate students an important part of their ongoing work. The National Science Foundation, for instance, has various projects and activities designed to strengthen the participation of underrepresented groups, including women and minorities, in science, engineering, and technology. Certainly, many of the authors in this volume have emphasized the importance of achieving a more diverse professoriate.

Through such efforts some progress has been made, but the challenge of fully including individuals with diverse backgrounds persists. As Antony and Taylor (Chapter Five) and Lovitts (Chapter Six) noted, educators must think carefully about who is being included and provided with opportunities for graduate education and who is being excluded and how. In the coming years, those committed to reforming graduate education must continue to commit themselves to ensuring the full participation of underrepresented groups. The quality of the future professoriate depends on such efforts.

Honoring Disciplinarity and Developing Interdisciplinarity

We believe that it is possible to honor disciplinarity while simultaneously developing and encouraging interdisciplinarity in graduate programs. The disciplines have provided a very useful framework for work in most universities, serving as a major organizing influence for research, teaching, and even the promotion and tenure structure. As Lattuca (2001) pointed out, "Academic departments that followed disciplinary lines provided a seemingly logical arrangement of scholarly activity. Disciplinary associations served to connect scholars to one another and to advance their given disciplines" (p. 2). Without a doubt, disciplines affect the kinds of work faculty members do, and therefore must be taken into account in preparing future faculty. Certainly, authors in this volume like Golde and Dore (Chapter Two), Hutchings and Clarke (Chapter Eight), and Walker (Chapter Twelve), who suggest approaches grounded in disciplinarity, have strong support for their positions.

At the same time, though, discipline-specific approaches do not always provide everything needed for quality doctoral education. Despite the tradition of the disciplinary focus, criticism of the heavy disciplinary focus is evident. Lattuca (2001) pointed out that over time "concerns about the proliferation of academic specialties prompted some educators to think about the problems associated with the disciplinary structure of colleges and universities and about developing coherent and integrated courses of study for students" (p. 6). For some academics, and in fact, for some of the authors in this volume, it is the specialization of the degree that raises concern, particularly when there is a simultaneous need for greater connectedness among scholars and greater awareness of blurring disciplinary boundaries that can only come from working across content areas and disciplines.

As a result, despite the importance of disciplinary perspectives, there is increasing recent emphasis on multidisciplinarity, transdisciplinarity, and interdisciplinarity, with implications for teaching, research, and graduate education (Klein, 1996; Lattuca, 2001). In this volume, for example, although the Carnegie Initiative on the Doctorate described by Walker (Chapter Twelve) is grounded in the disciplines, it addresses some of the issues of interdisciplinarity by focusing, in part, on students' ability to "transform" existing knowledge for successful communication across traditional disciplinary boundaries. Programs such as Woodrow Wilson's Responsive PhD (Chapter Eleven) have included interdisciplinarity in their basic tenets. More broadly, programs at major universities have emerged in recent years to produce interdisciplinary Ph.D.'s; interdisciplinary programs drawing on several areas to address environmental or technological issues are two examples.

We support innovative efforts to enhance graduate education that reduce the sense of total independence and compartmentalization that many doctoral students have experienced. However, in considering the place of interdisciplinarity in the preparation of future faculty, we also acknowledge the danger of perceiving disciplinarity and interdisciplinarity as situated in dichotomous opposition to each other. Rather, as suggested by Klein (1996), "Close inspection of boundary crossing reveals that disciplinarity and interdisciplinarity are productive tensions in a dynamic supplement, complement, and critique" (p. 4). Indeed, we believe, as suggested by many of the programs described in this volume, that disciplinarity and multi- or interdisciplinarity can work together in ways that meet the needs of a variety of graduate students. It is our position that seeking innovative options to approach this "productive tension" would enhance doctoral education.

Engaging in Experimentation

Doctoral education must have room for experimentation, and furthermore, those who struggle with innovative ideas and approaches should be rewarded. We applaud and encourage experimentation in doctoral education and urge those who are trying new strategies and developing new programs to discuss their ideas and experiences with colleagues across the campus and across the country.

Several of the action projects discussed in this volume are important not only for the innovative programmatic examples they provide but also for the research findings they are generating about the impact of experimentation in doctoral education. Creative programs that are set up in ways that gather information to help assess impact and relative success offer other institutions useful information for deciding the likely value of adapting that program. A particular contribution of the Re-envisioning Web site is the availability of extensive examples of innovative institutional initiatives designed to improve graduate education and the preparation of the future faculty.

Individual institutions can adapt these ideas as appropriate. We recognize that programs develop inside the cultures of specific institutions, departments, and groups of students, and that, given varying institutional cultures, not all programs evolve or work in exactly the same way. Nevertheless, opportunities for departments to look at examples and compare outcomes promote experimentation and new ideas. We call for continued experimentation and creativity of the kind already exemplified in the action projects described in this book. These national initiatives have been particularly helpful in providing for exchange and dissemination of information and strategies that can save time and make the best possible use of limited resources.

Incentives for creativity and innovation are also important. Institutions must find ways to reward faculty and leaders who spend time examining issues of doctoral education and finding efficient, effective approaches to enhance its quality.

Planning for Evaluation and Research

Improving graduate programs requires not only good ideas and innovation but also a commitment to evaluation and research. We envision these efforts occurring at several levels: ongoing evaluation of the culture in the department of specific doctoral programs; formative evaluation of innovative new action projects and summative evaluation of the outcomes and impact of these projects; and continuing research about the experiences of graduate students and the impact of graduate education on their careers.

Departmental Evaluation

Ongoing appraisal of the departmental culture experienced by graduate students is a particularly important responsibility of department chairs and faculty members. The culture of an institution or a department includes how faculty members and students interact, the norms and values that are honored, and the messages conveyed, implicitly and explicitly, about what is valued. Research studies reveal that graduate students constantly perceive messages about what kinds of scholars they should be, what constitutes good work, what faculty roles are most respected, and what kinds of future careers are most appropriate to pursue. The quality of graduate programs and the preparation of future faculty will be enhanced by regular appraisal of their cultures and impact on students. Involving graduate students with faculty members to conduct such departmental evaluation projects can provide useful learning opportunities.

In addition, departments should include the range of graduate student voices in the evaluation data. Individuals conducting the evaluation should direct special attention to the experiences of any groups of students who are underrepresented in the particular program—for example, women or students of color. Focus groups held once a semester or once a year, as well as surveys, can identify areas of concern and ways to enhance the graduate experience for all students. Such evaluation of the culture and environment as experienced by students might focus, for example, on topics such as the availability of information about formal and informal expectations, norms for student-faculty interaction, the advising process, how assistantships are assigned or allocated, and career exploration opportunities open to students.

One strategy departments should consider, if they are not already doing so, is conducting exit interviews with students who are departing early or graduating to capture their views of their graduate experiences, and where applicable, their preparation for academic careers. Surveys of graduates five or ten years after degree completion also are effective for learning about the usefulness of the program from those in the workforce.

Departments also should maintain data on completion rates and graduates' career paths. This information should be provided readily to both prospective and current students. If the institution also collects data about graduate students' experiences and perceptions, cross-departmental comparisons and exchange of ideas are possible. In addition, information from national studies may be useful to departmental faculty seeking to interpret local data and make appropriate adjustments. Following an evaluation process, avenues should be provided for students and faculty to discuss the results.

Formative and Summative Evaluation of Action Projects

The action projects and programs described in this volume illustrate another form of appraisal that is essential to the success of the movement to improve doctoral education. Even though many are in early stages, these action projects have already begun to evaluate their effectiveness. Most have built evaluation opportunities into their plans from the start—both for formative purposes, to ensure that information is collected along the way to allow for program adjustments, and for summative purposes, to provide data at the end to determine the extent to which the innovation is making a difference. Considering evaluation plans while a project is being conceptualized and during the hectic period when it is being initially implemented is demanding and time consuming. It is fairly easy to record the numbers of people involved in a program or gather perceptual and satisfaction data, but it is much more difficult to demonstrate that programs have deep impact on students, faculty, departments, institutions, and the overall quality of graduate education. Nevertheless, commitment and careful attention to embedding evaluation into innovation at all steps in the process will optimize the value of the projects and programmatic experiments both for the immediate participants and for others considering possible adaptations for their own programs and institutions.

Ongoing Research

Finally, we urge continued efforts to conduct research on graduate education, along the lines of the studies described in Part Two of this volume. Informed by research discussed here, we suggest a few important considerations in conducting research on graduate education. First, including many different voices and perspectives from inside higher education institutions and from stakeholders outside them is highly important. Second, using a variety of methods strengthens the credibility of collective findings about graduate education. Different designs and methods offer varying advantages. Survey research, on the one hand, enables a study to capture many perspectives; interview studies, on the other hand, provide the potential for researchers to probe in depth the complexities of students' experiences. Similarly, sometimes it may be crucial to use interviews or surveys to gather data at a specific period in the graduate experience; in other instances it may be more useful to use longitudinal methods to determine how perceptions or needs change over time. Third, research can be embedded into action projects as they occur. Besides formative evaluation about program development and implementation and summative evaluation of program outcomes and impact, action projects also may include plans to gather basic data to address other research questions. The Re-envisioning the Ph.D. Project (Chapter Ten), for instance, explicitly built in a research design to gather the views of multiple stakeholders about the doctoral degree and the process to attain it. In other words, as we hope we have illustrated in this book, research and action should go hand in hand in the movement to improve graduate education and the preparation of future faculty.

Handling Constraints of Time, Economic Pressures, and the Reward Structure

Efforts to prepare the faculty of tomorrow by necessity occur within the opportunities, constraints, and challenges of today. We recognize the context in which those engaged in doctoral education must function in the future. Among the major limitations are time, fiscal resources, and the reward structure. It is easy to propose that deans, faculty members, and students adopt the recommendations and strategies offered in this volume for improving doctoral education, but the reality of innovating, leading, and living with change is not easy.

Faculty and graduate students face increasing demands on their time. While they are fulfilling their traditional responsibilities, they also are facing expectations that they will spend more time thinking about and developing innovations for better graduate education. In these times of decreased institutional funding, there is little hope that faculty and graduate students can relinquish any responsibilities that might give them more time to focus on issues of improving doctoral education. In addition, at some institutions, the tenure system may not adequately recognize and reward the contributions, particularly of early career faculty, to such efforts.

The important lesson, perhaps, is that no single strategy or program is the "right" answer for improving graduate education and strengthening the preparation of future faculty. But taken together, the research and the program examples provide a number of good ideas. As they examine the needs of their own institutions and departments, deans, department chairs, faculty members, and students should be innovative in deciding what issues they most want to address and what combination of strategies may be most effective for improving the preparation they are offering to prospective faculty given both their goals and their constraints.

Conclusion

As this discussion illustrates, much currently is being done to strengthen graduate education in American universities and to ensure the quality of preparation for the faculty of the future. Deans and department chairs, faculty advisors, leaders in scholarly associations and foundations, faculty/instructional developers, employers who hire new Ph.D.'s, and graduate students themselves are involved in reforming graduate education and improving the preparation of the future professoriate. Researchers are gathering information and offering research-based suggestions for effective strategies. Leaders in institutions, foundations, and associations are developing action projects that invite the voices of multiple stakeholders into the discussion, experiment with creative strategies, and in the process, add to what is known about effective graduate education.

This range of activities reinforces our belief that the time is right for continuing serious thought and purposeful action to enhance doctoral education for prospective faculty. Graduate education for students aspiring to the professoriate is the crucial first stage of the faculty career. With the many demands on faculty members today, effective preparation for the faculty career has become more important than ever. Although the research studies and action projects highlighted here have accomplished much, the ongoing contributions of a wide array of stakeholders are necessary to continue to identify the most effective strategies, and of great importance, to get those strategies implemented. Efforts to build on the excellent research studies and action projects already under way will ensure that paths to the professoriate appropriately prepare the next generation of faculty for the challenges and responsibilities they will face.

References

Klein, J. T. (1996). *Crossing boundaries: Knowledge, disciplinarities, and inter-disciplinarities.* Charlottesville: University Press of Virginia.

Lattuca, L. R. (2001). *Creating interdisciplinarity: Interdisciplinary research and teaching among college and university faculty.* Nashville: Vanderbilt University Press.

Index